JUNGLE ACE

Potomac's
THE WARRIORS
Series

Acclaimed books about combatants throughout history who rose to the challenges of war. Other titles in the series:

JUNGLE ACE

Col. Gerald R. Johnson, the USAAF's

Top Fighter Leader of the Pacific War

JOHN R. BRUNING

Potomac Books, Inc.

WASHINGTON, D.C.

First The Warriors edition published in 2003.

Printed in the United States of America on acid-free paper that meets the American National Standards Institute Z39-48 Standard.

Library of Congress Cataloging-in-Publication Data

Bruning, John R.
    Jungle ace : Col. Gerald R. Johnson, the USAAF's top fighter leader of the Pacific War / John R. Bruning.—1st The warriors ed.
        p.   cm. — (The warriors)
Includes bibliographical references and index.
    ISBN 978-1-57488-694-8 (alk. paper)
    1. Johnson, Gerald R., 1920–1945.   2. Fighter pilots—United States—Biography.   3. World War, 1939–1945—Aerial operations, American.   4. World War, 1939–1945—Campaigns—Pacific Ocean. 5. United States. Army Air Forces—Biography.   6. Lightning (Fighter planes I. Title.   II. Series.

UG626.2.J363B78   2003
940.54′4973′092—dc21   200305222

Potomac Books
22841 Quicksilver Drive
Dulles, Virginia 20166

First Edition

10 9 8 7 6 5 4 3 2

For Jennifer, Barbara, Art, Bill, and Jerry

Your faith kept me strong

(Office of the Chief Engineer, General Headquarters Army Forces, Pacific, *Engineers of the Southwest Pacific,* vol. 6, *Airfield and Air Base Development* [Washington, D.C. Government Printing Office], p. 12).

CONTENTS

PREFACE

Let me introduce you to a very special man. Gerald Johnson rose from obscurity to become one of the great fighter leaders of the United States Army Air Force during World War II. All of twenty-four years, by 1945 he was an ace four times over, a full colonel in command of the hottest fighter group in the Pacific. He was a handsome, daredevil pilot who would try anything once—then try it again just for the visceral thrill of cheating death. He was a great ace, an incredible marksman, and a brilliant tactician. He was also complex man who loved to rebel while, at the same time, respecting authority. When the Air Force vested with him authority and leadership, he grew into the role, though he still found time to bend the rules a bit and have a little fun. Johnson went through life with his hair perpetually on fire.

Yet, when he is remembered by his pilot peers, they do not dwell on his 265 combat missions, his galaxy of medals, or even his 24 air-to-air victories. What they remember is a superb leader of men, who inspired all around him in the midst of some of the toughest fighting of the war. They remember an easygoing man who could laugh at himself, who could be quick-tempered at times but always did the right thing in the end. They remember the puckish sense of humor that Johnson displayed every time he pulled off one of his legendary pranks. Most important of all, they remember a man who cared deeply about his men and made their welfare his absolute top priority. They remember a man who, despite three combat tours in some of the most rugged areas of the planet, never once lost a wingman.

I first learned of Gerald R. Johnson when I was a kid. My dad brought home a copy of *Air Classics* that contained an article about his exploits in New Guinea and the Philippines. I recall being very impressed, and I kept the article with me even after I went to school at the University of Oregon. Later, when I discovered I had inadvertently gone to Johnson's college alma mater, I knew I had to write about this remarkable man. Through graduate school and beyond, I researched and studied Johnson's life. After writing my Master's thesis on him, I grew determined to write someday a full-length biography that would do his life justice.

This book is the fulfillment of that dream. It could not have been done without the help of hundreds of people—all of whom were more than happy to share with me their recollections of Johnson. I must thank especially the Johnson family for giving me open access to his letters, diaries, home movie footage, photo albums, and other memorabilia. To Generals John Henebry and "Sandy" McCorkle, Les Hardie, Wally Jordan, Carl Estes, Bill Runey, Bill Williams, Don Good, and Harry and Verla Huffman, I must say that this book could not have been completed without your recollections. There are many others who deserve thanks, including Jene McNeese, Marge Frazier, Clayton Barnes, Leslie Nelson, Bob Wood, Frank Beagle, Frank Holmes, and everyone from the 49th Fighter Group Association, Dave and Betty Knox, Ralph Wandrey, Albert Jacobs, George Alber, Ross Guiley, Erman Guistina, the Swift Family, Carl Martinez, historians Henry Sakaida, Dave Pluth, Jack Cook, and Eric Hammel and many, many more.

Special thanks are due to the folks at Brassey's. As always, Don McKeon has been both a teacher and a mentor. David Arthur did the lion's share of the editorial work, and did a terrific job. Julie Wrinn handled the production work immediately after returning from maternity leave. Julie, I hope this project didn't keep you from your own little one too much!

I need to also thank my wife, Jennifer. We met the year before I started researching Johnson for my Master's thesis, and she has put up with my devotion to his story for almost a decade. At times, we have had more photographs of Johnson and the 49th Fighter Group in our house than we have had photos of our own families! Jen, thanks for being the wellspring of my inspiration. I think I definitely got the better half of our marriage—you. How do you put up with me? How many people get to say they married their one true love? Luck has favored the foolish in my case.

Though she cannot yet read these words, I have to thank my little girl, Renee. She was born two years ago, just as my first book was wrapped up. Since then, she has put up with me and my roller coaster profession and has already shown impulses to follow in her daddy's footsteps. Like her old man, she has become obsessed with airplanes, and she constantly amazes my aviator friends by shouting out the names of the planes they flew during the war. Once, while visiting a local airport to see a B-24, she pointed up at the huge engine nacelle and blurted out "Double

Wasp, Daddy!" A B-24 pilot happened to be walking by at that instant, and was utterly dumbfounded by her comment. A two-year-old girl who can identify engines in a sixty-year-old aircraft. Now, that is some kid! Renee, you are my center—do not ever forget that.

More thanks are in order to a great group of people who have been as close as family to me over the years. Beth Gump, Jeff Hofstrand, Julie Coching, Dave Shen, Gary Wang, Debra Goldstein, Lori Miller, Alice Hart (wherever you are), Lis Shapiro, and Emily Pullins—even if some of us have lost touch, each one of you knows what you did for me during those crazy years in Saratoga. Pat Devaney, Stu Fonda, Kim Hiatt, JoLyn Taylor Rasmussen, Renee Van Hoeter, Colleen Welsh, Eric Stinemates, Tim Cushing, Nancy Anderson, and Professor Glenn May—you guys helped point a very confused young man in the right direction while at the University of Oregon. Whatever I have become is due in large part to your influence on me. An extra thought goes out to Susan and Jerry Taylor, whose home was the first into which I was welcomed after I came to the Pacific Northwest.

Mary Ann and Larry Beggs, my adopted Oregon parents, have put up with me and my off-the-wall-historian behavior for so long, I think sometimes they have come to regret giving me permission to marry their daughter on that rainy evening in the spring of 1991. Thanks for not losing faith in me, and don't worry, more grandkids are on the way!

Daryl Nichols—who ever would have thought those arguments in our U.S. History class would spark a friendship that has transcended everything from distance to war? You, Major Nichols, are my hero. Just remember to keep Tom in line!

To Mary Drew, I have got to say you certainly gave me a wake-up call at the coast way back when. You opened me up again and made me see who I was deep down, no matter what I was pretending to be at the time. Yeah, he'll never get married! Thanks for the swift kick in the rear; without it I may very well have become an absolutely wretched human being.

To everyone else who helped out or provided encouragement, I owe you all a debt I can only repay with the words in this book. I hope I have done justice to your memories. I hope I have captured the Gerald R. Johnson you remember and love.

Lastly, I must thank Gerald Johnson himself. Although we never met, his life transformed mine and put me on the path I am on today.

If you haven't met or heard of Gerald "Jerry" Johnson, find a cozy chair, settle down with a drink, and let me introduce you. This is a guy I know you'll want to meet.

"We gave up our boyhood, to drill and to train. . ."

❧

Irish Song "Patriot Games"

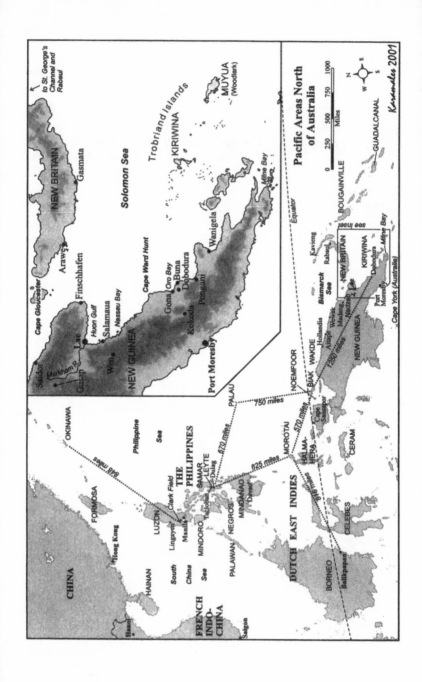

Pacific Areas North of Australia

Kerensees 2001

INTRODUCTION

New Guinea, October 12, 1943

The mission started on cue after breakfast, only to end in disaster by lunch. For Captain Gerald "Jerry" Johnson and his men of the 9th Fighter Squadron, the day would be forever etched into their memories.

It began well enough, with Jerry leading twenty Lockheed P-38 Lightnings into the air from their base at Dobodura, New Guinea in the pre-dawn darkness of October 12, 1943. Forming up into five flights—Red, Blue, Green, Yellow, and White—the squadron sped eastward out to sea until Kiriwina Island came into view. A small airfield had recently been established at Kiriwina, and on this morning the 9th used it as a refueling stop. By 10:20 A.M., they were back in the air, linking up with the "Jolly Rogers," a B-24 Liberator outfit that they would shepherd into Rabaul.

Rabaul, on the island of New Britain, had been the main Japanese base in the Southwest Pacific since its seizure in January 1942. Defended by thousands of veteran troops, hundreds of anti-aircraft guns, and hundreds of deadly Zeroes, Rabaul's Simpson Harbor gave shelter to the warships of the Japanese Eighth Fleet. On any given day, Allied reconnaissance photographs would reveal numerous heavy and light cruisers, destroyers, transports, and tankers scattered about the harbor, lying peacefully at anchor. Juicy targets, if the defenses could be penetrated—but that was a big "if."

In October 1943, the Fifth Air Force commander, Major General George C. Kenney, committed his forces to destroying Fortress Rabaul. The campaign's kick-off would be the October 12th raid, and every flyable bird with the range to get there would be thrown at Rabaul in a double-wave attack, designed to level the air defenses and smash the shipping in the harbor in one day. First in would be the B-25 Mitchells and Aussie Beaufighters, covered by P-38s. They were to sweep in low over Rabaul's airfields, strafing and dropping parachute fragmentation bombs—parafrags as they were called. With the Japanese fighter units hopefully suppressed, the B-24 groups of the second wave were to attack the warships in Simpson Harbor.

The night before, every pilot and crewman listened to the mission briefing, knowing that the plan depended on precise timing and accuracy. If surprise was achieved, the Japanese could be hit hard. If not, it would be a long, tough day. By the time the briefings were completed, every man knew just how important this raid would be. Kenney had ordered a maximum effort strike—some 350 planes. It would be the largest strike force yet assembled in the theater.

For the 9th Fighter Squadron, the "Flying Knights," the job was to escort the B-24s into Simpson Harbor, keeping the Zeroes at bay so the heavies could pound the shipping. They would leave Dobo just before dawn, fly to Kiriwina, and refuel. They would rendezvous with the Jolly Rogers over the Trobriand Islands, and provide high cover for them as they made their run over the target.

The first blow came around mid-morning, when the low-level bombers, Aussie Beaufighters and American Mitchells, raced over the Rabaul airfields at practically zero altitude. Surprise was complete. The bombers laced the strips with machine gun fire, chewing apart Japanese planes caught in the open or in revetments. As they passed over the runways, the bombers left a trail of parafrags blossoming behind them, looking like thousands of drifting jellyfish. When they hit the ground, the parafrags sprayed out millions of pieces of shrapnel, shredding trucks, planes, equipment, and men.

In minutes it was over, the bombers hugging the treetops as they raced to get out of harm's way. They hit the water of the Solomon Sea, gained some altitude, and at last began to relax as New Britain's coastline disappeared behind them. They had done their job; now it was up to the heavies. The next blow was about to come.

By 10:30, the second attack formation was spread across the Solomon Sea with parade-like precision. In its center, the B-24s clustered together in protective groups, their wingtips practically overlapping. Above them and on the flanks, Jerry and his five flights of Lightnings weaved protectively back and forth over the width of the bomber stream.

The trouble started forty minutes out of Kiriwina; at 20,000 feet, the attack force ran into a thin layer of clouds. Jerry led the squadron through them and up into clear sky, but the formations started to get ragged. Below them the bombers began to spread out, searching for ways through the cloud layer. Then the weather really closed in—blue sky became a rare sight as the bombers and fighters stumbled into a huge weather front.

Sitting high above the rest of his squadron, White Flight leader, 1st Lieutenant Ralph Wandrey, watched as Captain Johnson led his men into the storm. One by one, the 9th's flights plunged into the murk to disappear from view. The storm front looked absolutely solid to Wandrey, who nevertheless followed behind the last of the squadron and into the turmoil of the thunderheads. He too was soon lost from view.

Despite the storm, Jerry knew he had to push on. The bombers needed them over Simpson Harbor; otherwise, they would sitting ducks if any Japanese fighters survived the morning attack on the airfields. Knowing that was likely, he coaxed his men forward. With the rest of his squadron above and behind him, Jerry led his troops down into a gentle left turn, looking for a hole in the weather they could use to get on through. It proved to be a bad move. As he descended, he passed through a swollen ripe rain squall. Ice formed on the propeller hubs as wind and rain lashed at his aircraft. Behind him, the flight leaders tried to follow his maneuver, but soon had to chart their own courses, dodging and weaving through the worsening weather.

When Jerry and his flight finally dived free of one cloud layer, he circled around, waiting for the rest of the squadron to emerge behind him. He scanned the base of the thunderheads, but saw no sign of anyone in Red Flight's wake. His men were now hopelessly scattered and on their own.

Jerry quickly appraised the situation. To get to Rabaul, he could either fly through the storm, or go around it. Flying through it did not work, and as he explored the front, he realized skirting it would take too much fuel. They could get to Rabaul, but would run out of gas on the way home. Frustrated, and worried for his men, he aborted the mission and turned Red Flight back towards Kiriwina to wait for news of the other flights.

First Lieutenant Wally Jordan, Jerry's close friend since they had flown together in Alaska the year before, had Yellow Flight that day. As ordered, he followed his commander into the storm front, but quickly realized the effort was futile. He wheeled his men around, and through dead-reckoning, lead his flight to a Navy base at Woodlark Island. All of Jordan's men made it down safely.

The other flights weren't as lucky as Jordan's. Once Jerry led them into that gentle diving turn to the left, the scud forced the flights apart.

A couple of the flight leaders made steep right turns, which in the haze and muck of the storm, the elements could not follow. That foiled any attempt to keep the formations intact, and after that, the men just tried to get home.

Blue Flight returned to Dobodura minus its leader, First Lieutenant Theron Price. Green Flight came down at Dobo as well, but two of its members, First Lieutenants Ralph Hays and Frank Wunder, were missing. Ralph Wandrey and White Flight also made it back to Dobo, fortunately without loss. In the afternoon, Jerry led his men back from Kiriwina and settled in at Dobo, the last of the squadron to arrive there that day.

That night Jerry lay on his cot, alone in his tent, a pall of depression settling around him as the scope of the day's disaster began to sink in. He knew Jordan and Yellow Flight was safely at Woodlark, but three men were still gone—all of them experienced, senior lieutenants. Worst of all, nobody had even seen the enemy, let along fought them. Weather had killed these men.

It had been his decision to lead the men through the storm front, and he now wrestled with the guilt that decision had brought. Three men dead, three good friends whose families would have to be notified. He would have to write each pilot's family, a task he dreaded more than anything.

The living area was relatively quite that night. Most of the pilots were in the Officers' Club, nursing drinks and talking in hushed tones. A few miles away in the dispersal area, the 9th's ground crewmen worked on the remaining P-38s, getting them ready for the morning's mission.

Jerry slid off his cot and left his tent for the solitude of the stream that ran nearby. He stood staring down at it, wondering if he were fit to command. About a month before, he had been given the 9th after a summer of personal successes. He had bagged his third and fourth kills in July, became an ace in September, and earned his captaincy, all within six months of arriving in this fetid jungle hell hole.

The reality of his successes were lost on him that night, dwarfed by the realization that he was responsible for the day's disaster. It had been his decision to press on to Rabaul, despite the deteriorating weather. He knew that had the bombers continued on alone, which they sometimes had in the past, they could have been slaughtered by the hundreds of Japanese fighters based around Rabaul. He had too many friends in the bomber outfits to let that happen, if he could prevent it. With that in mind, he had gambled with his squadron, with the lives of his men. Now, knowing that three men were missing, probably dead, he could not help but question that decision. As he thought about this, his introspection filled him with doubts. Was he fit to command?

Jerry's sense of responsibility made him feel at least partially to blame for each man the squadron lost. Every time a friend went down to weather or Japanese fire, he suffered silently and alone. After all, as the command officer of the most successful unit in New Guinea, he simply could not show his emotions to his men. Instead, he stowed his feelings and always tried to be upbeat and give off an air of light-heartedness, even in the midst of a crisis.

On this night, though, all those half-buried emotions broke to the surface as he stood by that stream, alone in the dark with the sounds of the jungle all around him. Never mind that he was one of the top fighter pilots in the group. Never mind that his men practically idolized him, and were ready to follow him right to Tokyo if he asked. None of that mattered to him at the moment. On this single grim evening, Jerry had been rattled, and rattled bad.

Later, he wrote home to a family friend and related his thoughts:

My grass hut was beside a cool jungle stream, and one night as I stood there watching the moonlight dance on the ripples, something changed in my mind. At times I thought I was through. We had been fighting almost every other day, and one by one my pilots had gone to their death. I really thought I could no longer be their leader; that my nerve was gone and that I faced defeat. [Slowly, however], the dread and fear began to fall away. I was beginning to see that all my worry and concern was of little use in the accomplishment of my task; that men before me had feared and worried much more than I. I prayed to God that I might retain and strengthen this new source of courage which was Faith. I have never since wondered which way to turn.

That night, Jerry reached deep inside himself, and found out how much he could really take. He had come close to his own breaking point, but the experience gave him perspective, and he realized that as long he kept his perspective, he could continue to lead. Carefully, he packaged up all the emotions unleashed that night and stored them away. Later, in the comfort of a state-side bed, he would allow himself the luxury of grieving. In the meantime, Rabaul was to be hit again in the morning, and the Japanese were waiting.

October 15, 1943, 3:00 A.M.

"Hey! Any of you guys in here flying today?" yelled the OD (Officer of the Day), jarring Jerry out of a light sleep. Three A.M. Time to go to work. From the tent hut next door, the OD shined a flashlight around at each of the men.

"Any of you guys flying today?" he shouted again. Everyone hated being the OD, since the duty required running around in the middle of the night to wake up a bunch of surly aviators. It was a job almost as bad as garbage detail, maybe even worse, since at least garbage collectors did not wake anyone up.

"Hey, any of you guys flying today?" the OD repeated at the next tent hut. Jerry could see his flashlight bouncing around, a little spear point of light in the New Guinea darkness.

"Get the hell out of here, Willy," came a groggy retort. "Yeah, can't you do this a bit more quietly? Swifty is the only one in here flying today," came another.

Undeterred, the OD continued on his rounds, and as Jerry began shaking the sleep out of his system, his booming voice became more and more distant until it was lost amid the jungle noises that echoed through the night. Thank God.

❧

Jerry rose slowly, stretching carefully to get the blood flowing, before throwing on his clothes while trying not to disturb his tent mates, who were not on flight duty that morning. After sliding into his trousers, Jerry reached under his bed and retrieved his flying boots. Long ago, someone had discovered that scorpions loved to climb into aviator boots, so, as part of his morning ritual, he turned his footwear upside down and beat them together several times. That sort of treatment usually jarred any miscreant creatures loose, sending them scuttling for cover once they hit the wooden tent floor. On this morning, his boots were empty.

With his clothes on and his hair more or less combed—it never stayed in one place for very long, even when it was short—Jerry walked through the black New Guinea night to the mess hall to grab some pre-dawn chow. It was 3:10, and his day had just begun.

Breakfast was served by indifferent-looking enlisted men who slopped what passed for food onto tin trays. The pilots clustered together, gazing down at their meals and thought of the food their wives and mothers used to cook for them back in the States. They passed the time trying to top each other's stories of great home cooking, all the while practically gagging at the mess they were eating.

Breakfast at Dobodura consisted of pancakes that had sat for hours in a metal tub, surrounded by boiling water to keep them warm. They were warm, but they were also soggy and tasteless after sitting in that tub for so long. To help cover their unappealing pancakes, the men had tropical butter dished out to them from one-pound cans. The stuff was so repellent that long ago the men began calling it Marfac, which was a type of axle grease used on cars back in the States. Legend had it that the butter was so heat-resistant that even spooning some onto a hot griddle would not melt it. To go with the Marfac, the men had a syrup made from water and sugar, an unappetizing mixture at best.

Powdered eggs complemented the flapjacks, along with coffee so black it seemed to absorb light. To top the meal off, everyone got a few dripping wet pieces of bacon that flopped onto their tin trays like freshly-killed fish. No matter how long the bacon was cooked, it never got crisp and always seemed to be bursting with grease. Not a pretty sight, and certainly no one's idea for a last meal. Occasionally, though, it became just that.

After gutting out breakfast with his men, Jerry headed off to Operations to learn what would transpire for the day. The missions had all been scheduled the night before, but sometimes circumstances changed, which forced a new assignment. When he arrived, he soon learned that 49th Fighter Group Headquarters had just heard from Fighter Control that a Japanese raid was forming near Gasmata, New Britain. As a result, Group HQ canceled all the morning missions so that the 7th and 9th Squadrons could go on alert. For the 9th, this was something of a problem, as one flight was off at Woodlark Island searching for Price, Wunder, and Hayes, the pilots lost three days before. They were scheduled to return to Dobo, but they would not be back before mid-morning. Consequently, instead of sixteen birds ready in their revetments at the end of the field, the squadron could only muster twelve to deal with any incoming raiders.

After checking the latest news, Jerry and the other duty pilots climbed aboard a couple of jeeps and drove down to the Alert Tent, located in the dispersal area at the end of Horanda Airfield. Dobodura had two main fields, Horanda and Kalamazoo. Kalamazoo intersected Horanda about midway down the runway, so often, while the 9th was taking off, planes from the 7th Squadron were just getting airborne and crossing overhead. Needless to say, that took some getting used to.

The strips themselves were pounded dirt, for the entire base had been literally hacked out of the jungle. During rain storms, they became seas of mud. That would last only until the sun came out, since as soon as the weather cleared the strips would be baked hard again, and dust clouds would be kicked up every time a plane started its take off roll. The pilots hated to be the last in the squadron lineup, since the birds in front of them generated so much dust the tail-end-Charlies could hardly see the runway; it was like taking off in brown fog.

All in all, it was a horrible place to be, with the only saving grace being the width of the runway, which was large enough to allow four Lightnings to take off at once.

The jeeps deposited the men at the Alert Tent where they promptly settled down to await orders to scramble. The squadron's P-38s were all parked nearby at the end of Horanda Field, only a short run from the Alert Tent. Beyond the dispersal area lay the thick and foreboding New Guinea jungle, so dense that pilots who went down at the end of the runway could be missing for days in the bug-infested bogs and swamps. Search parties would have to be sent out to find them, hacking and slashing through the undergrowth as they pushed into the rain forest.

At the Alert Tent, Jerry and the men could look forward to hours of intense boredom. Half of the time, when orders to scramble did come, they would run down the plot, only to discover their target was nothing but a wayward Navy PBY, or a bomber whose IFF (Identification Friend or Foe) transmitter had failed. Only on rare occasions did an alert bring contact with the enemy, but those rare occasions could be some of the most intense moments these young men would ever experience.

While they waited for scramble orders, the men dozed on cots or chairs, listening to the outfit's portable wind-up phonograph. Unfortunately, they owned only a few records, so the same songs were played over and over until they could barely stand to hear any of them. Some of the men passed the time reading tattered paperback novels, which, of course, had the dirty parts underlined. Others wrote letters home. Lt. Leroy Donnell, a young pilot who would sometimes eat newspaper sandwiches when drunk, usually started a bridge game with Lt. Charles Kamphausen and another pair. Others would pull out bedraggled decks of cards and play poker on the hood of a jeep parked nearby.

Jerry had never been much of a gambler before coming to New Guinea. In fact, he had been morally opposed to it when he first joined the Air Corps, but his views had mellowed as he matured in the service. After he arrived in the theater in March of 1943, along with Wally Jordan and Tommy McGuire, he began to find poker a useful diversion that helped pass the slow time spent on alert.

He made a name for himself as an aggressive, wily poker player that spring. Once while on alert, Jerry, Ralph Wandrey, Tommy McGuire, and two others were playing draw poker on the hood of a jeep, betting with Australian currency. One Australian pound equaled about $3.22, and on this day the players were dropping £10 notes freely. As the pot grew, three of the players folded—it was just getting too rich for them. McGuire and Jerry played on, betting and raising each other until over $800 worth of Aussie money lay spread across the jeep's hood. Some joker had even thrown in some Dutch currency left over from 1942.

Finally, McGuire called, "OK, Jerry, what've you got?"

Jerry smiled sheepishly, laid down his cards and said, "Well, king high."

"Goddamn!" cried McGuire, throwing his cards dramatically onto the hood, "All I got is queen high!"

The other players sat in shocked silence. One of the guys who had folded had a pair of jacks in his hand—bluffed by two guys who did not even have a pair of deuces between them. What a way to lose!

After that, everyone took Jerry very seriously at the gambling fests.

On the morning of October 15, though, Jerry chose to stay out of the game. Instead, he leaned back in a chair and listened to Dinah Shore sing "Rum Bacardi" in a tinny voice on the phonograph. He had heard that scratchy record so many times he could probably sing it backwards from memory.

Around him, the men seemed to be in good spirits, especially given the last few days. After the disaster of October 12, the squadron flew another escort mission to Rabaul, only to be turned back again by the weather. Fortunately, no one was lost on that aborted flight. October 14 saw them flying searches for Hayes, Price, and Wunder, which turned up nothing—but did serve to remind everyone that if they themselves went down in the drink, Jerry and the 9th would do everything they could to find them.

"Can we listen to something else beside Dinah Shore?" someone asked. "I'm gonna puke if I hear that song one more time." Behind them, one of the other pilots fumbled with the small record collection and put another record on the phonograph.

Next to Jerry sat Ralph Wandrey, who had joined the squadron back in January. He would eventually end up with six kills and a captaincy before rotating home in 1944, sick with just about every jungle malady know to science. Beside Wandrey sat Lt. Bob Wood, a shy, reliable Californian whose father had died while Bob was very young. Behind Bob, Lt. Ray Swift, whom everyone called "Swifty," relaxed on a cot, reading a tattered paperback. Today, he was to fly as Jerry's wingman, an assignment he accepted with pride. Jerry in particular liked Ray, and whenever he could arrange it, he had him on his wing. Swifty would survive hundreds of combat hours in New Guinea and the Philippines, only to go home in 1945 to face tragedy. While on Luzon, word came that his wife had suffered a miscarriage, and Jerry arranged an emergency furlough for him so he could be with her.

They were good men, from all over the country. Wandrey was an Arizonan, Jerry an Oregonian. Bob Wood was a transplanted Californian, born in Massachusetts. Swifty hailed from Utah, with a good Mormon family background. They were easygoing, likable kids who were toughing out what would be the most difficult months of their lives.

At 8:00 A.M., their day started in earnest. Inside the Alert Tent, the phone on the tent's center pole began to ring. Jerry leapt from his chair, grabbed the phone and listened. Before he had hanged it up, his ten men were on their feet, making last-minute checks to their flying gear.

"Japs coming in from Gasmata from the Northeast. Let's go get 'em."

He had hardly finished when everyone began dashing to their waiting P-38s. Jerry ran along behind his men until he found his mount, #83, snug in its revetment. Waiting for him on the wing was his crew chief, Jack Hedgepeth.

"Everything ready, Jack?" Jerry called as he scrambled up the ladder and onto the wing.

"Yes, sir, fit as a fiddle!"

Jerry slid into the cockpit, where he sat on the waiting parachute and emergency life raft. The raft was quite literally, a pain in the ass—its air valve stuck out at such an angle that it always seemed to be poking extremely sensitive areas. After long missions, the men could sometimes barely walk, afflicted with what they called "Pilot's Ass."

On this morning, Jerry barely felt the painful little valve; he was so excited and focused on the coming mission. He settled right down, eager to get going, Jack hovering over him, strapping him in. With that done, the crew chief backed off, calling out as he slid off the wing, "Happy hunting, sir!"

Jerry leaned back, heard the canopy latch shut above him, then started the engines. The two liquid cooled Allisons quickly growled to life—the crew chiefs kept the planes warmed, primed, and ready throughout the morning's wait. Under the wings, Hedgepeth pulled out the wheel chocks and dragged them away.

Taxiing out of the revetment, the spindly-legged P-38 bobbed back and forth as Jerry gently worked the brakes. Behind him, seven other pilots did the same. Wandrey and Charles Ralph were left behind as reserve—Jerry would be leading only two flights into battle. Eight P-38s against a large formation of Japanese planes—it may have looked like long odds at first, but Jerry knew the other units around Dobo, including the 7th, would be scrambling as well. Indeed, minutes before, the P-38s of the 475th Fighter Group had rumbled down the runway in hot pursuit of the Japanese. With them was Jerry's old buddy from his days in Louisiana and Alaska, Tommy McGuire. McGuire would get two planes today, fighting with his new unit, the 432nd Fighter Squadron. Shortly after the poker game where Jerry had won $800, McGuire had transferred to the 475th in hopes of faster promotion.

On the runway now, ready to go. Swifty lined up on Jerry's right, while Lt. Grover Fanning and Bob Wood slid into view on the left. Red Flight was complete—in seconds, they would take off, four at a time, their flights already formed up before ever leaving the ground.

Jerry nodded once, then opened the throttles. The Allisons whined as he began his take off roll, dust billowing out behind his Lightning. Three thousand feet later, his flight lifted off the ground; hydraulic systems whirring as landing gears retracted. Right behind them came Blue Flight, led by Leroy Donnell. His wingman was Lt. John McClean, who would later die after doing a victory roll over Biak in 1944. The other Blue Flight element was led by Lt. Milby Marling, whose wingman was Donnell's bridge partner, Charlie Kamphausen.

Together the eight Americans climbed to 22,000 feet, looking for the Japanese as they flew northward over Oro Bay, searching the sky for the telltale dots of enemy aircraft. The battle began at 8:25. Red Flight caught sight of them first—counting out about forty bombers and fighters, coming in from the northeast. The bombers were arrayed in a neat Vee of Vee formation, while slightly above them, the bomber's escort of about twenty Zeroes had their hands full as they tried to fend off the P-38s of the 475th Fighter Group, which had been the first to engage.

Jerry led his men down from 22,000 feet into the fight. By the time he arrived, the Zeroes were scattered all over the sky, doing what they could to keep the Americans off the Aichi D3A Vals, fixed-geared dive bombers that usually saw service from Japanese aircraft carriers.

Jerry and Swifty dove behind the formation of Vals, and with Swifty covering his back, Jerry selected a target and hammered it with his .50s and 20 mm cannon. The Val staggered under the fusillade, burst into flames, then dropped straight down to crash into the sea. Swifty, watching from above and behind, saw the Val hit the water.

After that first pass, Jerry pulled up and away from the bomber formation and covered Swifty as his wingman closed in on a bomber. From dead astern, Swifty opened fire and saw his bullets chop the rear gunner into bloody pieces. The poor man's head came tumbling back through space and impacted against the Lightning's nose, leaving a red splotch that the ground crew would later have to scrub off. Though sickened by the sight, Swift nonetheless kept firing. His rounds cut along the fuselage and tore into the engine. A small flash of flame and the Val rolled over on its back and plunged into Oro Bay.

Two passes, two bombers. With Swifty climbing away, Jerry put his nose down and targeted another Val. This one tried to get away by diving, which was a clear rookie mistake. Nothing, save a P-47 Thunderbolt, dove faster than a P-38, so he shortened the distance in mere seconds. At close range, he opened up with all guns. The Val started smoking almost immediately, but the canny pilot managed to roll out of Jerry's line of fire. The P-38 roared past the Aichi, still in a steep dive, and Jerry soon lost sight of it. He claimed it as a probable upon return to Dobodura.

Just off the water, Jerry leveled out and went hunting for more Vals, Swifty faithfully covering his tail. Instead of bombers, they stumbled across a Zero chasing another P-38. Jerry slid behind the unsuspecting Japanese plane and began to fire. The Zero sparkled like a Christmas tree as .50-caliber rounds sliced into its wings and fuselage. In seconds, it was over—the Zero, belching flame and smoke, nosed over and smacked into the gray water of Oro Bay. When Jerry swept over the Zero's last resting place, only a few burning pieces of wreckage remained on the surface. There was no sign of the pilot.

Climbing back into the fight, Jerry ran across two Vals, which he and Swifty attacked without success. Just as they finished their runs on the two bombers, another Zero appeared on the scene. Jerry took a snap shot at it, but missed, and it disappeared before either he or Swifty could re-engage it. Finally, on the dregs of his ammunition, Jerry stalked another Val. He pressed the firing button and felt the vibration in the seat of his pants as his four .50s churned out eight rounds a second. His bullets stitched across the Val's left wing root, blowing holes into the hapless bomber's fuel tank. A spark, a glow of flame, then suddenly the Val exploded, blowing debris into a wide arc around the dying bomber as it spun crazily, trapping its crews in the fiery confines of the cockpit. The two Americans watched as the Val plunged into the ocean below, pieces of wing and fuselage fluttering down behind it like a silvery tail.

Jerry toggled his throat mike. "Hey, Swifty. I'm out of ammo. Let's call it a day."

Jerry winced with pain as he shut off the mike. His neck, shoulders, and back were covered with sweat, and every time he used the radio, his perspiration would short the throat mike. After months of that, a small round burn mark right below his Adam's apple had been seared into his skin. Just another reminder that their equipment was not designed with the tropics in mind.

With Swifty alongside him, Jerry turned for Dobodura, low on fuel and without a single round left in his guns. Together, they had shot down four planes and had probably nailed another one—not a bad day at all.

While Swifty and Jerry were shooting up the Vals, Red Flight's other element, Grover Fanning and Bob Wood, dropped their tanks and dived into the melee. Instead of going for the bombers, Wood and Fanning struck out after the escorting Zeroes. They made five passes at various aircraft until each pilot had flamed one, then continued to chase the Japanese as they ran for home. They eventually lost sight of the retreating formations, and turned to join another dogfight, but arrived just as the last enemy plane hit the water below. Out of targets, Fanning and Wood returned to Dobo, exhausted but satisfied with their performance for the day.

As Red Flight mixed it up with the fighters and bombers, Lieutenant Donnell led Blue Flight down to have a crack at the bombers. On the way down, Charles Kamphausen's P-38 suffered engine trouble. One fan's temp gauge sagged downward as it began running rough. He pulled out at 20,000, watching as his flight mates descended into the growing dogfight, hoping all the while that his engine would start running smoothly again. He hovered over the fight, keeping one eye on the sky around him and one eye peeled on his temp gauge, urging it higher with every passing second.

Kamphausen's element leader, Milby Marling, followed Donnell and McClean down into the dogfight, but as Donnell continued to dive towards the Vals, Marling took off after a couple of Zeroes. By himself, Marling soon found more trouble than he needed when a pair of Zekes dove down after him. He chandelled, pulling up and away from them in an effort to disengage. By keeping his speed up, he soon left the Japanese fighters behind, struggling to catch up. When far enough away, he reversed course and came back at the Zeroes in a classic slashing attack. As he opened up on one, both Zeroes broke into his attack, then slid on past under his nose, spoiling his shot. He did not even try to maneuver with them; Marling knew better than to meet the Zekes on their own terms. Instead, he leveled off, kept the throttle firewalled, and pulled away from the two Japanese fighters. Before they could turn around and get in behind him for a shot, he was nothing but a speck in the distance. A few seconds later, Marling came back around again, this time, firing from long range. Again the Japanese pilots ducked under him, ruining his pass. This happened one more time before, on his final pass, he managed some hits on a Zero. Hoping to finish him off, Marling let go with another burst, but the enemy pilot Immelmanned out of his fire, and Marling lost sight of him. At that point, low on ammo, he headed for home.

Meanwhile, Donnell and McClean tore into a formation of fat, slow Vals and had a field day. Donnell got behind a pair of Vals that were scooting for home a few hundred feet off the water, selected one and picked it off from dead astern. He swung his nose a bit, and the other Aichi drifted into his gunsight. He lightly touched the trigger—a sheet of flame spouted from his Lightning's nose as his tracers zipped through the sky and lanced into the Val's fuselage. For a second, it appeared that the two planes were connected by four glowing red threads of fire.

Above Donnell, a Zero spotted the plight of the Val and dived to save the wounded bomber. Donnell, however, spotted the Zeke and broke into his attack, ducking under him. He shook the Zero loose a few seconds later, but by then the damaged Val was nowhere to be seen. Without his quarry in sight, Donnell disengaged and returned to Dobo.

On Donnell's heels came young John McClean, eager to score his first kill. Just above the wave tops, he caught sight of a lone Val staggering home. He dived on the Japanese plane, closed in from six o'clock, and poured a long burst of cannon and machine-gun fire into it until it finally splashed into the Solomon Sea north of Oro Bay. As McClean continued along, studying the floating remains of his kill, seven Japanese aircraft crashed into the water around him, victims of the P-38s and P-40s fighting above him. With all that aluminum falling out of the sky, McClean decided to bug out; He landed at Dobo shortly before 10:00 A.M.

While Donnell and McClean were busy at sea level, Charles Kamphausen fumed at 20,000 feet, waiting for his engine to quit acting up. Finally, his temperature gauge climbed again, and he plunged into the fray. As he dove, a Zero spotted him and sped toward him in a 90-degree deflection pass. Kamphausen broke into him, forcing the Zero to meet him head-on. The Japanese pilot accepted the challenge, and stayed stubbornly on course. Both opened fire, and Kamphausen's concentrated fire began scoring hits at 400 yards. They continued to close, Kamphausen hosing the Zero down with steady streams of lead. Four .50s and a 20mm cannon threw out so much lead and explosives that no Japanese plane, frail as they were, could survive a full burst. Kamphausen's aimed true this time, and his bullets found the Zero's unprotected wing tank. The Zero's left wing erupted in flame as the tank ignited, throwing the stricken fighter out of control. It fell off into a dive, burning as it went, trailing a long tail of smoke and flames, and exploded just before it hit the water.

With the Zero destroyed, Kamphausen surveyed the situation. Far below, the waters in and outside of Oro Bay were littered with burning Japanese planes. Wreckage and debris peppered the surface for twenty miles around Cape War Hunt, and tendrils of smoke drifted in the air over each crash site like headstones marking a grave.

In the distance, a dogfight was still underway, so Kamphausen sped for the action, but by the time he got there, the last of the enemy planes had been shot down. Rather than heading for home at this point, he joined up with another pair of Lightnings and stalked the retreating Japanese. Flying north towards New Britain for almost 25 minutes, the trio finally overtook a small formation of Zeroes running for home on the wave tops. They dived to the attack with Kamphausen picking out a lone, dirty-green Zeke. The Japanese saw the P-38s coming and broke hard, forcing Kamphausen to take a 90-degree deflection shot. At 150 yards, he squeezed the trigger and felt the gratifying vibration of the guns through his seat. His bullets smacked home, tearing the fragile Zero apart in the blink of an eye. Flames shot out from the wing tanks, then the Zero exploded right off the water, showering the ocean with bits of debris.

Kamphausen was just about to make a pass over the wreckage, so that he could capture it on his gun camera film, when another Zero popped out of the clouds above him. He reacted to it, but his maneuvers came a split second too late. The Zero's bullets peppered his right boom and wing, and Kamphausen could feel the '38 shudder from the hits. Before things could get any worse, the other Lightnings showed up and chased the Zero off. It was a close run thing, as the Zero's accurate fire had taken out the right inter-cooler. Low on gas, and now damaged, Kamphausen called it a day and returned to Dobodura, where he landed at 9:45.

It had been a banner day for the pilots of the 9th. The eight pilots claimed ten Vals and Zeroes, fully a quarter of the attack force. The 475th also had a field day, coming home with no less than 36 victory claims. While the numbers were unintentionally inflated (there were only forty Japanese in the air), the results were clear: The Japanese had paid dearly for this attack on Oro Bay.

That night, in the comfort of the Officers' Club, Jerry relaxed with his men. They had had a wild fight that morning, and the search flight had also tangled with some Zeroes on their way home, but in both cases they had kicked the crap out of the Japanese and brought home twelve scalps for their effort. That meant twelve more red Rising Suns to add to their scoreboard mounted out in front of the club. That was cause enough to celebrate.

Jerry and his men were weary, but all except Ralph Wire, the squadron's attitude case, who was sitting sullenly by himself next to the radio and nursing an Aussie beer, were in high spirits. Tomorrow they would be on alert again, probably all day. After that, who knew? In New Guinea, the pilots lived day to day, sometimes hour by hour. One thing was for sure, though: Kenney would not give up on Rabaul. They would see Simpson Harbor for sure before the month was out.

The night wore on, and the chatter grew as the men reviewed the day's fighting. Much flying of the hands was done, as each man went through his part in the action, recounting in great detail the destruction of a Val, or a head-on pass with a Zero. A few began joking that they had actually escorted the lone remaining Val home, just to make sure he returned to Gasmata and told all of his buddies about how tough the Yanks really were. By daybreak the next morning, the stories would grow even bigger.

As they talked, their drinks were drained and new ones ordered. Though the pilots slated for duty in the morning were taking it easy at the bar, the men not scheduled to fly were under no such restrictions. Sooner or later, these nights would end in song. The men had their own term for it: Sing-Sing, a pidgin-English term picked up from the local natives. Jerry was not surprised when, from one corner of the club, a well-oiled tongue let loose with a tune. It did not take long for the song to spread through the bar as other men joined in, singing in loud and tipsy voices. Most were off-key, which they tried to compensate for with sheer volume and lustiness. Jerry sat and laughed as he recognized the squadron's favorite tune, *Bastard King of England*, an utterly filthy ditty taught to them by Aussie pilots when the outfit was stationed at Darwin back in '42.

Outside, and up on a little knoll overlooking the "O" Club, the squadron's enlisted men gathered to listen to the budding Sing-Sing. They loved the songs that the pilots sang, and would often stay out late into the night, frying fish they'd caught in the local stream as they listened and laughed.

Inside, Jerry hesitated a minute, then threw caution to the wind and joined in. He had a sweet tenor voice, groomed through long practice in church and school choirs. If his mother could only see him now, all his talent wasted on this stuff. . . .

> *Oh, we sing the song of an ancient king*
> *Of a thousand years ago*
> *Who ruled the land with an iron hand,*
> *But his mind was weak and low!*
>
> *He loved to hunt the royal stag*
> *Out in the royal wood*
> *But most of all, he was exceedingly fond*
> *Of pulling his royal pud!*

Laughs all around, as the men regaled in the song's sheer bawdiness. For a minute after the song concluded, Jerry thought about how truly crude the words were, chuckling as he did so. He supposed that had he heard it back before he joined the Air Corps, he would have been mortally offended; now, he was singing with the loudest of them. His father, the minister and lawyer, would certainly turn purple with shock and rage if he heard it, let alone Barbara, his fiancée. Had the Army changed him that much? He brooded on that, thinking back to his life in Eugene. High school, camping trips, Barbara, Jene McNeese, they all seemed so distant, so untouchable, their memories cursed by the searing reality of New Guinea and combat.

As their commander lost himself in thought, his men struck up another song,

> *Don't give me a P-38, the props, they counter-rotate*
> *They're scattered and sittin' from Burma to Britain*
> *Don't give me a P-38!*
> *No!!*

The revelry continued, but Jerry was far away.

PART ONE

Of Innocence Lost

ONE

Chrysalis

For Gerald Richard Johnson, the long path that ultimately led him to the New Guinea jungles began in Akron, Ohio in June 1920. Born to H. V. and Hazel Johnson, Gerald was the second of five children. His twin brother, Harold, beat him into the world by only a few minutes, and for years the two kidded each other about being "two minutes younger" or "two minutes older." The other children included Ralph, the next oldest; Juanita, whose auburn hair earned her the nickname, "Red," and Art, the youngest boy, who would eventually become one of the most respected attorneys in the Pacific Northwest.

Jerry's father, H. V., was a take-no-prisoners, bull-moose of a man whose towering frame and rough features belied his farming background. His huge physique, combined with a thunderous voice, could intimidate anyone, and he used both to his advantage. He could bend anyone to his will, and those who resisted, he could break. Those two features made him a powerful adversary years later in courtrooms throughout Oregon.

H. V. grew up on a farm in Owensville, Indiana. Long hours of field work had built his imposing body, and the muscles he developed stayed with him long after he had fled the land for the legal profession. Even into middle age, he retained the strength of his youth. Once, in the summer of 1935, as H. V. approached forty, he took his wife and kids to a rodeo while on their way home from a vacation in Oregon. Sometime during the show, a bull broke out of the ring and into the parking lot, where it spotted Juanita. Before Juanita could get out of the way, the beast charged her. Terrified, she took flight, running past H. V. who was sitting behind the wheel of the family's Nash. Calmly, he watched as Juanita tore by, the bull close behind and gaining. As it passed him, he leaned out the window and smashed the bull square on the snout with a vicious left jab. Stunned by the blow, the bull staggered to a stop, allowing Juanita to escape by throwing herself into the Nash through the passenger-side door. Before the bull went any further, a couple of cowboys lassoed it from behind and brought it under control.

Years before, H. V. had wanted to make a living on that arm. As a young man fresh off the family farm in Indiana, he dreamed of a baseball career. One of his brothers provided encouragement when the Yankees signed him to a contract. Though he played only for a short time, the mere fact that his own brother had made it to the major leagues infused H. V. with wild determination. He went to Akron, where he signed up to pitch for a local semi-pro club. H. V. soon learned he had nearly everything it took—heart, grit, guts, and unbridled love for the game— except pro-quality talent. It took only a few months before H. V. admitted that he did not have a big-league arm. Still, he refused to give up. Instead of quitting, he pushed himself harder, trying to compensate through sheer force of will. His will soon proved stronger than his own body. He put everything he had into every pitch, pushing himself to his physical limits and beyond. He pitched games after game, ignoring injuries and exhaustion, playing through the pain as he fought for his dream. At times, he even pitched entire doubleheaders, staying on the mound, firing his southpaw bullets over the plate until every nerve in his arm throbbed with pain. He'd walk away from those games with his arm hanging limply at his side, feeling like jelly from all the abuse. Eventually, his arm failed him and forced his retirement. He never lost his love for the game, though, and years later he reveled in coaching his sons, teaching them what he had learned in his days on the mound, chasing his major-league dreams.

With his baseball career behind him, H. V. tried higher education next. He enrolled at a small West Virginia bible college, where he studied to become a minister. Though he loved school, and his church, he never did graduate, thanks to German submarines.

In April 1917, America entered World War I. Like most young men of the age, H. V. was caught up in the patriotic outburst that the declaration of war had brought to the country. He left the classroom for the drill field, enlisting in the Army in the summer of 1917. He served for a year or so without ever getting out of the United States. When the war ended in November, 1918, he was discharged and returned to civilian life.

Fresh out of uniform, H. V. returned to Akron, where he got married and landed a job at the Firestone Tire Factory. Hours of mind-numbing labor in the factory only stoked his ambition, and soon H. V. had convinced a local judge to let him read the law under the judge's tutelage. To pay the bills, he kept working for Firestone, and spent his evenings studying Ohio law.

Hazel, his wife, watched her husband drag himself through this routine, doing whatever she could to help out. Late at night, she would stand behind her husband as he studied at the kitchen table by candlelight, ready to dash cold water on him if he nodded off. Other times, she would lay wet towels across his face to keep him awake. Whatever she could do, she would do it, and they got through this tough time in their marriage together.

The day finally came when H. V. gave notice at Firestone. A few days before, he had passed the Ohio bar exam; he was officially a lawyer now. He set up a private practice in the Akron suburb of Kenmore, and embarked on a distinguished legal career that spanned nearly half a century. He did it without ever going to law school—or even earning an undergraduate degree.

The family was happy in Kenmore. H. V.'s practice thrived, even as the family grew with the addition of Ralph, Red, and Art. In the late 1920s, he served as mayor for a term, which helped to enhance his practice and to see him through the Great Depression a few years later. The family even purchased a plot of land at a local lake, hoping to build a summer cottage there someday. On weekends they would sometimes drive down to their new land to clear brush and pick blackberries.

In the summer of 1935, the Johnsons took a vacation out west to visit H. V.'s brother Carl, who owned a farm in Yoncalla, Oregon. The lush Willamette Valley instantly attracted H. V., who found his farming roots hard to shake. He and Hazel began to talk of moving to Oregon, opening another law practice, and perhaps buying a farm. The family liked the idea, but figured it would never happen. After all, by then H. V. had become a well-established man in Kenmore. He was both respected and trusted, which helped his law practice grow despite the Depression. H. V. also served as a minister in the local First Christian Church, making the family's roots in Ohio that much deeper.

One afternoon in June 1936, H. V. returned home early from the office and announced, "Well, I've sold my law books! We're moving to

Oregon." The decision caught the entire family by surprise, but soon all looked forward to the change.

The next few weeks found the family scurrying around in preparation for the move. The house sold quickly, and H. V. turned his practice over to a friend. In August, they rented half of a railroad boxcar, stowed their belongings in it, and watched as it pulled out of the Akron station, Oregon-bound.

The next day, they were on the road, heading west in the family's Nash. On arrival in Oregon, they stayed with Carl Johnson, H. V.'s farmer brother in Yoncalla. The kids loved the farm; they played with the animals, hunted in the nearby woods, and spent hours target shooting with their .22 rifles.

While the kids played on the farm, H. V. and Hazel house-hunted in Eugene, a mill and rail town of about 20,000 located in the southern Willamette Valley. It took several weeks before they found the right one—a white four-bedroom, two-story house, with a semifinished basement and a covered front porch, one lot in from the corner of West Broadway and Jackson Street. By the time school started that fall, the family had moved their belongings up from Yoncalla, and had settled into their new home.

That fall, Jerry started his junior year at Eugene High School. At first, since they were the new kids at school, he and Harold did not make many friends. H. V. watched his boys struggle through their first month of school, and decided to try and help them out. He suggested that they try out to be the school's yell leaders—male cheerleaders. The twins agreed it was a good idea, and a few days later they were in the thick of the competition for the two open slots.

During a school assembly the final candidates led cheers and demonstrated their school spirit. When Jerry and Harold came before their classmates, they were initially greeted with lackluster applause. Undaunted, Jerry and Harold went through their practiced routines, barking out a cheer that most of the students chose not to follow.

Disappointed with their response, Jerry yelled out at them, "Hey! What's the matter? You haven't even broken your G-string yet!"

The gym erupted in laughter, and when the twins tried again, everyone cheered lustily. From that one comment, they had become school heroes. Ironically, the class misunderstood Jerry's comment. He was a violin player, and back in Kenmore, he and his orchestra friends used to wish each other luck by saying, "Go break a G-string!"

Shortly after, Jerry and Harold were voted in as yell leaders, becoming, in their two remaining years, the best ones the school ever had. During games and rallies, the boys would be in front of the home crowd, leaping and cavorting about with such infectious enthusiasm, that people fondly recalled their performances decades later.

Jerry had no trouble making friends after he became a yell leader. His gregarious personality soon replaced his initial shyness. Everyone seemed to be drawn to him and his easygoing, happy-go-lucky manner. He seemed to excel at everything he tried, and whatever he did, no matter how difficult the task, he made it look effortless. His friends always marveled at that, and his unconcerned ways.

It did not take long for Jerry to get involved in school clubs. He joined the choir, became a member of the High Y society, played in the orchestra, and joined the Pack Rats. The Pack Rats became the center of his social life through high school. They were a climbing and hiking club that got together on weekends to go on outings in the Cascade Mountains. Through the club, Jerry grew to love hiking and ice climbing, and his best friends were the ones from the club he spent his weekends with in the mountains east of Eugene.

In high school, Jerry befriended a handsome, but somewhat awkward kid named Jene McNeese. Jene's family lived around the corner from Jerry's, and the two boys were together constantly. They would hunt, fish, or hike on the weekends, hitching rides to the Cascades and back. Sometimes, when it rained heavily during the winter, they would sit in the Johnson's basement, target shooting with their .22 rifles. Jene and Jerry stayed friends all through high school, and then into college. After Jerry left for the service, Jene went to Alaska, where he worked in the heating business. Jene joined the Navy in 1944, where he served aboard the destroyer *Haynesworth.*

Jerry learned to drive late in his high school career, which unleashed a terror upon the quiet streets of Eugene. Behind the wheel, Gerald Johnson was nothing short of a menace. He loved to speed, tearing through town in his dad's car, hell-bent to make every green light between his house and the school. With speed came recklessness, which caused most of his friends to avoid riding with him whenever possible. Once, while returning from a ski trip in the Cascades, Jerry nearly wrecked a fellow Pack Rat's car. On a foolish whim, John Skillern gave Jerry the keys to his father's car, which Jerry proceeded to wring out thoroughly on the narrow, icy roads back to Eugene. At one point, with the gas tank nearly dry, Jerry sped into a roadside gas station, slammed on the brakes only as he reached the pump islands, skidding to a stop mere inches from another car on one side, and the gas pumps on the other.

In fact, Jerry was no stranger to recklessness. As a kid, he loved to perform crazy stunts on his bicycle to awe his younger brother, Art. His best stunt, which clings to Art's memory even sixty years later, involved a steep hill and no hands. Jerry would find the tallest hill around, pedal down it madly until the wind whistled in his ears and the threat of a speeding ticket became real. Then he would slide up, put his feet side by side on the seat and stand up. He'd bend over slightly, so he could still keep his fingers on the handlebars, reveling in the challenge and the danger of his stunt. At twelve, he was already living on the edge, growing ever more addicted to the adrenaline rushes his wild antics provoked. As an adult, though he had long since graduated from his beat-up Schwinn to a bright silver P-38, he never lost that love for adrenaline.

TWO

The Would-Be Dentist

Jerry and Harold graduated from high school in June of 1938. After a summer spent camping in the Cascades, hunting deer and fishing in the local rivers, they began college at Eugene's University of Oregon—the Fighting Ducks. The year before, when he submitted his application, Jerry had decided to major in pre-med, planning to go on to the Oregon Health Sciences University and study dentistry. In truth, being a dentist did not thrill Jerry—he had picked it only because a friend of the family was one and made a great deal of money at it.

Pre-med or not, Jerry really did not know what he wanted out of life as he started college. He knew that he needed an education, but he never figured out what he would do with it. Every time he considered his future, he would end up tossing out every career option he thought of. At times, he could grow quite exasperated brooding over this matter, and he would start telling anyone who asked that he planned to be a potato farmer. He was usually kidding, but at times, not having a goal to shoot for made him feel rudderless.

His dad, always a dominating figure in his life, wanted him to become a lawyer or a minister, as Harold intended. H. V. could be quite overbearing in this regard, pushing his young sons into the direction he wanted them to go, whether they objected or not.

Frustrated with his thoughts on the future, Jerry set his feelings down in his diary one day,

> I've been trying to think what I really want to do in my search for a type of work for life. I don't really care for a profession—I want to work and be outdoors. I want my training and ideas to be used, but not just to make money. I want to raise a real family and make people happy and to work from sunrise to sunset. God gave us minds and bodies to build homes and live with one another the world over, not to beat the other

fellow or to lay away a store for ourselves. I don't want a free education, or a free profession. I want to accomplish things myself so that the things I do myself may be marks that my wife and my children may be proud of.

H. V. ensured one thing: Jerry's education would not be free. H. V. helped Jerry and Harold with some of their college costs each term, but not all of them; Jerry had to work to stay in school. Since high school, he had delivered papers for the *Eugene Register Guard,* a job he continued into college. To supplement his meager paycheck from the newspaper, he picked up odd jobs: babysitting, hauling siding, or washing cars. Whatever it took, he would do it. H. V. watched him, pleased that his son was determined to do what it took to stay in school. Unfortunately, his grades never did please his father, and for three years, his GPA hovered just under a B-average.

A few weeks into his first quarter as a Duck, Jerry and his friends took a Saturday off to go picnic at Old Baldy, a butte a few miles northeast of town that had a great view of the valley. Jerry, Jene McNeese, and a few other boys bicycled out to the butte, each carrying a sack lunch and a Coke bought at the corner store for a nickel. At Old Baldy, they left their bikes at the base of a trail and began the hike to the butte's barren crest. Halfway to the top, Jerry and his friends broke for lunch amongst a pile of boulders, shaded by huge fir trees.

As it turned out, they were not alone that day. In a nearby clearing, sitting on some boulders, several local girls were eating lunch, too. While checking the girls out to see if he knew any of them, he caught sight of an unfamiliar face. She was a brunette, medium height, immaculately dressed in climbing pants and a thick blouse that gave her an outdoorsy, rugged look. Her face, though, conveyed none of that. Instead, as he watched her, he sensed she was light of heart, ready to laugh at anything, her gestures thoroughly feminine. As she talked, her dark hair bobbed around her shoulders, and he liked that small, flirtatious movement. He grew fascinated with her, watching her for the rest of the afternoon, intrigued by her contrasting qualities.

After lunch, he decided to attract her attention. Though Jerry had never been serious about any girl before, he never had any problem getting dates. Handsome and fun to be with, most of the girls he had met were captivated by him. This time, though, the tables were turned, and he did not know how to deal with it, so he spent the day making a fool of himself. He tried to show off to this brunette, dashing amongst the boulders, loudly hunting rattlesnakes. He would pause and crack a joke, making sure his voice would carry to her group of friends. When that failed, he fell back on his yell-leader training, capering about on the rocks with amazing athleticism.

It did not work; she did not even notice him. Jerry left Old Baldy that day, not sure what had gone wrong, knowing only that, for the first time, his courage had failed him. He never did get up the moxie to just go and introduce himself. Jene McNeese witnessed Jerry's spectacle, laughing to himself at the way his best friend had behaved. Finally, on the way down the butte, he confessed to Jerry that he knew one of the girls who had been eating lunch. Jerry convinced him to track down the brunette's name, and by the next day, after church, Jene had secured the information. The girl's name was Barbara Hall, and she was a student at University High School.

Armed with this information, Jerry plotted his approach. He wanted to meet Barbara more than anything, so he went to extraordinary lengths to make it happen. He borrowed his dad's car that Monday, and after classes at the university, he drove down Alder Street just as Uni High let out, looking for Barbara. He did this for over a week, without catching a single glimpse of her. Finally, one afternoon he grew tired of the game and just asked a passing kid if he knew her.

"Sure," said the boy, "But she always leaves school from the back door."

Thoroughly chagrined, Jerry swung around the back of the school just in time to see Barbara heading down the back stairs. Somehow, he screwed up the courage to introduce himself, and the two clicked immediately. They talked a good while, and Jerry escorted her through the cemetery out behind the school as she walked on home. A few days later, he asked her to a dance at the university. Though her mother was not at all pleased with the attention her daughter had drawn, Barbara was delighted to accept his invitation. She was a senior at Uni High and planned to attend the U-O in the fall of '39, intending to go on to the Oregon Health Sciences University in Portland and become a nurse.

From that one dance, a steady romance blossomed. As 1938 wound to a close, Barbara and Jerry were seeing each other almost every weekend.

They would study together, go to movies and dances, all the while having a tremendous time getting to know each other.

Barbara's mother stood by, watching the romance develop, suspicious of young Gerald Johnson, whom she considered to be "too much fun." To her, any male was a threat to her two daughters, and she never once liked any of the boys Barbara or her sister Jane brought home. Jerry, however, worried her more than most. He was so fun-loving—with his effortless charm and gentle sense of humor—that she always thought he was up to something, be it plotting mischief or figuring out how to skirt her authority. In truth, he usually was; Jerry had a puckish sense of humor, and he seemed to always be involved in some form of deviltry. Once, Jerry showed up at the Hall house in the middle of the night, scaled the front wall, and sidled along the second story roof to Barbara's window. He tapped at the glass until Barbara came to the window seat in her night clothes. Delighted to see Jerry, the two sat and talked through the open window for some time, until suddenly, Barbara's bedroom door flew open and Mrs. Hall put an end to the shenanigans. After that incident, Mrs. Hall watched Jerry even more closely.

While Jerry ran the gauntlet of Mrs. and Mr. Hall on each date, Barbara and Jerry's family got along famously. H. V., for all his imposing nature, could also be quite gregarious and charming. He soon had Barbara under his spell, and she always impressed him. When Jerry began openly talking of marriage a few years later, H. V. and Hazel could not have been happier. By the time Jerry left Eugene for the Air Corps, Barbara had practically become a member of the family.

By 1940, Jerry had developed another passion outside of Barbara: flying. Jene McNeese had learned to fly the year before, and he took Jerry up with him on a number of occasions. In fact, Jene would sometimes give Jerry lessons, though that ended after Jene let him land, and the ensuing near-crash scared the hell out of both of them. Undeterred by his horrible landing, he applied for CPTP training at the university in the fall of 1940. CPTP—Civilian Pilot Training Program—was a federally-funded course that taught thousands of young Americans to fly in the years before Pearl Harbor. CPTP was designed to create a vast reservoir of skilled pilots that could be tapped by the Navy and the Army Air Corps should war come to the United States. It worked just as planned, and after Pearl Harbor some of the best fighter pilots to emerge from the war had first learned to fly through their college's CPTP.

One of Jerry's proudest achievements came at the end of that quarter, when his pilot's license arrived in the mail. He promptly went flying whenever he could afford it, taking up friends and family with him to enjoy the ride. One of his earliest passengers was his brother Ralph's girlfriend, Kay Mallory. Kay and Ralph dated throughout 1940, their senior year in high school. One night, when Kay ate dinner at the Johnson house, Jerry asked her if she wanted to go flying. Eagerly, she accepted, captivated as she was by Jerry's natural charm.

That evening he took her up in a two-seat biplane just before sunset. The sky was tinged with red, and they flew around clouds reflecting a soft pink that gave the flight a touch of the dramatic that Kay never forgot. Kay graduated later that year, went on to college, and eventually became a reporter for the *Salem Capital Journal*. As a journalist, she had the chance to fly in everything from hot-air balloons to blimps and helicopters, but even fifty-six years later, nothing ever topped that one early evening flight with Gerald Johnson in the crimson-streaked sky over Eugene.

Eugene changed that fall. As the world erupted in chaos and bloodshed, America began preparing for war. The first peacetime draft in history was enacted, which took some of the young men from the town, sending them to remote parts of the country most had never heard of before their draft notices arrived in the mail. Others, especially at the university, decided to go in before they got drafted. By October, the number of men leaving school grew from a dribble to a steady stream.

Jerry watched the change with growing interest, especially as many friends left Eugene for the Army Air Corps. At first, he was skeptical that America would join the war in Europe, though his friends were under no such illusions. First to go was Tom Taylor, a classmate from Eugene High and the U-O. In 1943, while on a mission to Lille, France, Tom Taylor's B-26, *Dry Martini*, was attacked by Focke-Wulf 190s. One of the German fighters made a head-on pass at Taylor's Marauder, riddling the cockpit with cannon and machine gun fire. Tom took a 20mm round right in the chest and died before the copilot could fly the damaged bomber back to England.

Aaron Cuddeback, a neighbor of Barbara's, went next. He tried to enlist, but the Army rejected him because he couldn't look cross-eyed. After that, he spent weeks practicing in the mirror before going back and retaking the physical. The Air Corps accepted him the second time around. Assigned to a B-17 group just before the war, he became one of the early members of the Eighth Air Force in England. He and his crew began flying missions in early 1943, a time when the men had a one-in-three chance of seeing home again. The first missions were rough, and Aaron was awarded the Purple Heart before his fifth mission. Then, in March 1943, anti-aircraft fire crippled his Flying Fort over Hamm, Germany. He coaxed the bomber out over the sea, where he finally had to ditch it. The other crews from his bomb group saw Cuddeback's crew get into life rafts, but they were never picked up. Somewhere in the rain-swept grayness of the North Sea, Aaron and his crew drowned.

Don Good, a friend of the Johnsons who had also dated Barbara, went next. He joined the 3rd Attack Group just in time to be shipped out to Australia in the crazy weeks following Pearl Harbor. On his first mission, to Lae, New Guinea, five of the seven A-20 Havocs the 3rd Attack sent out were shot down. Good's plane and one other managed to limp back to Australia, their aircraft full of holes. Don would later be shot down in 1943, but was rescued by an American PT-boat after having lost his crew.

Dave Curtis, a neighbor and classmate of Jerry's, also joined up. He wound up flying AT-6 Texans as a training instructor for a few months after he won his wings. After the war broke out, he joined a night-fighter squadron and served in the Southwest Pacific, where he ran into Jerry in the Philippines in 1944.

Finally, it was Jerry's turn. Towards the end of fall quarter, 1940, he received a letter from the Oregon Health Sciences Institute, informing him that his application had been denied; his grades were just not good enough. Though the failure stunned him at first—he had never failed at anything before—he soon realized that dental school was a false goal anyway. He had no burning desire to be a dentist—it had been just something to shoot for while he tried to figure out what he really wanted to do with his life.

Jerry considered his future, and came to the conclusion that he wanted to fly more than anything else. He could not deny it any longer, especially now that dental school was not an option. A few days later, in November 1940, he visited the Air Corps recruiter on campus. The officer ran him through a routine physical, passed him, and signed him up. Jerry walked away with mixed emotions—excited at the prospect of becoming a military pilot, or "war pilot" as he called it, but terrified at the prospect of breaking the news to his parents and to Barbara. He had not told anyone that he wanted to join the Army, and presenting a fait accompli was going to be tough.

As he feared, when he told his parents that night, his father blew up at him. H. V. thought that joining the Army was the worst possible career move his son could make. He still clung to the hope that Jerry would come around to his way of thinking, and go to law school or become a minister. Flying for the Army did not figure into his plans for Jerry at all, and the fact that the decision had been made without his input infuriated him even more.

It took several days for the Johnson family to return to normal after Jerry broke the news, but his father eventually reconciled himself to his son's career in the Air Corps. He figured that Jerry would only be in for a few years, then afterward he could go to law school. In a few more years, his son would join the family firm. With that in mind, H. V. slowly grew quite proud of his son's military achievements before the war, thinking they were but the first steps to a legal career.

᪥

Jerry's time in Eugene swiftly came to an end midway through his junior year at the University of Oregon. At the end of 1940, he received orders to report for active duty at Vancouver Barracks, Washington on March 12, 1941. His final weeks were spent winding up his college work and preparing for his new life in the service.

Just before he left, Jerry became an Eagle Scout, and a ceremony was held in his honor. He even got his photograph in the *Register Guard,* the paper he delivered for so many years. As a result, he left Eugene on a high note, confident that his success in his adopted hometown would serve as a springboard to success in the service.

THREE

Jackpots and Dodos

On Wednesday, March 12, 1941, Jerry stood with his parents outside Vancouver Barracks, saying good-bye as gracefully as he could. His mother was not taking the impending separation well. She stood beside her son, crying openly as he tried to reassure her that he would be OK in Uncle Sam's care. Finally, just as he left to go join the other men, his father shoved $25 into his hands, and his mom added another $6. Jerry thanked them both, hugged and kissed them, and then walked into his new life.

Jerry and his new comrades spent that first day with a battery of doctors, who prodded and poked and poured over every inch of their young bodies, looking for any medical problems or physical defects that would prevent them from flying. By the end of the day, Jerry was sore and worried. He had been examined thoroughly, but had no idea if the doctors passed him. Rather than dwell on it, he and Ronald Hillman, another recruit from Eugene, went into town for dinner and a movie.

Jerry and Ronald ate breakfast in town the next morning, and then headed back to the recruiting office on the base. Word had not yet arrived from the hospital on their physicals, so Ronald went over to the dentist to have a tooth filled. Jerry just fretted, waiting for word to come. Finally, he and Ronald learned that they had both passed their physicals. They were on their way to the air.

Later that day, Jerry met another recruit named Floyd Baumgartner. Floyd had grown up in Salem, just up the road from Eugene. For the last few months, he had been working in a tuberculosis ward before deciding that he wanted to fly. As the two began chatting, they discovered they had met each other a few years before, when they were in high school.

Jerry and Harold had been up in Portland for a school function one weekend. Rather than returning with their classmates, they stayed late to catch a couple of bands. Later, they hitchhiked home. It had been

Floyd and his girlfriend who had driven them through Salem as they worked their way back down to Eugene.

Floyd and Jerry quickly grew close as they discovered they both shared the same values and many of the same outlooks on life. Jerry confided in his diary one night, "Floyd is a <u>very</u> fine boy and I know we will enjoy being together. He is an exceptionally decent, rational fellow."

For the rest of that first week in Vancouver, Floyd, Ronald, and Jerry spent their evenings in town or in Portland, going to dinner and seeing movies. The night before they left for their new assignment, Ontario, California, Jerry went out on the town. When he returned a little after midnight, he discovered some other newly-arrived cadet had taken his bunk. Miffed at the injustice of that, he took the top bunk, easing between two mattresses since he had no sheets or blankets. He didn't even bother to get out of his clothes. A few hours later, he awoke, chilled from the cool spring night, feeling grimy in his street clothes. It was still dark, but he slid off the bunk and padded along the floor of the barracks until he reached the door. Outside, he wandered about the base, chatting with some of the guards at the gate until he felt sleepy again. He spent the rest of the night huddled in a small room next to the barracks' boiler, warm but uncomfortable.

The next day, Tuesday, March 18, Jerry and Floyd climbed aboard the train that would take them to Primary Training. Earlier in the week, they had resolved to stick together as much as possible, so they shared a sleeping compartment on the trip to California. They left that morning bright and early.

About 1:30 that afternoon, the train pulled into Eugene and stopped at the station, which was just a few blocks from the Johnson home. When Jerry stepped from the Pullman and onto the platform, his folks and Barbara were there to greet him. They chatted nervously for a few minutes, giving Jerry one last time to say good-bye to his loved ones and his hometown.

The whistle blew, a conductor called out; it was time to go. He gave his mom and dad a final hug, kissed Barbara, then jogged back to the coach. His family watched him disappear inside. For H. V. and Hazel, it was an emotional moment—their first child had left the nest.

Inside, Jerry returned to his berth and opened the window. Half sitting, half standing, he leaned out the window, looking back along the rear of the train and waving to his family standing on the station platform. Next to his folks stood Barbara, who was waving anxiously, as was his mother. Soon, though, the train followed a bend in the river and he lost his view of the platform. He slumped back into his seat, excited but afraid at the same time, at the dramatic change his life had just taken. Outside, the landmarks of his youth slipped past as the train moved forward. First came the U-O, its stately buildings spread along Franklin Boulevard, then the Mill Race, which he could just make out from the window on the other side of the car from where he sat. Following along came Villard and Hilliard Streets, both of which connected with Fairmount. Jerry had used both of them to get to and from Barbara's house for nearly three years. Then all the familiar sights vanished as the locomotives pulled Jerry south.

The train pulled into Sacramento that night, and the passengers were given an hour in town. Jerry, Floyd, and a few others wandered through the neighborhood around the station, gawking at the many Chinese and Mexicans rushing about. Jerry had rarely seen anyone who was not white, so this first glimpse of California made it seem very exotic. After eating at a Chinese restaurant, complete with gold dragons and Tong symbols, they returned to the train. The next day, Wednesday, March 19, 1941, they reported for duty at Ontario. Their training had begun.

When Jerry and his fellow cadets arrived, they found the base at Ontario crude and incomplete. Construction work continued all over the base, but there few permanent buildings were finished, and no concrete sidewalks installed. The sidewalks would have been much appreciated by the cadets, as the spring rains had turned the area into a sea of mud. To help keep everyone clean, the construction crews laid out wooden planks over the waterlogged ground, so that the men could get from the barracks to the mess hall. Even so, mud clung to everything and everyone, making it that much tougher to prepare for morning inspections.

Primary Training at Ontario was run by a private aviation company, Cal Aero Academy. They were given a handsome government contract to teach cadets to fly PT-17s—graceful biplanes that were both easy to control and very forgiving of mistakes. When the class arrived that Monday, the PT-17s with their bright blue fuselages and yellow wings attracted immediate attention. The men could barely wait to get a chance to fly them.

Thursday, 4:55 A.M. Jerry lay in his cot, his three roommates snoring around him. Without warning, a shrill bugle's blast cut through the early morning air. Time to find out what the Air Corps was all about.

Jerry and his roommates dressed hurriedly in their gray-green coveralls and leather flight jackets, then assembled in the muck of the company street. Greeting them that morning was a lieutenant, who explained their situation after they had fallen in.

"You men are now Jackpots and Dodos. You will speak only when spoken to, and all I want to hear is 'Yes Sir,' 'No Sir,' and 'No Excuse, Sir!'"

The cadets stayed stock still in company formation, listening intently.

"Further, when I ask you to sound off, you will do so in the following manner: Each of you will say, 'New Flying Cadet' then state your last name, your first and middle initials, and tack a 'Sir' at the end of it. Got that?"

The company chanted out, "Yes, Sir!"

"Sound off!"

Up and down the line, the men shouted out their name. When Jerry was next, he belted out, "New Flying Cadet Johnson, G. R. SIR!" It was to become a morning ritual.

The lieutenant continued, explaining that, as Jackpots, they were to walk and march everywhere on base with their arms stiffly down at their sides. Swinging their arms was not tolerated. Further, any upperclassman they encountered had every right to haze them, especially if the harried Dodo forgot to salute, or did so improperly.

After explaining the rules, the lieutenant ran the men through fifteen minutes of calisthenics. When that routine ended, the men shuffled off to the mess hall, where the cooks served breakfast promptly at 5:30. Around the tables, the cadets wondered when they would get a chance to fly. It was the overriding topic of conversation of the morning. Unfortunately, none of them would be flying for a while.

Two hours of drill, the staple of any Army training program, followed breakfast. The men marched, countermarched, about-faced, and double-timed all over the base, tramping through the muck the spring rains had created. Two hours of that after breakfast gave some of the men a bad attitude, and complaints were heard throughout the mess hall at lunchtime. Jerry listened, but kept his mouth closed. It was a good thing, for he and his comrades were in for another two-hour drill session after lunch.

Drill mercifully ended at 3 P.M. For Jerry, marching around did not phase him a bit. He simply put his mind in neutral and followed orders as he had been taught on Oregon's Hayward Field during his ROTC days. His roommates, however, continued to gripe for the next week about all the close-order drill.

After drill the men broke up into groups to play either football or baseball. Jerry, being short and skinny, generally avoided football, so, for two hours that first full day of Army life, Jerry played baseball. After sports, the men had forty-five minutes to clean up for dinner, which was served between 5:45 and 6:00 P.M. Lights Out came at 9:00 P.M., giving the men about three hours to study or write letters home following dinner.

The next morning, after breakfast, Jerry hastily scrawled a few letters home. He wanted to write and describe what he had seen so far, and he knew he would be too tired to do anything but sleep after dinner. Today, they were going on an all-day marching fest.

Four hours of marching just about wore the men out. By 11:00 A.M., Jerry was sore and his lymph glands in his groin had swelled up. In four hours on the march, they had been granted only a couple of fifteen-minute breaks. At 11:00, though, the upper classmen released the Dodos for lunch. Jerry crowded into the mess hall and simply devoured his meal. When he finished, he was still hungry.

There was no letup in the afternoon, as they drilled for another hour before being issued their socks, shirts, and ties. By dinnertime, everyone was ready to drop with exhaustion. It had been a long day, marching and drilling in the chilly spring air. While the nearby mountains still had snow on them, the weather remained clear, so at least the men did not get rained on or snowed on during their ordeal.

After dinner, Jerry sat at his desk, barely able to lift a pen to write in his diary. Sore all over, and still famished despite eating two huge meals plus breakfast, he had just enough energy left to scrawl a few hasty lines in his diary, then perhaps head for a shower afterwards. Just as he finished his diary entry, in walked the Inspection Officer. Jerry "Popped To" then yelled, "Attention!" His roommates jumped up and went rigid, and as the IO walked among them, each man sounded off. He examined their barracks, then departed. As soon as he left, the men relaxed.

That proved to be a mistake, since a second IO stalked into their quarters just a few minutes later, catching Jerry completely by surprise.

He forgot to yell "Attention," which got his roommates in trouble for not Popping To properly. That ended the evening on a sour note, and after the second IO left, Jerry took a shower and hit the sack. It had been a long, long day.

On Friday, the cadets were lined up and given their vaccines, which made many of the men sick. Jerry's arm burned from his shots, and by early evening, he developed a fever and a bad headache. The next morning, Jerry and his roommates weathered their first S.M.I.—Saturday Morning Inspection. Jerry managed to avoid having any demerits, as his bed and living spaces were well-tended.

Later that day, after lunch, he was heading back to his quarters when someone came up behind him and covered Jerry's eyes with two, clammy hands.

"Guess who?" came a voice from behind him.

Jerry was not in the mood to play games, and this routine irked him. He still felt sick—his headache had yet to clear up, his arm was still sore, and his fever had not broken. On top of that, he was feeling particularly down that morning, probably just homesickness, since this was the first time Jerry had been away from home for any period.

"Guess who?" came the voice again. Jerry thought it had a familiar tone to it, but he could not figure out who it was. He turned around and squirmed loose from his visitor's hands. Instead of a fellow cadet, the mystery person turned out to be Howard Hall, Barbara's older brother. Jerry was so happy to see him, he gripped Howard's hand and shook and squeezed it heartily. "I could have hugged him!" Jerry later wrote to Barbara. "Instead, I nearly squeezed his hand off."

Seeing Howard, whom Jerry called Scrap Iron, cured his homesickness for a few hours. He took his old chum down to the flight line, showing him around the hangars and the aircraft while Howard busily snapped photographs of everything. Three hours later, they parted company, promising to see each other as much as possible. Since Howard was going to school at Cal Tech, he was not too far away. As it turned out, they saw each other nearly every weekend, and had it not been for Howard's friendship, Jerry might not have made it through training.

The next day was Sunday, which meant the cadets could sleep in—until 7:30. After breakfast, they were excused from duty to attend church. Jerry wound up walking all over Ontario in search of a First Christian

Church. He finally gave up, going instead to an Episcopal service, which he found boring and ritualistic. He returned to the base just in time for afternoon drill, and the usual mandatory baseball game.

And so it went for the first week of training. The men drilled until the very sight of a parade ground made them ill. They marched until they all felt flat-footed and sore, but through it all, they grew tough and hard. They also learned to respond to orders instantly.

While Jerry appreciated the need for drill, his roommates did not. Every day he sat and listened to them gripe and complain. It got so bad that Jerry grew angry and withdrawn. Finally, needing to vent, he fired off a letter to Barbara describing the situation,

> Say, honey, I can't figure these fellows out. We've been in the Army one week now and just because we drill every day, they are complaining. They say, "You can't fly an airplane with stiff muscles. We joined the Air Corps to fly. What good will this drill ever do?"
>
> That is the complaint of about 95% of the men here—I can't hardly understand them except that they don't realize the real good of drill. After all, we will be lieutenants and must be able to organize and train men. Drill and calisthenics teaches alertness and coordination, and develops senses and muscles. I really like the whole works.

Worse still for Jerry, the men in his quarters all liked to party, drinking and smoking whenever they could, which led them to brag about their sexual adventures. Jerry couldn't stand this—as the son of a minister, he emerged from the cocoon of his childhood to find himself unprepared for the fluidity of morals in the real world. In those initial days of training, he tried to measure everyone's actions by his own moral yardstick—and he found nearly everyone, save Floyd Baumgartner, wanting.

To Barbara, he wrote of his roommates,

> They're nice fellows, but have always had their own way. All three of them drink and smoke and have little moral scruples. They're talk (conversation) is very clean, however, but they're playboys.

Chained to his adolescent sense of morality, Jerry soon isolated himself from the rest of his class. He made things worse by excelling quickly in drill and the morning formation, which got him promoted to Cadet Captain before the first week had ended. Every morning, he drilled his classmates and led them through their calisthenics in the company street. He noted the grumbling this caused as he took over his new role, writing in his diary,

> Today we drilled and I was acting Cadet Captain. I'd just as soon be a minor officer—there's too many fellows who don't appreciate having one of their own classmates drilling them.

Just short of a week into training, his roommates ended up in hot water. During the afternoon football and baseball games, the three cadets sneaked away and returned to their quarters to take a nap. Unfortunately, a passing lieutenant happened to notice them sprawled out on their bunks, and gave them a thorough dressing down. He shouted and ranted until he got them in the company street, then he drilled them mercilessly for two hours. When he finally let them go, he gave each man twenty-seven demerits. It took only fifty to wash out, so the trio was in deep trouble. Jerry had to suffer through a night of more bellyaching about the Army as a result. All three figured that, if they washed out, they could go to Canada and join the R.A.F.

Jerry did not do himself any favors by siding with the lieutenant on this one. He kept silent through all their complaints, then wrote home to Barbara, venting again. The incident left him even more isolated, and helped to secure his reputation as an outcast.

It did not help that his only friend washed out during the second week. Floyd Baumgartner, a fellow Oregonian from Salem, had teamed up with Jerry during their indoctrination at Vancouver Barracks in mid-March. The two stayed together throughout their stay in Vancouver, then sat with each other on the train to Ontario. The two spent the trip chatting about their girlfriends, families, and friends, and as they got to know each other, both realized that they shared the same conservative values. Neither smoked or drank, and both were determined to remain loyal to their girls. For Jerry, Floyd was a perfect friend to help him get through the intensity of flight training.

On the morning of March 29, Jerry and his classmates eagerly assembled down at the airfield. All were excited to get into the air for the first time, and the mood on the flight line was nothing short of electric. Even the bad weather—high clouds and occasional drizzle—failed to dampen the cadets' enthusiasm. They had been divided into groups of five, each group under the direction of a flight instructor.

Jerry was scheduled to be one of the last to fly that morning; Floyd was one of the first. He went up with Mr. Walters, their instructor, who took him on a short tour of the local area. When they landed, Floyd flung back the straps, slid out of the cockpit and fell onto the tarmac, where he retched up breakfast in front of all his classmates. Clearly, Floyd and flying did not agree, though he gave it one more shot the next day. On this second flight, he returned green with airsickness again, though fortunately he did not throw up.

With a final gesture of frustration, Floyd walked unsteadily up to Jerry, announcing, "There's no damn way I'll ever get in that tin kite again!" That was the end of Floyd Baumgartner's aviation career. He washed out the next day, and Jerry never saw him again.

By the time the class got its first few minutes of flight time, they had been sent to Oxnard to ease some of the overcrowding problems at Ontario. The Oregon contingent, plus about fifty others, all went one Saturday afternoon at the end of March. When they arrived at Oxnard, they discovered that the barracks did not yet have any water lines installed, which meant that the men could not stay there. Everything was new or under construction at Oxnard, so the base was pretty torn up as construction crews hurried to finish things up.

Jerry's class ended up bedding down in the town's old high school, about twenty blocks from the new base. For the next two months, the men would sleep, live, and eat at the high school. To get to the flight line and the hangars, a Cal Aero Academy bus shuttled them back and forth every morning and afternoon. It was an awkward situation, but it did have its advantages. Most gratifying was the distinct lack of upper classmen prowling their living spaces, looking for any reason to "Jack up" the cadets. Hazing had not been particularly common at Ontario, but the Texans from the upper class could sure be obnoxious on occasion, and Jerry for one was glad to be rid of them.

Of course, the lack of annoying Texans came at a price. The high school had no hot water, so the men would emerge from their showers, teeth chattering, goose bumps covering their flesh. That took some getting used to, but it sure woke everyone up in the mornings.

In the final days of March, Jerry finally began his flight training. In between rain storms, he and his classmates were able to spend about an hour a day in the air. He loved the PT-17, finding it easy to fly, solid and forgiving. His first flight really excited him, as Jerry had never flown with more than one or two planes in the sky around him. On that first hop, though, dozens of other Stearmans flitted about all around his PT-17. This turned out to be a fact of life in Primary, and at times almost fifty planes would be in the air over the field, forcing the cadets and instructors to keep a sharp eye on the airspace around them, lest a collision occur.

On Monday, April 7, Jerry arrived on the flight line at Oxnard after spending a wonderful weekend in Los Angeles. He had gone into the city to stay with some old family friends, who took him to see Duke Ellington's band. He listened to the music, eating ice cream and drinking hot milk and enjoying himself immensely. He returned to the high school on Sunday night, exhausted but happy.

That post-weekend glow soon wore off when he stepped off the Cal Aero Academy bus and walked over to his waiting instructor. Usually, Jerry was the last of his group to fly in the mornings, but today, he checked the duty board and found his name listed first.

Mr. Walters, his instructor, came up to him and said, "Johnson, you ride with Mr. Fernald this morning."

Jerry nodded, wondering what brought on the switch as he went to go get his parachute. When he returned to the flight line, Fernald had already started the PT-17 and had it idling on the taxiway. Just before he climbed aboard, Jerry discovered the reason for the instructor switch: this flight was a check ride. Every cadet underwent periodic checks, where the instructors would make sure the students were getting the hang of flying, or developing at the desired pace. With barely three hours of air time, the check ride caught Jerry completely by surprise.

Knowing his future in the Air Corps could be on the line, he slipped into the cockpit shaking like a leaf. When he settled in, he could not find the safety straps. He twisted around looking for them, all the while under the impatient glare of Mr. Fernald, who sat in the PT-17's front seat. Finally, his hands found the straps, but as he brought them across his lap, he realized that they had not been adjusted. He wasted several more seconds playing with the straps, until they fit snugly across his body.

By that time, though, Jerry's confidence was totally blown; he was so rattled he could not do anything right. When Fernald's voice come through the Gosport tube, telling him to go ahead and taxi out to the runway, Jerry promptly took control of the PT-17 and killed the engine. For several eternally long seconds, he fiddled around in the cockpit until the engine roared back to life, all the while feeling Fernald's cold stare reflecting off the mirror mounted on the upper wing. His problems were not over, either. A few seconds later, after easing out onto the taxiway, Jerry accidentally killed the engine again. That blew whatever poise the young cadet had left, setting the stage for a terribly sloppy flight.

Jerry finally managed to get the PT-17 into the air. He was so preoccupied with taking off that he forgot the standard procedures the cadets had to follow after getting off the ground. After banking away from the field at 200 feet, Jerry kept the PT-17's nose up, and before he realized his error, he had flown himself right out of the traffic pattern. Behind him, Fernald called out through the Gosport tube, yelling at Jerry for the error.

For the next forty-five minutes, Fernald ran the young Oregonian through all the basic maneuvers: coordinated turns, Crossroad S's, and Eights. Each time Jerry executed one of these maneuvers, though, his nerves jangled and destroyed his coordination. He muddled through, but the PT-17's nose wandered all over the sky.

Jerry fouled up even at the end of the flight. After Fernald told him to land, he forgot all about the traffic pattern again and put the Stearman down on the runway improperly. Realizing what he had just done, Jerry shook his head out of frustration as he taxied back to the flight line. When he climbed out, the other four Jackpots stood nearby, watching him sympathetically. They had seen the whole performance, which made Jerry even more depressed and humiliated.

As he headed back to deposit his chute, Fernald came to Jerry and said, "You're trying too hard. Practice your maneuvers, and learn the traffic pattern, for God's sake." Without another word, Fernald flunked him.

The next morning, Walters took Jerry up in the Stearman and gave him most of the hour to practice his maneuvers. His Crossroad Eights were better this time, and his coordination had improved, mainly because he was not nearly as nervous as the day before. Still, Jerry handled the controls stiffly, which made his flying rough and unpolished. After the hour was over, he returned to Ontario, entered the traffic pattern, and landed.

When they were back on the ground, Walters patted Jerry on the shoulder and told him, "You fly safe enough and you handle the plane all right, but you don't quite have the precision we want."

That evening, Jerry returned to his quarters at the old high school to clean windows, sweep, and dust in preparation for an inspection. As he worked, he considered his future. He was damn close to washing out of flight training, and the thought of that terrified him. Yet at the same time, he had been acing all the ground school courses, including meteorology, which was a major achievement considering that a third of his class flunked the first exam. He had received a 92 percent.

No matter how well he did in ground school, it did not get him anywhere if he could not cut it at the controls of a Stearman. He loved to fly, loved that sensation of freedom that being aloft gave him. That night, he decided that if he did wash out, he'd try for bombardier's school, or go into photographic reconnaissance—anything to get a chance to stay in the air. Bombardier school sort of appealed to him, actually, as he figured he would be safer dropping bombs than flying fighters. Wartime experience was to disprove that assumption.

After inspection that night, he scrawled a couple of hasty notes to his parents, writing quickly so he could finish before Taps. He related the bad news, then went on to write,

When you fly, you're traveling at 105 mph and they want your tach to hit 1750 rpms—not 1740 or 1760—you must fly at 500 feet—not 510 or 490, or even 5 feet above or below 500.

I may be able to hit things off better and may solo Thursday. I wouldn't be surprised or disappointed if I didn't make it. I've found that it doesn't do any good to worry. Either you can fly like the Army wants it or not. I'm going to relax and just fly. If I don't make, all right, if I do, then that'll be all right too.

JACKPOTS AND DODOS   29

Of course, I think about what folks at home might think if I wash
out. I like to fly better than ever, but I feel pretty empty right now.

His roommates did not help his mood much when they greeted him
by his new nickname, Captain Eagle. A few days before, Barbara had
sent Jerry his Eagle Scout ring, which he wore with pride the day it came
in the mail. Upon seeing that, someone started calling him Eagle, which
later became Captain Eagle when Jerry started drilling the company every
morning. Though it was meant in fun, there was an underlying meanness
about the nickname that unsettled Jerry, and it reminded him that he
had yet to truly fit in.

After breakfast the next morning, Mr. Walters took him up for more
turns and maneuvers. This time, Jerry and the PT-17 seemed to click.
He put the nose right where he wanted it at all times, blowing through
his maneuvers without any of the awkwardness of the day before. He
relaxed at the controls, easing his way through Lazy Eights and coordinated turns, feeling for the first time how it was to really be a part of
the aircraft. All it took, he discovered, was to not out-think his own
natural abilities.

After the practice session, Walters sat down with Jerry and reviewed
the flight. "If you keep flying like that, Johnson," Walters said, "You
shouldn't have any trouble with your next check ride. You flew really
well today."

Those few words threw Jerry out of his gloomy mood, and he was
practically walking on air for the rest of the day. The compliment restored
his confidence completely, and the lesson he learned that day in the air—
namely, that to fly well he needed to feel the plane and lead it with his
natural coordination—turned out to be the best and most important
thing he learned in training.

Thursday the 10th of April came, but Jerry's pre-check ride jitters
did not. He practically bounded into the PT-17, eager to show Fernald
that Monday's dismal flight had been a fluke. He did just fine, staying
relaxed, not over-concentrating while remaining loose and precise on
the controls. He ran through the check list, taxied out onto the runway,
and opened the throttle. The PT-17 ran along the tarmac until Jerry
brought the nose up, lifting it into the air. This time, he remembered
the traffic pattern. He climbed out to 200 feet, leveled off at that exact

altitude, then executed a quick medium bank to the left. After turning 90 degrees, he straightened his wings out and checked the altimeter. He pegged it at 200 feet. Now that was precision! His confidence growing, he pulled the stick back just a hair, sending the Stearman into a nice steady climb to 500 feet. Behind him, Fernald smiled. The kid was learning.

After getting out of the traffic pattern, Jerry ran through the usual routine, executing Crossroad Eights and S's, coordinated turns, and following the proper procedures in the traffic pattern. He made a perfect landing at the end of the check, taxied over to the flight line, and cut the switches. Though he was dying to know how he had done, he kept calm, going through the post-flight routine with a coolness he was just beginning to develop. Finally, he flung back the safety straps and pulled himself out of the cockpit.

Behind him, Fernald pulled off his helmet and goggles, and as he did so, he saw Jerry looking up at him from the bottom wing, trying hard not to look too anxious. Fernald flashed him a big, reassuring grin, then gave him the thumbs up signal.

Jerry had made it! Bombardier school never entered his mind again.

FOUR

I Wanted Wings

Jerry made steady progress through the rest of Primary Training at Oxnard, with only one more bump along the way. Towards the end of April, he caught "checkitis" again and failed another flight evaluation. He rebounded quickly, however, knowing this time that brooding on the setback would only make things worse. He passed the second check with flying colors.

Indeed, two weeks into flight training, Jerry had become Mr. Walters's star pupil. He soloed with just 4½ hours in the PT-17, and everyone who flew with him complimented him on his pillowy, three-point landings.

As Jerry developed into a confident, accurate pilot, Walters began to trust him more and more. They got to know each other a little, and Jerry discovered that his mentor had two sons and a daughter. He had been happily married for years, something that Jerry admired, since he wanted to marry Barbara as soon as both his family and hers would consent.

One day, while out practicing in the Stearman, Jerry heard Walters's voice come through the Gosport tube, "Hey, Gerald!" he called, "Let's go see if my wife is home yet. She's been out of town for a while."

Jerry turned the controls over to his instructor, who banked away from the airfield, flying towards a subdivision a few miles away. The noise of the approaching PT-17 obviously reached the Walters's home long before the plane came into view, for Mrs. Walters came rushing out onto the back porch and stood there waving at them when they passed overhead. They buzzed the house a few times, getting lower and lower on each run, waving madly as they went by. For Jerry, that kind of low-level flying really got his blood going.

A few days after his flight over the Walters's home, Jerry wrote home to his mother describing the flying he had been doing.

In spite of all the romance you might think is here, it is all work. After roaring around for two and a half hours in the morning, you don't much care how you fly. You do coordination rolls until your sense of coordination is all shot. Then you do spins, stalls and chandelles until you think you'll go crazy. Yet none of us want our feet on the ground—we want wings to get up into the blue, a little closer to heaven.

Towards the end of April, Jerry showed up at the flying field after breakfast, ready for his next lesson, only to discover a sleek, strange-looking plane parked near one of the hangars. Naturally curious, he walked over to the plane, which turned out to be a German Messerschmitt Bf 110C, a twin engine fighter-bomber used extensively during the Battle of Britain. This particular example had been shot down in North Africa and captured by the British, who sent it on to the United States for the Air Corps to evaluate.

The story went that the 110 had been hit by a single .50-caliber bullet. The round went through the rear of the fuselage, killed the rear gunner as it passed through him, hit and killed the observer, then ricocheted off the radio equipment and struck the pilot. The pilot managed to drop his flaps and belly-land the 110 on the desert floor. It turned out to be his last act, for he died of his wound a short time later.

Jerry marveled at the construction of the Messerschmitt, taking note of its clean lines, solid construction, and powerful armament. He had heard nothing but bad things about German aircraft—that they fell apart easily and could not outperform American types. This "up close and personal" encounter with the German fighter caused him to change his perception, giving him a healthy respect for what figured to be his future enemy.

Jerry's spirits remained high during the waning days of Primary Training. His grades in ground school were outstanding, his flying impressed everyone, and he had even found a few men who respected his abstinence from smoking and drinking. One, a middle-aged major who had served in the Air Service during the First World War, really helped Jerry through the hard time he was having with his fellow cadets. He took Jerry aside one afternoon and talked to him about his own feelings on the matter.

"Gerald," he began, "I have always said if I hadn't smoked my first cigarette, I wouldn't be smoking this one now. It is a dirty, filthy habit.

As for this drinking business, leave it alone. Let those who want to drink do so, but if you don't care for it, just leave it alone and you'll be a lot better off."

With Jerry's life finally coming together in Oxnard, it seemed only natural that some sort of crisis should crop up in Eugene. It came in the form of Mrs. Hall, Barbara's extremely conservative, over-protective mother. While cleaning the house one day, she discovered one of the letters Jerry had written to Barbara a few weeks before. Rather than putting it aside for her daughter, Mrs. Hall sat down and read it. Unfortunately, Jerry had made a reference to kissing Barbara under a full moon, and when Mrs. Hall's eyes ran across those words, she erupted in anger. When Barbara came home from the university that day, Mrs. Hall confronted her. Barbara admitted to kissing Jerry, not seeing anything wrong with it, especially since they had been dating for three years.

Mrs. Hall, though, thought differently. She forbade Barbara from having any more contact with Jerry, then ended the conversation by shouting, "Now that you've kissed a boy, I don't care what happens to you!"

When Jerry found out what happened, he could not believe Mrs. Hall's reaction. He also could not believe that she would rifle through Barbara's mail. For several weeks, though, he forced himself to wait out the situation, hoping it would get better. He still wrote to Barbara regularly, but he sent the letters to Art, who delivered them to Barbara away from her house.

Finally the situation got so ridiculous that he appealed to his father for help. H. V. stood right up for his son, went over and talked with the Halls and sorted everything out. Nevertheless, there remained much ill will between Mrs. Hall and Jerry. It would crop up again and again in the coming two years, causing Barbara a great deal of pain.

A month later, at the end of May 1941, Jerry and his class graduated from Primary, and moved on to Basic Training. At first, rumors abounded as to where they were going to be sent. The class ahead of them ended up at Randolph Field, Texas, so some of the cadets expected to go there as well. Jerry, however, had heard they would be sent to Moffett Field, near San Francisco. He hoped that it was true, as his old friend Dave Curtis was stationed there as a second lieutenant. Dave had joined the Air Corps a few months before Jerry, and had already finished his training.

In fact, Curtis was an instructor now, which gave Jerry all the more reason to want to go there. He thought it would be great to have an old friend as his teacher.

Both rumors proved to be false, and the class ended up at Bakersfield, California. Hot, dusty and primitive, construction of the base was just beginning. There were almost no permanent facilities yet—no barracks, no mess hall or rec center, nothing. As a result, the men lived and ate in dirt-floored tents, which were arranged in long lines not far from the runways. Between the heat—the temperature hovered around 115 degrees—and the living conditions, Jerry and his classmates were miserable.

To beat the heat and the discomfort of living in tents, the cadets would pour out of camp en masse every weekend and head for the Motel Inn, a local spot where the men would rent rooms and relax by the pool. Jerry went there nearly every weekend, staying cool and enjoying the comforts of a real bed.

On Friday and Saturday nights, the Motel Inn could get pretty rowdy when the cadets began to drink. One night, with the liquor flowing freely, a fight broke out between a couple of tipsy pilots. Before the locals could control it, a full-fledged barroom brawl ensued, and the place was badly damaged. Among other things, somebody had managed to destroy the Inn's juke box. Fortunately, nobody was seriously hurt, though the fight caused quite a stir at the base, and many of the participants were sternly disciplined.

While the weekends were spent unwinding in Bakersfield, Jerry and his classmates continued to fly during the week. They flew new planes, gangly Vultee BT-13s, the Air Corps' newest single-engined basic trainer that soon earned the nickname, "Vultee Vibrator." The BT-13s had more power and more instruments, and with its low-wing, all-metal construction, the cadets felt like they were really beginning their military flying at last. Even more impressive were their new instructors, all of whom were Air Corps lieutenants. At Primary, their teachers had been civilian contractors, so this new change gave them much more perspective on their chosen service.

Jerry breezed through the flight training at Bakersfield without a single failed evaluation. He had conquered the cadet's worst fear, "checkitis," by relaxing and letting his flying come naturally. He went through the paces, learned cross-country navigation, more advanced aerobatics, and the use of the dizzying array of instruments now before him on the cockpit's instrument panel.

One day, while flying with another cadet named Besby "Frank" Holmes, Jerry was practicing instrument flying when he decided that he wanted to try a roll. Sitting in the back seat, Holmes did not think that was such a good idea. Jerry was under a black hood that blocked all vision from the cockpit. To attempt such a complicated maneuver, without any outside reference points, was a very tricky undertaking. But, like Jerry, Holmes was never one to refuse a challenge.

Jerry studied his instruments intently as he rolled the BT-13 over on its back. Suddenly, just as they got inverted, a terrible stench engulfed Frank in the back seat just as he heard Jerry cry out in disgust. Quickly, Frank took the controls and righted the airplane, even as the odor grew worse. What could it be?

With the wings level again, Jerry threw back the hood and opened the canopy, coughing and gagging as he did so. As it turned out, whoever had flown the plane before Jerry and Frank had used the "Relief Tube" then had forgotten to make a note of it to the ground crew. Thus, the tube had not been emptied, and when Jerry flipped the plane over, its contents rushed out and spilled all over Jerry in the front cockpit.

Thoroughly disgusted, Jerry and Frank returned to the field and landed. Later, once thoroughly scrubbed and showered, the two pilots had a good laugh over their misadventure. Frank went on to become an ace in the Solomons, where he took part in the Yamamoto assassination mission.

Relief tubes aside, Jerry soon mastered the complexities of the BT-13, unlike some of his fellow cadets. Some of them simply could not adjust, including two of Jerry's roommates from Primary, and eventually they washed out. Several others could not control their behavior on the ground during their off-duty hours, and they were also booted from the program. One of Jerry's acquaintances from Oxnard became a victim of his own sexual successes. He developed a case of gonorrhea, which he failed to hide from his superiors. He was sent to Moffett Field for treatment, and never returned.

With the ranks thinning, Jerry and the remaining pilots spent more time with their instructors. Lt. E. G. Berry was Jerry's teacher in Basic.

A good man with a thorough knowledge of the BT-13, he really loved to put Jerry through the paces when they flew together. Usually, Jerry's alertness and lightning reactions helped him to counter any of Berry's favorite tricks—like suddenly chopping the throttle, or throwing the plane into a spin without warning. Occasionally, though, Berry could catch Jerry off guard. Once, Berry dropped the BT-13's flaps 20 degrees, then firewalled the throttle. "Your airplane!" he called over the intercom, and then left Jerry to his own devices. Jerry played with the controls, trying to figure out what to do, but managed only to stall the Vultee. While trying to recover from that, the plane half-rolled and dropped into a spin. Berry laughed, took over the controls, and taught Jerry how best to deal with that situation.

By the end of Basic, Jerry had blossomed into a truly exceptional pilot, who had full confidence in his own ability. As his confidence grew, so did his willingness to try outrageous things in the air. When not under the watchful eyes of any instructor, he loved to get a little reckless with his BT-13. He became aggressive and daring, accepting any challenge that came his way in the air, be it flying under a bridge, or shining his ass over Bakersfield.

Over Bakersfield one day, Jerry and a cadet named Harry Huffman were busy practicing formation flying with their instructors, learning to stay at a constant speed and a constant distance with each other. Suddenly, Jerry's BT-13 rocketed up into the beginning of a chandelle, then snap-rolled right over Harry's Vultee. Jerry rolled right over his wingman, ending up tacked onto his opposite wing as if nothing had happened. Harry sat dumbfounded, staring at his grinning comrade, while both instructors threw back their heads and laughed.

Harry and Jerry became fast friends soon after that incident. Jerry still had some problems fitting in with his comrades, and Harry was a natural loner, so the two gravitated to each other and developed a deep, mutual respect. Harry hailed from the shadows of the Long Lake dam, just outside of Spokane, Washington. He had grown up on a farm just downstream from the dam's spillway, on a stake of land his grandfather had homesteaded at the turn of the century. Part Cherokee Indian—his grandmother was a full-blooded member of the tribe—Harry had a warrior's spirit and was always ready for a challenge. The two developed a chemistry that brought out their natural competitiveness, both on the ground and in the air. Fifty-four years later, Harry vividly recalled how he and Jerry would even get into foot races around the base to see who was the faster sprinter. They usually tied, since both were so similar physically, being on the short side at around five six, with skinny builds and short legs.

In August, Harry and Jerry, along with the rest of the class, moved on to Advanced Training at Luke Field, Arizona. The rigorous training program had thinned their ranks, but the survivors knew that if they could just hang tough for a few more months, they would be commissioned officers. Advanced Training was the last phase of their cadet days, and if they made it through, they would join an operational squadron.

Jerry survived the next few months easily, making the transition from the Vultee Vibrator to the North American AT-6 Texan without a hitch. Through more formation flying, navigation flights, and night operations, he added another ninety hours of flight time by graduation in October. When he finished training, his total flight time amounted to 211 hours and 20 minutes.

Jerry had one last brush with trouble before finishing training. In early October, a P-64 arrived at Luke Field, which the cadets were allowed to fly. Designed to be a low-cost export fighter for countries like Mexico, the P-64 was nothing more than a souped-up, armed version of the AT-6. Still, it had more power than the trainer, and that caught Jerry off guard a bit when he tried to fly it. While coming in to land at the end of his first flight, he kept the power on for too long during his final approach. He hit the runway going way too fast, causing him to bounce back into the air. The '64 waddled back into the air, nose high and shuddering on the verge of a stall. To Jerry's credit, he did not panic. Instead, he gently brought the nose down, gave it a bit more power to inch it away from stall speed, then, as he wrote later, he "painted her on in."

A few weeks later, Jerry graduated from training and received his wings and his commission as a second lieutenant. His folks, beaming with pride, came to the ceremony to take part in their son's success.

With graduation, however, came worry. Jerry and Harry fretted over where the Air Corps would post them. Both were dying to fly fighters, so they prayed they would get assigned to a pursuit squadron. They both admitted, though, that the odds were against such an assignment.

When the orders finally arrived, Jerry and Harry eagerly scanned the lists to see where they would be placed. They first noticed that about half the class became "plowbacks." Thirty-eight men, including Wally Kupfor, one of Jerry's surviving roommates, got orders to report to Minter Field at Bakersfield, where they would serve as instructors. Another forty-four stayed at Luke, also becoming instructors. Thirty more men discovered that Hawaii would be their next assignment. Going with that contingent was Darwin K. Carpenter, an acquaintance of Jerry's from Monroe, Oregon. He ended up flying B-17s during the war, winning the Silver Star for heroism under fire at the Battle of Midway. Many of the others ended up in New Guinea, flying P-39s out of Port Moresby in the darkest days of the 1942 campaign.

Harry and Jerry initially were scheduled to remain behind at Luke Field to become instructors. Their disappointment was hard to swallow, but their orders changed a short time later. Instead of staying at Luke, the Army ordered ten men, including Jerry and Harry, to join the 57th Pursuit Squadron at Paine Field, Washington.

Jerry could not have been happier. Not only was he to be a fighter jock, he would be doing it in his beloved Pacific Northwest. Light at heart, he packed his few things the next day, then followed his parents home in his new Plymouth, wondering all the way what life in a pursuit squadron would be like.

FIVE

The Green Death Squadron

After a short leave in Eugene, Jerry reported for duty at Paine Field, just outside of Seattle, on November 16, 1941. He was greeted by the squadron commander, Maj. Loring Stetson, a short, odd-looking man who attacked life at full speed, with boundless energy. Later in the war, Stets, as everyone called him, served overseas and made ace fighting the Germans as the commander of the 33rd Fighter Group. But here, before the war, Stets quickly endeared himself to his new men with his terrific sense of humor and his fun-loving outlook on life. At his heart, he was all fighter jock—play hard, fly hard, and forget the ticky-tack spit-and-polish crap. He was a pilot's pilot, a man they would follow anywhere, and in time Jerry would come to learn that Loring's leadership style always brought out the best of everyone under his command. In the 57th, Stets first proved that he was a great leader.

Jerry spent the first few days with the 57th studying the tech orders on the fighters he would soon be flying, the Curtiss P-36 Hawk and P-40 Kittyhawk. Between cram sessions and frequent rainstorms, Stets took him up in a PT-17, then in a AT-6, to see just what kind of pilot Jerry was. Satisfied at Jerry's skills, Stets let his newest pilot get flight time on the squadron's few non-fighter types while he came up the learning curve on the '36 and '40.

December 1941 brought rough weather and bad news from across the world. In Russia, the German army threatened Moscow, the heart of the Soviet Union. In the Libyan desert, Rommel was running amok, shattering the latest British offensive, code-named Crusader. Worse news came out of the Pacific, where the diplomatic relations with the Japanese continued to deteriorate.

War with Japan was imminent, or so the Army believed in those first few days of December. The 57th went on 24-hour alert status, ready to intercept any attacking planes bound for Seattle or the vital naval shipyard at Bremerton. Not that the 57th amounted to much. In the entire 54th Pursuit Group, meaning the 57th, 42nd, and 56th Pursuit Squadrons, only three P-36s and three P-40s were operational—not much of a force to repel a Japanese attack.

As tensions mounted during the first week of December, and while the men anxiously waited at the field for any news of an attack, Stetson asked for volunteers to go to "Plumb." Jerry immediately volunteered, knowing that Plumb was the code name for the Philippines. By Friday, December 5, he had settled his remaining debts, prepared to sell his car, and had all of his personal gear ready for a trans-Pacific journey. Stets gave him one last leave that weekend so that he could go home, say good-bye to his family, then go to Portland and see Barbara, who had started nursing school there in September.

Jerry left for home Saturday morning, and arrived late that afternoon. On the 7th, he went to church with his family, and while there ran into his best friend from high school, Jene McNeese. Jene gave him a hearty send-off, hugged him and wished him well. As Jerry left for Portland that afternoon, his mother pressed a small package into his hands. He opened it and discovered his mom had bought him a beautiful portable radio. Jerry carried it with him wherever he went during the next year.

While driving to Portland that Sunday, Jerry learned of the attack on Pearl Harbor. He hurried back up to Paine after a brief stop to see Barbara. When Jerry got back, Paine was in chaos. Middle-aged WPA construction workers busied themselves all over the field, digging foxholes and slit trenches to protect everyone from a bombing attack. Even the pilots of the 57th were pitching in. Jerry had time only to park his car and dump his gear in the Bachelor Officers' Quarters (BOQ), before he headed off for a long shift of digging holes and filling sandbags.

The war accelerated everything: replacement personnel started to pour in to help bring the squadron up to full strength, while occasional dribbles of new P-40s found their way to the group as well. Training became quite intense, and Jerry's leisurely study of the tech manuals came to an abrupt end when Stets ordered him to solo in the P-40. The day after Pearl Harbor, Jerry officially turned fighter pilot, riding a Kittyhawk into the sky over Paine Field, making touch-and-go landings for about an hour. Later that afternoon, he took another P-40 up over the Seattle skyline, getting the feel for the plane's characteristics. After getting some more time in it, he decided he liked the Kittyhawk, though he felt it was underpowered.

Jerry and Harry flew constantly for the next few days, getting into the air whenever the weather cleared and an available fighter was sitting on the tarmac. The pre-war restrictions on flying time, a cost-saving measure implemented years ago, were quickly forgotten as everyone tried to prepare for war. Around them, the Northwest had gone into panic mode. Slit trenches were being dug, volunteer "home guard" units were being formed, and the region's universities made plans to use their underground steam tunnels as bomb shelters, should the Japanese attack.

Caught up in all the activity, Jerry wrote home, counseling his family on what they should be doing:

> How are things in Eugene? I hope everyone is cleaning their guns and covering their windows.
>
> If you get any bombing raids, remember, always lie flat and preferably in some hole away from buildings.

Around Paine Field, the frenetic activity unleashed by Pearl Harbor continued unabated, but it started causing problems. A week after the attack, the first tragedy struck the "Green Death Squadron."

On the morning of the 14th, Jerry and Harry Huffman, who by now had become inseparable friends, took off from Paine in a pair of Kittyhawks and flew out over the Puget Sound. For two hours, they rat raced all over the sky, taking turns chasing each other in mock dogfights. They really gave those Kittyhawks a workout that day, twisting and turning, diving and Split-essing as each tried to evade the other's attacks. Finally, low on fuel, they formed up and returned home.

Over the field, both pilots spotted two odd-looking clouds of smoke at the end of one runway. They circled overhead for several minutes, watching the fire that had produced all the smoke. Then, with their fuel nearly exhausted, they used the smoke to gauge the wind and put their P-40s down on the strip.

After they had parked and deplaned, someone from the squadron told them what had happened only a few minutes before they had showed up back over the field. Some fool had ordered three P-40s to take off on a short runway, while fully loaded with gas and ammo. Weighing about 9,000 pounds in that condition, the Kittyhawks needed every inch of runway to claw their way into the air. They did not make it. Two crashed in the weeds at the end of the strip, while the other just got off the ground before running into the tree line. The P-40 cartwheeled over the treetops, exploded in flames, then tore itself apart as it tumbled through a small clearing. It came to rest, broken and battered, some 600 yards from the initial point of impact. Flames claimed all three pilots, who were charred beyond recognition as their fuel and ammo cooked off.

Just like that, Jerry had lost three friends. It was hard to take, all the more so since the trio all hailed from Portland, and Jerry felt a bond with them as fellow Oregonians. Unfortunately, it would not be the last accident in the 57th—not by a long shot.

Two days later, Phil Shriver knocked on his door at the BOQ and said, "Jerry, five of us have just been ordered to California. We leave at 11:00 tonight." Shriver and the other four men were all from Jerry's graduating class, so he spent the rest of that night rounding up the other half of his classmates, then saying their good-byes in a subdued send-off party. When they left, only Harry, Jerry, and three others remained of the original contingent from Luke Field.

Combined with the deaths of the three pilots on the 14th, the departure of those five familiar faces really cut the legs out from under Jerry. He spent the next few days fighting a strong case of the blues. He even wrote out a will, detailing exactly which of his close possessions would go to his brothers and sister, and what went to Barbara. The deaths of his comrades had shook him, made him feel mortal. The same thing would happen again a few months later in Louisiana.

That night, after writing out his will, he collapsed into his bed in the BOQ, lost in thought. He looked around him, noted his Spartan quarters, and wished he were back home on West Broadway, in his own bed. Since the war began, he had not had much time to decorate his new home, which fostered his feelings of emptiness on this night. He had put out a few photographs of Barbara and his family on his desk, and hung a raccoon tail from the light fixture, but other than that, the walls remained bare and sterile. It just served to remind him that he was a long way from home.

His mother's radio sat beside him on the night stand, and on impulse he reached over to click it on, thinking that it might ease his loneliness.

With some fiddling, he picked up a Portland station he used to listen to in Eugene. He eased back into his bed, listening to the music as he thought of home and Barbara. Abe Lyman and the Californians were singing, *Until Tomorrow, Goodnight Sweetheart*, and the melancholy words lapped over him, giving his mood a sweet but painful edge of nostalgia. Over and over he told himself that he would, sooner or later, marry Barbara, whether her mother approved or not. If he could do that, even if he died while overseas, he would be happy, knowing he had finally made her his wife.

Christmas day came, but celebrations were few as the grim news flowing out of the Pacific dampened everyone's spirits. From the Philippines to Malaya, the Japanese inflicted crushing defeats on the Americans and British. At home, blackout restrictions had doused the city lights, making the atmosphere that much more dreary.

Jerry spent Christmas on the base as aerodrome officer. He flew in the morning, but spent the rest of the day and night trudging from guardpost to guardpost, crunching through ice and slush as he checked on the sentries. A biting arctic storm had blown through the area the night before, leaving in its wake ice-covered puddles and frost on all the cars and buildings. The night was bitterly cold, and Jerry cursed, because having the duty prevented him from even having a decent dinner. After all, it was Christmas, war or no war. He hoped that the new year would bring better times.

At the end of December, the 57th moved east to Geiger Field, just outside of Spokane. For Harry, this move could not have made him happier. His new posting was just a few miles from his childhood home, and his high school sweetheart, Verla. He and Verla had dated since he had turned sixteen. Harry had been helping his father deliver some hay to Verla's farm when he had spotted her for the first time. She had made unloading the hay especially difficult, as he kept looking around for her every few seconds. A short time later, they went to a local roller rink together, which started a romance that lasted over fifty-four years.

When Harry returned to his native area in the weeks following Pearl Harbor, he proposed to Verla, and married her on January 7, 1942. They went down to the courthouse in Spokane, and were married by a justice of the peace.

The new bride and groom returned to Harry's small, off-base apartment to discover Jerry waiting for them by the door, looking like a lonely, lost puppy. Since Jerry had spent nearly every day, and most nights, with Harry since they joined the 57th, his arrival on their wedding day was not terribly unusual. Somewhat reluctantly, Harry invited him in, and the three spent the rest of the afternoon together.

After dinner, Harry and Verla began to wonder whether Jerry would leave. He had spent many nights sleeping on Harry's couch as a way to avoid the sterility of his BOQ room at Paine, and now at Geiger. When Jerry began making himself comfortable on the couch, Harry knew he had to move fast.

"Jerry, get out of here. It's my wedding night for God's sake!" he whispered to his pal.

"That's OK, just let me sleep on the couch."

"NO! I'm taking you back to the base."

Reluctantly—very reluctantly—Jerry said goodnight to Verla and let Harry drive him back to the BOQ, where he spent the rest of the evening writing in his diary. Harry went back to his apartment to his new young bride.

That night, Jerry wrote, "Have visited with the Browns and the Huffmans, they make me feel right at home in Spokane."

He might have added, even on their wedding night!

The 57th stayed in Spokane for only a few weeks. The snow and bad weather finally drove them south—far south—to Harding Field, just outside of Baton Rouge, Louisiana. There, for next four months, the squadron trained at a frenzied pace.

In Baton Rouge, Jerry again lived on base, spending his nights with the Huffmans several times a week. By this time, he had long since ceased passing judgment on his peers, and was much more popular with them as a result. His natural sense of humor came out, and his fun-loving side made everyone think he was just full of beans.

He used to avoid eating dinner on the base whenever he could by showing up at the married pilots' homes just before dinner time. His buddies were obliged to take him in and have their wives set an extra place for him at the table. It got to be a fairly routine event, and the Huffmans especially were always ready for Jerry's evening arrivals.

After a few weeks of this, the other pilots began calling Jerry a mooch, and teased him mercilessly about being a freeloader and a skinflint. Finally,

Jerry announced that he had had enough. To show his gratitude, he would take everyone out to dinner in Baton Rouge.

Jerry wasn't really a mooch, he'd just grown up in a household where guests were frequent. Nearly every week, the Johnsons would open their home to friends or family, who'd sleep on the downstairs davenports. Out on his own for the first time, Jerry assumed everyone had the same level of hospitality.

That night, six of the pilots and their dates or wives, gathered at the Huffman residence to wait for Jerry's arrival so they could go out on the town. He showed up—driving a limousine. Somehow, he had finagled a rental without a driver, a duty which he performed with relish. He showed up at the door wearing a chauffeur's hat, ushering everyone to the waiting car, playing his role to the hilt. With six couples packed in the back, Jerry and his escort for the evening, the limo was fairly bursting with fighter pilots and good-looking women.

Jerry drove on into town, looking for the restaurant where he had made reservations, when suddenly Harry yelled out, "Hey, Jerry! You're going the wrong way!"

Sure enough, he had made a wrong turn. Not wanting to waste any more time, Jerry turned the wheel hard over, sending the limo into a wild skid, then drove it right over a median. He plowed over some grass, and finally spun out on the opposite side of the street. Now going in the proper direction, he floored the gas pedal and nearly pulled everyone's back teeth out as the limo roared down the street. A few minutes later, frazzled but intact, Jerry escorted his friends into the best dinner spot in town. It took him weeks to pay off the debt incurred by that evening.

At the airfield, the squadron practiced nearly every day. By this time, the 54th Group had picked up a mish-mash of aircraft. Besides some P-40s, they had scooped up the cast-away Bell P-39 Airacobras from the 31st Fighter Group, which had left them at Paine Field when they were redeployed at the end of 1941. Amongst the P-39s were a variety of models, including a few YP-39s—pre-production types that had no business in an operational squadron. Still, they used what they had, and those YP-39s performed well for the next several months.

By this time, Jerry had made another good friend in the squadron. Early in 1942, Stets made him B Flight's commander, and one of his new charges was an older pilot named Wally Jordan, a classic hard-charger. Wally was tough, bristly, and irascible, a man who loved a good time and was always ready for a party. At twenty-six, Wally was a few years older than most of the other pilots in the 57th, and he had a good deal more experience in life. Born in San Francisco, his family moved to Denver when he was young, where they stayed until 1926, when his father abandoned his family. Looking for a new start, Wally's mom brought the family out to Long Beach, California, a city that Wally would call home for the rest of his life.

Out of high school, Wally worked various jobs, including one as a ticket taker at the Fox West Coast Theater, where he fell for one of his coworkers, Elaine. A drop-dead gorgeous brunette, she always turned heads whenever the Fox corporate execs came for previews. At the time, Elaine was trying to make it in the movies, so she hoped to convert the attention she garnered into a shot at an acting career. Unfortunately, though, despite having a beautiful face and upper body, the Fox executives never gave her a chance, since she had, as Wally put it, "A big butt and wide hips. That just didn't play in Hollywood in those days."

Wally and Elaine married a few months after the war started, but it was not more than a couple of months after their wedding that Wally realized he had made a mistake. Other than sex, they had nothing in common. He spent most of his tour with the 57th trying to figure out what to do with her.

One day, Jerry, Wally, and six other P-40 pilots were over the Mississippi River on a training flight. Jerry led the eight-ship formation, with Wally as his wingman. He stacked the Kittyhawks in a right echelon, then took them down the river and began buzzing the barges chugging along below. After a low-level pass on a barge, Jerry suddenly turned into the rest of the echelon and raced right in front of everyone. That was a bad move, since to follow him, half the pilots had to cross under their wingmen to stay in formation. With Kittyhawks going every which way, the echelon got all tangled up. The pilot on Wally's right tried to cross under him, but got too close. His propeller chopped apart Jordan's right aileron, then tore up the underside of the fuselage.

At first, Wally had no idea what had just happened. The controls felt mushy, and the Kittyhawk began to wallow. That was when he looked out over the wing and spotted the remains of his aileron fluttering in the slipstream. With damage like that, he figured it was time to bail out.

He rolled back the canopy and prepared to jump, calling on the radio to tell Jerry his condition.

Just before slipping a leg over the side of the cockpit, Wally decided he ought to give the P-40 one more chance. He began playing with the stick, and to his surprise he found that the battered plane responded sluggishly. Slowly, he wheeled the Kittyhawk around and returned to Harding Field. He landed very cautiously, having to keep the stick pushed all the way over to the left to keep the wings level.

After he parked, as Wally was busy getting out of the cockpit, Stets jumped onto the wing and looked at him. Hands on hips, he belted out, "Yeah, we don't need all these ailerons and things in these airplanes!" Together the two burst out laughing.

The squadron had a big meeting a few days later to discuss the accident. They went through the details, and all concerned learned what had gone wrong. Jerry knew he never should have cut into the formation as he had done, and while he was not disciplined for his mistake, he never made it again.

Mistakes, however, continued. While landing after a training hop one afternoon, Jerry lost control of his P-40 and ended up stuffing the nose into the runway. He wasn't hurt, but he badly bent the prop and the nose.

Landing mishaps were common with the P-40, because if the pilots did not land hot, it would stall out and ground loop. It took some practice to keep the speed up to avoid that burbling stall, and some pilots crashed several times before they learned their lessons.

Wally also had his run in with that problem after the squadron deployed to Eglin Field, Florida, for gunnery training early that spring. While coming in to land, he ran into a terrible crosswind just as he painted the Kittyhawk onto the runway. The wind blew him sideways for a second, then he overcorrected and bobbed over the other way. He wound up bouncing, weaving, and sliding all over the field, until he managed to come to a stop. Stets watched the whole thing, and when Wally climbed out of the Kittyhawk's cockpit, he went over and talked to him.

"Jordan," he said, "That was the worst landing I've ever seen in my life where somebody didn't ground loop the airplane."

Wally grinned sheepishly, thinking that at least he had held it together.

The squadron went through intense gunnery training at Eglin, using both ground targets and a towed sleeve. Against the sleeve, each pilot used different colored ammunition, so after they made their runs and the target tug dropped the sleeve on the ground, everyone could figure out just how many hits he had scored.

Jerry wanted to be the best shot in the squadron, going all out to hit that wire-mesh target. On one pass, he dove down on it, holding his fire until he could practically touch the thing. Then, he opened up with a quick burst just before breaking away from the sleeve. Unfortunately, he was too close and broke the wrong way. He flew right into the tow cable, his propeller chopping it up, then spinning one length of it around the nose and hub like a web.

He throttled back and limped home to Eglin, where he made a perfect landing. As usual, Stets was there to greet him.

"What the hell happened to you?" he demanded.

Jerry flashed him a huge grin and shot back, "Just got a little close!"

While at Eglin, the 57th often saw a B-25 squadron practicing take-offs at one of the local satellite fields. In the course of their training, some of the pilots in the 57th caught sight of a series of white lines painted across the runway the B-25s used. Nobody could figure out what they meant, so the pilots kept a lookout for the B-25 crews at the local officer's club, hoping to ask them about it. None of the bomber guys ever showed up, and the issue remained a mystery until mid-April, when those same B-25 crews launched the famous Doolittle Raid from the aircraft carrier *Hornet*. They had been practicing their short take-offs on that runway, and the white lines showed them just how much space they would have aboard the *Hornet*.

After gunnery training at Eglin, Jerry and the rest of the squadron returned to Harding Field. Harry and Jerry did not stay long though. Stets detached them to San Antonio, Texas in early April to run some experiments with an observation squadron.

Together, Jerry and Harry flew over to San Antonio in P-40s, where they met the commander of the observation and artillery spotting outfit. The CO was convinced that their little Stinson L-4 Grasshoppers could avoid any kind of interceptors, and he wanted to prove it. He figured that the nimble L-4s could duck and weave out of the way of any attacking fighter, especially since they flew so low to the ground.

During next few days, the two fighter jocks took turns making dummy gunnery runs on the L-4s, and quickly proved that the observation planes would be sitting ducks. Though more maneuverable, the L-4s were so slow that they could not get out of their own way, let alone from under the guns of an attacking Kittyhawk.

With the experiment completed, Jerry talked a couple of the spotter pilots into loaning Harry and him their Stinsons for an hour. Not completely trusting the two brash fighter pilots, the spotter guys insisted on going along. That proved to be a mistake. For an hour, Harry chased Jerry all over the place as they grab-assed at zero altitude. They wrenched those L-4s around buildings, between trees, and under power lines as they played and rat raced. Finally they set the Stinsons down in a pasture and climbed out to claim bragging rights. Behind them they left two badly-shaken spotter pilots, green with fear and motion sickness, regretting that they ever asked to come along. A few days later, Harry and Jerry returned to Harding Field.

It was not long before Harry and Jerry were immersed in their squadron's routine, flying training missions nearly every day through the latter days of April. By now, they were the old hands in the outfit, and as part of their duties they had to help train the newer replacement pilots that had been brought in to fill out the squadron's ranks.

On April 22, 1942, Harry, now a flight leader, took off from Harding in a P-40 to give one of the replacement pilots some instruction. Leading three other P-40s, they practiced various formations for a while, until Harry put them in line astern and began a steady climb towards some cloud cover. Harry passed through the cloud first, then, as he came out, felt something go wrong with the controls. He struggled with the stick, but could not get the Kittyhawk's nose to move. He was stuck in the climb and his speed was falling off. If he could not wrestle the nose down, he would soon stall.

Suddenly, Harry was slammed around in the cockpit as the P-40 was racked by a violent collision. Behind him, the greenhorn had not seen Harry slow down, and before he could react, he had rammed into his leader's tail. The rookie's prop tore through Harry's stabilizer, and hacked its way into the fuselage just behind the end of the cockpit, before the aircraft broke free of each other and fell off into spins.

It took Harry only a split second to realize his P-40 was doomed. He reached over his head and yanked the canopy jettison lever. Nothing happened. In front of him, the ground spun crazily up towards him, getting closer and closer.

Trying to stay calm, he pulled the lever again. No luck. The canopy stayed sealed shut. Harry reached for the hand crank and began pumping it madly. The canopy moved about eight inches, then jammed. Harry was trapped.

"Oh God," he cried, terrified, "Please don't let me die. Please don't let me die."

Panic welled up in him. He reached up again, grabbing the canopy's lip and pulled. It didn't move. He tried again, this time propping his feet on the instrument panel and pushing backwards with every ounce of strength he had. It wasn't enough. The canopy moved just a hair, then jammed again.

"Oh my God. Please!" desperation cracking his voice.

He yanked again. Somehow he was thrown free, but as his body was flung through the narrowly open canopy, his right foot got caught. The slipstream tore him loose, almost ripping his foot from his leg. As Harry fell away from the doomed fighter, he lost consciousness.

He came to only a few seconds later. Above him, his parachute blossomed out, and he felt the nasty jerk as it opened with a whooshing sound. He looked down to gauge how far he was from the ground, but caught sight of his foot instead. It hung limply, blood spraying out from under his ankle at such a rate that he knew he'd die of exsanguination if he did not do something about the bleeding fast. He squeezed his hands around his right thigh the rest of the way down, hoping to cut off as much circulation as he could.

Harry came down hard in a farmer's field with his parachute collapsing around him. He began working his way from under the parachute canopy, hurrying as he scrambled away from the tangle of silk. He only a had a few more minutes to make a tourniquet, for soon he would lose consciousness.

Suddenly, arms were pulling him free. He looked up, dizzy now from loss of blood, to see a teenage farm boy helping him out. The boy soon realized the severity of Harry's injury, and he did not waste any time applying a tourniquet himself. The kid saved Harry's life in those frantic few minutes. Afterward, Harry passed in and out of consciousness, remembering vaguely that an ambulance had rushed to the scene and taken him to the base hospital.

The news of Harry's accident tore through the 57th and sent everyone into a depression. They gathered together that day, waiting for news of their comrade. The next day they did the same, hoping their friend would be OK. Finally, the group's father figure, Sergeant Major Battle, came through the door. Tears welled in his eyes and unabashedly streamed across his forty-year-old cheeks as he broke the news to his boys. The doctors had amputated the foot—Harry Huffman would never fly again.

During the next few days, Sergeant-Major Battle gave the pilots daily updates on Harry's condition. One by one, the men fearfully went to visit him, but most of the time Harry was asleep or too medicated to recognize them. Eventually, Harry was moved to a hospital in New Orleans, where he could get more specialized treatment. Along with his foot injury, his right leg bone had been shattered, and doctors feared he would lose it too. Verla, still in a daze over the accident, followed her wounded husband to New Orleans, her father-in-law with her for support. She ended up spending the summer in the city, living with friends who treated her wonderfully.

Harry, though, lost his leg. More than the loss of a limb, the reality that he would never fight the Japanese, never get a chance to avenge Pearl Harbor, tormented him. He was a fighter pilot, pure to the core, and he had wanted a "crack at the Japs" more than anything else in his life. Now he would never sit in a cockpit again. The sheer injustice of it tore him apart inside; it would take years for Harry to make his peace with it.

After the operation, Jerry and some of the other pilots drove into New Orleans to see him. They came into his room, Jerry in the lead, and found Harry lying asleep, looking wan and waxen from his ordeal. They stood by, regarding him, waiting to see if he would wake up. When he did not, they crept quietly out of the room, figuring he needed all of his rest.

Jerry paused at the door, looking back at the man who had become his best friend, the man who wanted to fight for his country more than anything. He would never get that chance now, Jerry knew. And for the rest of his life, he knew Harry would feel like he missed something he was supposed to be a part of—World War II. Then, Jerry turned from the room and headed back to Harding with his friends. He never saw Harry again.

Sometime during the night, Harry awoke to a torturous scream. In the room next door lay Rynne Doggett, a buddy from the squadron. On May 18th, Rynne had crashed his P-40, and before help arrived flames had totally engulfed him. He now writhed in agony in the room next door, his flesh seared beyond hope.

"Just let me die," he screamed, his voice scratchy and broken. He coughed and gagged, then screamed again. His lungs had been burned, and every breath brought stabbing pain.

"God, let me die. Please. . . ."

Harry closed his eyes and tried not to listen, praying for his buddy's sake it would be over soon.

Rynne's screams continued.

PART TWO

Frozen Wings

SIX

The Backwater War

For the next month, Harry and Rynne remained on everyone's mind. Around them, a nasty spate of accidents continued to claim their buddies. Several more pilots from the group crashed and died, and the young guys who had only recently been in college or working a good job were at a loss how to handle it.

Frank Beagle, the 57th's accident investigation officer, and one of the better pilots in the unit, had a particularly difficult time. He gradually learned to harden himself, to contain his emotions so that he could continue to do his job. The other pilots learned it as well. The deaths of the friends were making them hard and, in a way, preparing them for the horrors of combat.

In June, the group received orders deploying them to the West Coast on temporary duty. Leaving the bulk of the ground crew behind, the pilots packed their overnight kits and flew to southern California. Following them in civilian DC-3s pressed into military service were the crew chiefs and a scattering of armorers and radio men.

The 57th Squadron deployed to San Diego's Lindberg Field, where they flew combat anti-submarine patrols along the coasts of Baja and California. The 42nd went to Los Angeles, while the 56th flew out of Santa Ana. Their stay in the sun, however, turned out to be brief. Just after they arrived, the Japanese launched their combined attack on Midway and the Aleutians. In the far north, Dutch Harbor was attacked, which prompted fears that Alaska would be next.

Suddenly, the 54th Fighter Group, now equipped with sixty-five Bell P-39 Airacobras, received orders detailing them to the "Asiatic-Pacific Theater." Not knowing exactly where they were to be sent, the squadrons all followed the group commander, Colonel P. K. Morrill, up to McClellan Field, outside of Sacramento. There they drew winter flying gear and learned they would be going to Alaska and the Eleventh Air Force.

For Jerry, the trip north in his P-39 gave him one last chance to see Barbara. Ordered to Portland, and then to Spokane, Jerry took his flight north into Oregon and over Eugene. He buzzed his family's home—really cutting the treetops on a couple of passes—then headed up to Portland. Unfortunately, his family was off having a picnic, so they missed his display, though the neighborhood talked about it for weeks afterward.

In Portland, Jerry wasted no time seeing Barbara. He caught her in the Oregon Health Sciences Institute nursing dormitory, pulled her away from her friends and broke the news to her. He was going into battle.

Then, with time running short, Jerry proposed to her. She accepted at once and gave him an old Hall family heirloom, a ruby-encrusted ring. He put it on his dog tag chain and swore that he would never take it off. He kissed her good-bye, leaving her until the morning, when he hoped to tie the knot before he continued on with the rest of the squadron.

Then Mrs. Hall stepped in and spoiled everything again. She had come up to Portland in hopes of saving her daughter from a marriage of which she did not approve. That night, in Barbara's dorm room, Mrs. Hall insisted that they delay the marriage until after Barbara graduated from nursing school. Barbara resisted, and the two disagreed terribly. Finally, worn down by her mother's persistence, Barbara relented. Before Mrs. Hall could savor her victory, though, Barbara cut her off at the knees.

"Mother, if Jerry dies before I can marry him, I will never, ever forgive you."

The next day, Jerry left Portland, buzzing Barbara's dorm room so low that witnesses said he flew between two buildings. Disappointed that he could not marry her yet, he nevertheless knew that, sooner or later, Barbara would be his wife.

Secure in that thought, he tore down the Columbia Gorge, hugging the water with his throttle wide open. A week later, he was in a combat zone.

SEVEN

Three Missions to Kiska

First Lieutenant Gerald R. Johnson spotted the convoy while it was still miles off. It was not a large one, just a friendly gunboat mothering home a couple of coastal luggers. Small, yes, but Jerry was never one to let an opportunity for some low-level hell-raising escape him.

Checking around, he saw that his squadron mates had long since left for their base at Kodiak Island, Alaska. Sure that nobody he knew would see him, he firewalled the throttle, pushed the stick over, and his Bell P-39F Airacobra plunged towards the water below.

Jerry leveled out expertly, just above the whitecaps, the P-39 going flat out. Seconds later, he spotted the convoy again, their masts peeking over the horizon. He aimed for the gunboat. It quickly filled his canopy, the superstructure well above his wave-hopping P-39. Then, with a blur, the Airacobra roared over the vessel, just barely clearing the aerials and masts while the boat's crew scattered for cover. Jerry pulled up and away, looking behind him and laughing to himself. The fun was over now. It was time to get home. Back at Kodiak Island, Jerry parked his sleek fighter among the trees alongside the runway. He cut the switches and climbed out onto the wing, wondering if anyone had seen his latest low-level stunt.

By this time, September, 1942, Jerry had quite a reputation in the 54th for wild flying, something that did not always sit well with his commanding officers. Though the 54th's new commander, Colonel Sandy McCorkle, regarded Jerry as one of his best pilots, at times the black-haired Oregonian went too far. Every now and then, McCorkle would have to rein in his wild child, tempering his enthusiasm with a little discipline. In general, the colonel hated to play the "heavy," preferring instead to let his men enjoy themselves and do their jobs with a minimum of interference. The one exception came after one pilot from the 57th augered in at Fort Richardson while slow-rolling over the airfield. The pilot dished out at the bottom of his roll, hit a tree stump, then tumbled across the field in a flaming cartwheel that spread wreckage in every direction. The accident was so horrifying that McCorkle forbade any more aerobatics below 5,000 feet. This, of course, was a rule that Jerry could not help breaking.

A half hour after his latest flight, Jerry sat on his cot, growing increasingly worried that the Navy gunboat might have reported him. He shuddered to think what would happen if he was caught again. Only a few weeks earlier, Jerry buzzed the field at Kodiak while inverted, a stunt that landed him in deep trouble with superiors. He was grounded and confined to quarters for a week. Shortly after that episode, Colonel Phineous K. Morrill, the outfit's old CO and present commander of 11th Fighter Command, called the squadron together and ordered that nobody attempt any aerobatics below 5,000 feet. Just as he finished, he looked over at Jerry and pointedly asked, "You got that, Johnson?!"

As Jerry struggled to write a letter home to Barbara, trying not to think about consequences of his latest buzz-job, his roommate Charles Griffith bounded into their quarters.

"Put that away. You won't be writing for awhile," Grif announced as he waved at the pile of stationery Jerry had stacked on his desk. Grif went on to tell Jerry that Colonel McCorkle wanted to speak with him.

Silently, he put his pen and paper away, grabbed his hat and headed to see the colonel, praying that the punishment would not be too severe. Fortunately, as Jerry saw it, McCorkle only wanted to send him into combat, not put him under house arrest again.

That night, several of the men from the 57th Fighter Squadron, 54th Fighter Group packed their gear and prepared to move out in the morning. With McCorkle in the lead, they had been temporarily assigned to the 42nd Squadron (also part of the 54th) as it moved out from Kodiak into the Aleutian Islands, in order to help fight the Japanese at Attu and Kiska.

The next morning, the pilots, Jerry included, got going. They first went to Cold Bay, where the squadron stayed for only a day before moving on to Umnak in the Aleutian chain. There, they got their first real taste of war. Though they had been in the theater for the entire summer, nobody in the 54th had yet seen an enemy plane. Finally, that was about to change.

A few days after the 42nd arrived at Umnak, the Lockheed P-38 Lightnings already based there launched a strike against Kiska Island, a Japanese-held stronghold that had been captured earlier in the summer of 1942. Jerry and a few of his friends waited down at the airstrip for the strike to return. When the fighters returned home that day, it was clear to all that Kiska was no milk run.

One P-38 zoomed low over the field, its landing gear only partially down, which Jerry captured on film with his 16mm movie camera. Coming around to land, only the P-38's nose gear had fully extended, making the landing an iffy proposition at best. Still, the Lightning pilot's luck held as he pancaked onto the strip and skidded on the plane's belly to a safe stop. After inspecting the P-38, Jerry noted in his diary, "It had some nice holes in the wings and tail. . . ."

Later that night, Jerry dwelt on those holes. It was his first encounter with a battle-damaged aircraft, and he knew that he would be thrust into harm's way any day. He worried about that, and the conditions that the Eleventh Air Force had to fight under—the aging planes, the horrible weather, the lack of resources. It set him in a maudlin mood, and he confided in his diary,

> I feel if we get through this campaign in the Aleutians that we needn't worry about anything else. The ships are getting old and worn. Almost all our flying is over the sub-zero Arctic waters. If I fall in the drink, I won't be surprised. We all know it may happen, but flying fighters is our chosen job. The Japs don't offer the danger or threat to the pilots here as this damned weather and the miles of ice cold water. . .

September 10, 1942 brought Jerry closer to battle. The 42nd Squadron moved up to the new airstrip at Adak Island, code-named "Fireplace." A few weeks before, a battalion of engineers had drained a lagoon, built a dam across the river that fed it, then flattened out the lagoon's sandy bottom. With the sand compacted, they laid PSP (pierced steel planking), which completed the runway. The strip always had a layer of wet sand underneath the PSP, which most of the pilots liked, since it helped slow them down on landing. During the frequent storms, however, the field would flood, causing all sorts of problems. Sometimes, the standing water could get up to four feet deep in the dispersal areas, forcing the base to close down.

At Adak, the men lived in tents lined up along barren hills that overlooked the airfield. McCorkle and Major Wilbur Miller, the 42nd Squadron commander, chose Jerry as their third tent mate after Miller discovered their young Oregon hot-shot had been an Eagle Scout. Both officers figured he would be able to spruce the tent up and help make it more livable, since neither knew much about "roughing it."

Jerry assessed their tent and decided that it needed a wooden-frame door to help keep the elements out at night. For the first few days after arriving on Adak, he wandered around the new base in search of lumber. Lumber, however, was scarcer than good scotch on Adak, as Jerry soon found out. It took hours of foraging before he found enough two-by-fours and plywood to make his door. As he found each new piece, he would take it to the tent and put it in a nearby pile. By the 14th, he had quite a cache of timber stacked up outside the tent. Before he could turn it all into something useful, however, duty called.

Jerry awoke in the pre-dawn hours of September 14, ready for his first combat mission. In case the Japanese got him, he wanted to say a few last words to his family, so Jerry scribbled a couple hasty sentences in his diary a few minutes before take-off. He wrote,

I'm all set to go on my first attack, and I don't feel more excited than when I go on a hunting trip at home. Now it's 5:00 am, and we'll take off as soon as it's light. If anything happens to me, I've had a pleasant life. . .

Then it was time to go. Just as dawn broke over Adak's sand and metal-matted runway, the 54th's twelve P-39s lifted from Fireplace, formed up and headed west, the rising sun silhouetting their slender forms. The target, Kiska, would be bombed by Consolidated B-24D Liberators, while four P-39s provided close escort. The other eight fighters, led by Colonel McCorkle, would sweep in low over Kiska a few minutes before the bombers arrived, suppressing anti-aircraft batteries and clearing the area of any enemy fighters.

Shortly after the rendezvous with the B-24s, McCorkle signaled his seven comrades to follow him. Together, the P-39s headed for the deck, gaining speed as they made their final approach to their target. On this mission, McCorkle chose Jerry as his wingman, for though he was troublesome at times, he was one hell of a fighter pilot.

With their Airacobras right down on the water, the men of the 54th Fighter Group went into their first battle. Kiska appeared on the horizon, and its barren hillsides soon grew large as the small formation barreled on toward the coast. Just short of "feet dry," alert Japanese anti-aircraft crews spotted the water-hugging Airacobras and unleashed a stream of tracers at them. Fiery red dashes filled the sky around McCorkle and Jerry, who swung out away from each other as they each lined up on an anti-aircraft site. McCorkle watched as Jerry unleashed all his guns, including the 37mm cannon, on his target. The Oregonian's rounds splattered all around the AA gun, tearing it and its crew to bits.

Ignoring the remaining ground fire, the colonel led his men right into the harbor, where they stumbled onto a huge Japanese submarine sitting at anchor, surrounded by a brood of midget subs. The colonel went after the big one, his deadly 37mm cannon pumping shells into the gray-black vessel. Jerry followed behind him, walking his rudder to spray the I-boat with cannon and machine gun fire. Seconds later, they were over the boat, looking for other targets, racing for the desolate hillsides around the harbor. When they hit the coast, Jerry caught sight of a cluster of buildings, which he sprayed with gunfire. When he finished his run, he spotted several Nakajima A6M2-N Rufes—the famous Zero, equipped with floats—tangling with a pair of P-38s from another outfit and some P-39s from his own squadron. Before Jerry could join the fray, though, the P-38s had collided with each other, plummeting in flames into the Arctic waters. Seconds later, Jerry's comrades Lts. Gene Arth and Winton Matthews flamed the Rufes.

Disappointed that he did not get a crack at the enemy planes, Jerry pointed his P-39 back towards Kiska proper, looking for good targets. He hugged the terrain, flew down a ravine, then alongside a hill until he rolled over a ridge and came upon a tent set up in the open. As his P-39 approached, men boiled from the tent, sprinting down the hillside. Jerry opened up, reporting later that he could, "see the fire from my guns knock them over just like a scythe."

With no other friendly planes in sight, Jerry called it a day and sped for the coast. As he reached the water, another large submarine came into view. This time, though, he held his fire, thinking that it might be a friendly. He glanced once back over his shoulder, spying the smoke and flames rising from the bowl around Kiska Harbor, then headed for home.

After landing safely at Adak, Jerry and McCorkle returned to their tent, discussing the morning's events with great interest. Suddenly, Jerry stopped cold in front of their quarters, looking around for his pile of wood. It was nowhere to be seen. While they were in action, someone had foraged his own stash. The sheer injustice of the theft struck Jerry hard. He grew angry and his dark eyes flashed cold. Without a word, he went into the tent, dumped his flight gear, checked and reloaded his pistol, then slid it into his shoulder holster.

"I'm gonna go get me my boards back," Jerry told McCorkle in an even, controlled voice. With that, he headed off into the Adak hills. He returned a few hours later, carrying his lost wood. He dumped it down next to the tent, stepped inside and stripped off his holster and Colt .45. Then he noticed McCorkle staring at him, and said simply, "Got my boards back."

Nobody ever touched Jerry's scrap wood again. By the next evening, Jerry built the door frame for his tent, and just as he intended, it helped shield them from the bitter Aleutian wind.

Eleven days later, Jerry was back in action over Kiska. Again he flew on McCorkle's wing. This time, though, instead of coming in from the east, the colonel led his men around Kiska to strike from the north. To ensure surprise, McCorkle kept the squadron right on the deck, even after they made landfall. The P-39s raced down canyons and ravines until the squadron scattered so as to approach the harbor from many different directions.

When the squadron broke up into elements, Jerry followed McCorkle off to one side: their target, the island's radar facility. As they began to line up for a strafing run, Jerry spotted a sailor running for an AA gun. He banked his wings slightly and cut loose with his machine guns, tearing the man to pieces. Seconds later, McCorkle opened fire on the radar facility, his cannon fire blowing enormous chunks out of the buildings. Then it was Jerry's turn, and his machine guns raked the smoking remains, knocking over the radar aerials and leaving them a tangle of wires and poles.

McCorkle continued on, flying to Reynard Cove in search of AA guns to suppress. Meanwhile, Jerry had been so absorbed in his attack on the radar site that he lost his element leader. Alone, he searched for targets along the coast until he spotted a P-39 circling just under a cloud. Jerry turned and climbed to join him, his P-39, which he named *Scrap-Iron,* knifing through the frigid air.

Suddenly, a float Zero popped out of the cloud's bottom and began a firing pass at another P-39. Jerry watched in horror as the Rufe's wing cannon's opened up, sending tracers arching through the sky. He steepened his climb, his engine howling as he firewalled the throttle.

Seconds later, the Rufe filled his gunsight, and his full array of .30- and .50-caliber machine guns chattered away as he pressed the trigger button on the stick. His fire tore into the float Zero, and bits of metal blew off as the machine guns did their deadly work. The Rufe staggered, its wings wobbling, then started a dive just as Jerry zoomed past it, still in a steep climb.

To keep the Rufe in sight, Jerry flipped inverted, then split-essed for another pass. By the time he came around, though, the float plane was long gone, heading for the water in a steep dive, smoke trailing behind it. Though he did not see it crash, several bomber crews who witnessed the fight later reported that the Rufe splashed into the sea just off the coast of Kiska. Though Jerry was sure he got the Rufe, he received no official confirmation.

Three days later, the 54th lost its first pilot over Kiska. Major Wilbur Miller, the commander of the 42nd Squadron, was shot down during an escort mission as he tried to protect a bomber flight from more float planes. He was last seen in his life raft, but was never picked up. The loss hit Jerry particularly hard, since Miller was one of his tent mates. That night, he sat alone, staring at Miller's belongings. He wrote in his diary:

> The tent is quiet and lonely. Over there on the table is the picture of his wife and two children. He was fortunate to have a family. Many of us will die and not even have wives. There is his slouch hat and corncob pipe, and his harmonica. Seems like he should be here.

October 1, 1942, a time to avenge Miller's death. Jerry, Art Rice, and two other men from the group were ordered to escort another B-24 strike to Kiska. A flight of P-40s was also supposed to cover the bombers, but en route to Kiska they all aborted, leaving just four Airacobras to shepherd the vulnerable Liberators.

The small formation continued on to Kiska at 16,500 feet, flying through scattered clouds. Just before the bombers began their run over the harbor, Jerry spotted a glint of sunlight on the canopy of a Japanese fighter, which he called out on the radio. The formation watched the lone plane, but it veered well clear of the Americans, so the bomb run was completed without interception.

The quartet of Airacobras weaved protectively over the B-24s, keeping their airspeed between 250 and 300 mph as the pilots scanned the skies for any other intruders. From his perch, Jerry watched the bomb run, keeping one eye on the sky around him, and one eye on the explosions walking along Kiska's docks and harbor facilities. The Liberators had really plastered the target this time, much to everyone's satisfaction.

The Americans turned for home, unhindered save for scattered anti-aircraft fire. Jerry and his comrades ignored the ugly black smears, reasoning, "By the time you see them (the bursts), they are harmless." On the way out, though, that lone Rufe decided to make a run at the last box of Liberators. Jerry's earphones crackled with a call for help from a distraught bomber crew. He searched the sky below him until he found the Rufe, already beginning a firing pass at the B-24.

Quickly, Jerry rocked his wings to signal his wingman, Lieutenant Malcolm Moss, then rolled *Scrap-Iron* on its side and turned towards the Japanese fighter. He reached it just after the Rufe finished a gunnery pass on a Liberator from dead astern. It started climbing over the B-24 it had singled out, getting ready to make another pass. That was when Jerry and Moss swept down on it, catching the Japanese pilot by surprise. Jerry opened on with all his guns at long range, hoping to scare the Rufe away from the bomber, but his guns fired only a split-second burst before all seven jammed. His guns had frozen in the bitter cold over Kiska!

Still, Jerry kept his P-39 pointed at the Rufe, which he briefly considered ramming. Instead, he blazed past his target, passing so close he could clearly see the Japanese pilot in the cockpit. He banked away from the Rufe, a mistake that allowed it to take a snap shot at him. Tracer rounds zipped by, just off either wing, and one round put a hole in his propeller blade just above cockpit level.

With the Rufe behind, Jerry pulled up and tried to disengage so he could try and get his guns working. The Japanese pilot stayed on his tail, climbing after him as Jerry charged and recharged his guns. When the Rufe started to gain on him, he turned into it, forcing a head-on pass. As the two planes tore at each other, Jerry prayed that his guns would work. Later, he wrote, "It was a funny feeling 'cause I didn't know if my guns were going to fire."

The Rufe quickly came into range, and Jerry jammed his entire hand down on the trigger. His four .30-calibers barked in reply, sending out a stream of bullets that ripped into the Rufe's cowling and wings. Simultaneously, the Japanese pilot opened up as well, his tracers filling the sky around the P-39. Neither pilot would break, and the planes hurtled towards each other on a collision course, each one spitting tracers at the other.

Finally, just a split second before impact, Jerry shoved the stick forward and plunged beneath the float plane. As he did, he looked back over his shoulder to see the Rufe spiraling down, a long tongue of smoke and flame trailing behind it. Lieutenant Moss's voice filled Jerry's earphones, "You got the son of a bitch, Johnson! Let's go home!" Far below, the Rufe plummeted into the sea.

Like his first encounter, Jerry received no official confirmation of this kill, though newspapers back in the States reported the victory. Exactly what the issue was with this kill is not clear. To have one officially credited generally required a witness to the plane's demise, or gun camera footage showing its destruction. In a series of 1996 interviews, Colonel Sandy McCorkle, Jerry's group commander, said that he did not remember Johnson ever claiming a victory in the Aleutians. It could be that Jerry never filed the necessary paperwork, or that the paperwork was lost. Usually, after a mission in which enemy aircraft were encountered, USAAF pilots filled out a brief statement, which in the Pacific was called an Individual Combat Report. No such statements exist in the 54th Fighter Group records for any of the unit's combat missions, so the question of Jerry's two claims over Kiska, and why they weren't officially credited, will remain a mystery. Official or not, he was convinced he had two kills and the Stateside papers related the story of the two air battles. For the next three years, the Japanese flags on the side of his aircraft would always be two greater than his official score.

Bad weather hampered the Eleventh Air Force for the next few weeks. A few strikes were made against Kiska but, more often than not, the weather forced the fighters to abort. Jerry flew no further combat in the Aleutians as a result.

October 16, 1942 would be a day the entire outfit remembered, though not because it went into combat. That morning, the pilots gathered down at the Alert Tent, waiting for word to intercept any Japanese snoopers sent Adak's way. Bored and frustrated by the frequent willywaws that dumped sleet and snow on their tents and turned their strip back into a lagoon, the men were going stir-crazy from lack of flying, and the waiting made things even worse.

That's when Lt. Bob Neal decided to play Russian Roulette. From his shoulder holster, he drew out his .38 revolver, pulled out all but one shell, then spun the barrel. Gun to his head, he pulled the trigger. Click. That attracted some attention, and soon most of the pilots in the tent were watching him.

He spun the barrel. Click. Once more. He pulled the trigger and blew his head off right in front of all his friends. The tent erupted in chaos as bits of brain and blood splattered everyone nearby.

Jerry left for the States a few days later, that incident his last bitter memory of Adak and his first combat tour.

PART THREE

Jungle Wings

EIGHT

New Guinea Dog Days

In late October, Jerry returned to Harding Field, ahead of many of his comrades who had remained in Alaska. His reunion with the 54th's ground crew proved brief; the next day, he received orders sending him to the Fighter Command School at Orlando, Florida.

Jerry arrived in Orlando just as Harry Huffman finished up his course work there. Though the two were at the school together for a couple of days at the end of October, they never ran into each other. Harry left for his new assignment as a fighter control officer in Seattle before the two could meet. In fact, Harry did not even know that Jerry went to the school until 1996.

Jerry remained in Orlando for the next few months, learning the intricacies of directing friendly fighters onto hostile radar blips. Though he enjoyed the work and found it very interesting, he did not get to fly nearly as much as he wanted. When he graduated in December, he looked forward to returning to his fighter squadron.

After a short leave to Eugene, Jerry rejoined the 54th Group at Harding. McCorkle and the rest of the men had only recently returned from Alaska, so the entire outfit was at last reunited. As it turned out, Jerry would not be with the 54th much longer. In January, Colonel McCorkle had received a request for several P-38-qualified pilots who were to be sent to the South Pacific. In some cases group commanders used such requests to off-load their problem cases; McCorkle did nothing of the sort. Although he had no men with time in Lightnings, he selected four of his best pilots for the duty. Among them was First Lieutenant Gerald R. Johnson. McCorkle could not have made a better choice. Of the four pilots he chose, three scored at least five kills and became aces.

At first, Wally Jordan was not on the list to go with Jerry and the others. The thought of mucking around the ZI (Zone of the Interior, or continental U.S.) while his buddies were in the thick of things overseas nearly drove Wally crazy. He wanted to be where the action was and, through a bit of subterfuge, finally got his way. One of the other pilots McCorkle had chosen for the duty had recently married. He had no interest in seeing combat now that he had a young bride, so he and Wally swapped Form 5s and switched places.

That was how Wally Jordan, Gerald Johnson, and Thomas McGuire Jr. all ended up in the Southwest Pacific. After a month-long stay with the 329th Fighter Group in California, where they learned to fly the P-38, the men, less Ed Baulch who was McCorkle's fourth choice, climbed aboard a converted B-24 Liberator at Hamilton Field to begin the long journey into combat.

The trio arrived at Archer Field in Australia at the end of March 1943, and from there they were sent to a backwater hellhole called Camp Muckley. It did not take long for Jerry and his friends to detest the place and its officers thoroughly. The base was run with a by-the-book-approach that was light on intelligent thought and heavy on obnoxious discipline. For three combat veterans, used to the lax approach to regulations, dress, and discipline, the atmosphere at Muckley could not have been more stifling. Unfortunately, they could only wait it out, spending the month hoping their new orders would come through.

Whenever possible, Jerry fled the base in the afternoons. Early during his stay, he ran across two young twin boys, who must have reminded him of the way Harold and he used to be together back in Eugene. He struck up a conversation with the lads, and he soon had their rapt attention as he told them of his exploits in the sky. He ended up springing for ice cream, then helped the twins repair their bikes, both of which had flat tires. Toward sunset, he said farewell to his new young friends and trudged back to camp, where the martinets awaited. Though only a brief interlude, Jerry's afternoon with those twins helped break up the boredom and monotony of Camp Muckley.

A few nights later, towards the end of their stay there, Wally Jordan broke down and opened a quart of Yellowstone sour mash bourbon that he had squirreled away back in Santa Ana and smuggled in from the States. Together, he, McGuire and Jerry polished that bottle off as they chewed the fat into the long hours of the night. They laughed over the sign in the O Club at Fort George Wright, which the group found waiting for them after they arrived in Anchorage back in June 1942.

Bemused, they had stood at the bar staring at it, reading the words, "All Air Corps Colonels Can't Drink Unless Accompanied By Their Parents."

They teased each other light-heartedly, giving McGuire hell for his infamous brush with a flock of gritty Russian ferry pilots. Back in Nome, McGuire and the 56th watched as hundreds of P-39s were flown into Siberia as part of America's Lend-Lease arrangement with Stalin. The Russians would come to pick up the fighters, sometimes spending a day or two in the area while waiting for decent flying weather. One night, McGuire began storming around, claiming that he could outdrink any "Damn Commie" who dared to take him on. The Russians took him up on his offer, and promptly drank him under the table with vodka that they had brought over from the Motherland.

McGuire laughed off the harassment, then turned back to talking shop. He complained that since the 56th stayed at Nome during their whole deployment, the closest he had come to combat was when a local tavern keeper irritated one of McGuire's buddies. The offended pilot pulled out his Colt .45 pistol and sprayed the bar with gunfire. That night the three men bonded in a way that solidified their friendships for life. Fifty years later, Wally Jordan remembered that night very vividly as one of the best he spent with Jerry and Tommy during the entire war.

A few days later, the pilots got their revenge on Camp Muckley's harassing officers. As part of the daily routine, they had ordered, the camp's inhabitants had to undergo morning calisthenics—just like the regimen Jerry underwent as a cadet. Each morning Wally, Jerry, and Tommy would gather for the ritual, going through the motions, griping all the way. One day, several of the camp's officers decided to join the pilots in their morning exercise. They happened to choose the day that Jerry was leading the calisthenics, which turned out to be a bad move. Jerry picked up the pace and ran his group through a ferocious series of exercises that left Muckley's pests panting for breath. Revenge exacted, Jerry, Wally, and Tommy left for New Guinea a few days later.

❧

Dobodura, New Guinea, April, 1943. Around them, Jerry, Wally, and Tommy saw an airstrip at war. The packed-earth runway, dusty as it may have been, was wide and long, hacked straight out of the jungle. Scattered around the field, connected by a snakelike series of taxiways, were revetments that housed everything from P-38s to B-26s and A-20 Havocs. P-40s, P-39s, a scattering of Aussie Wirraways, a Beaufighter or two, and some C-47 "Gooney Birds" with men unloading supplies from their bellies completed the scene. For the three Alaska vets, this was where the action was.

They reported for duty with the 9th Fighter Squadron. Known as the "Flying Knights," the 9th had been in the Southwest Pacific theater for over a year. The squadron, along with the rest of the 49th Fighter Group, arrived in Australia shortly after the outbreak of the war, and was greeted with a scene of unimaginable chaos. Orders were lost or countermanded, parts, planes, and personnel arrived, and then disappeared, apparently at random. Nobody seemed to know what to do with them, or where to put them. Finally, after a number of moves, the 9th ended up at Darwin in the spring of 1942 to defend that battered port from further Japanese attack.

Through that spring and on into the summer, the 9th had battled hard, giving much worse than they got. Even postwar Japanese accounts give grudging credit to the defense put up by the 9th, a defense that cost the Emperor some of his finest Navy pilots. As the Darwin situation stabilized, another crisis erupted, this time in New Guinea. With Port Moresby under constant air attack, a crackerjack unit was needed to help stem the tide. The Airacobras of the 8th Fighter Group stood alone in the skies over that vital base, fighting the increasing formations of Betties and Zeroes with tenacity born of desperation. Still, the Airacobra proved no match for the nimble Zero, and the 8th suffered a steady stream of losses. One pilot later recalled, "We got our asses kicked." Enter the 49th Fighter Group. Equipped with rugged P-40 Tomahawks, most of the outfit's pilots were blooded combat veterans. Some of the group's men had escaped from the Philippines or the disaster in Java, and had attached themselves to the 49th to avenge those defeats.

They did not have long to wait. Through the fall of 1942 and into early 1943, the 49th helped to defend the fragile Allied toehold on New Guinea. They flew constant intercepts, making quick passes at Japanese bombers as they did their best to dodge the Zero fighter escort. Again, the group exacted a heavy toll, but suffered their share of losses as well.

When the three Alaska vets arrived in April 1943, the 49th had a sterling reputation, and the 9th was considered the elite outfit in the Fifth Air Force. Recently reequipped with Lockheed P-38 Lightnings, the Flying Knights could at last meet the Japanese on more than equal terms. Fast, rugged, and surprisingly maneuverable for a twin-engined fighter, the P-38 had long ago earned the undying loyalty of its pilots. They loved its powerful armament—four .50-caliber and a 20mm cannon in the nose—and its rugged construction. The second engine was just icing on the cake, since losing one did not mean that they would end up in the drink or some unexplored jungle hell hole. The P-38 flew well on one engine and could get them home, an advantage envied throughout the theater by the P-39 and P-40 pilots with their single liquid-cooled Allisons.

The three Alaska vets soon became known as the "Eskimos" by the squadron's old hands. At first, their arrival engendered some resentment, since all three were first lieutenants. Promotions in the squadron were hard to come by, and the 2nd looies who had been breaking their tails for months in the squalid conditions at Dobo could not believe what HQ had sent their way. With three new first lieutenants, fresh from the States, they would never get promoted. That resentment lasted only until Jerry and Wally began talking about Kiska, the weather, and the "Japs" up there. As word spread through the squadron that they had been in action and had scalps to their credit, the tension disappeared and the men were welcomed into their tight weave of friendships.

As the old hands of the 9th soon found out, 5th Fighter Command had sent them three true characters. Jerry blossomed here in the front lines of the South Pacific air war. He chatted and joked, pulled pranks, and soon became quite confident, and even developed a little swagger. Since he kept volunteering for missions, sometimes flying three times a day, his newfound friends christened him with the nickname, "Johnny Eager," which was eventually shortened to just "Johnny."

Jerry's easygoing and unabashed nature soon endeared him to the men in the squadron. Even more endearing were some of the young Oregonian's idiosyncrasies, which caused quite a stir around camp when first displayed. To the amused shock of his tentmates, Jerry did not have a self-conscious bone in his body when it came to trotting between the showers and their quarters. Most of the guys would hike on over to the showers (upturned 50-gallon drums) with their towels wrapped tightly around their waists in an almost comical sense of prudishness. Jerry, on the other hand, would strip down bare, throw his towel over his shoulder, then march out into the blazing sun in all his glory, unconcerned by the stares of astonishment that he attracted as he went.

Tommy McGuire proved to be an even wilder sort. Full of nervous energy, he just could not sit still; he would be up, scooting around from place to place, words spilling from his mouth at a torrential rate, carrying on conversations with two or three guys simultaneously. In fact, Tommy turned off some of his comrades; he could be tough, abrasive, and obsessively stubborn at times, which contrasted starkly with Jerry's fun-loving and mischievous nature. At times, Tommy grated on people's nerves like sandpaper; worse still, his flying needed work. When he first joined the outfit, his energy and aggressiveness made him an erratic pilot. Once he settled down, though, he was a tiger in the air. That took some time, however, and it was not until Tommy was transferred to the 475th Fighter Group that he really developed into an outstanding pilot.

While Jerry usually did not drink much, and was far more mellow than Wally Jordan, the two pilots did have some common qualities. Wally was tough in a jagged sort of way, whereas Jerry was resolute. Wally has been described as irascible, while Jerry was fun-loving and diplomatic. Like Jerry, though, Wally was pure fighter pilot—aggressive, determined, and unafraid of the "Nips." Thoroughly unflappable, Wally could be as quick with a one-liner in the O Club as he was at escaping from a belly-landed fighter. Like McGuire, he turned some people off, such as one of the squadron's old hands named "Jump" O'Neil. O'Neil watched with chagrin as Wally beat him to Captain, something that Jump thought he deserved more than Wally did. After that, he would always address Wally as "Captain" in a sneering, almost derisive tone. "I don't know what that guy's problem was. . . ," recalled Wally years later.

❧

When Jerry first arrived at Dobo in April, 1943, the 9th Fighter Squadron had some serious problems. P-38s were in short supply, thanks to the fact that the Fifth Air Force remained at the bottom of Hap Arnold's priority list back in Washington. Though the Fifth's commander, Lieutenant General George C. Kenney, fired off message after message pleading for planes, parts, personnel, and reinforcements, his cries went largely unheard. Every now and then, Arnold would mollify Kenney by sending him a new batch of planes, or a new fighter group, and the thin trickle of equipment dribbling into Australia from the States would, for a short time, become a torrent. All too soon, though, the pipeline would dry up again, and the Fifth would be right back in the same desperate position.

For the 9th, this meant that getting replacement Lightnings tended to be a real headache, and the squadron remained underequipped throughout that spring. Supposedly allotted twenty-five aircraft, the Knights usually had around twenty Lightnings on hand, with many of those unserviceable. By mid-April, the squadron had a polyglot collection of aircraft: old P-38Fs cast-off from other units, early P-38Gs, and some newer G-15 models filled out the roster. The latest G variant proved to be a pain for the ground crews, as their tachometers failed at an alarming rate, and spares were nearly impossible to come by. The tach in the G-15 model was different from all of the other P-38 versions, which further complicated the logistics problem.

Despite these obstacles, the ground crews performed miracles. They worked out in the open through the long, dangerous New Guinea nights, replacing engines, repairing battle damage, checking hydraulic systems and such, keeping the Lightnings in the best shape possible, given the rugged conditions and spare parts problems. For the ground crew, their day began at first light when they drove down to the revetments to pre-flight the fighters for the morning missions. Usually, the crew chiefs would stick by the planes to help strap in the pilots and see them off. Work continued throughout the day, as the men labored away on any unserviceable P-38s. Only after dark would they return to the camp area for some quick chow—their first since breakfast—then they would shower or bathe in the local stream. Cleaned up and fed, their day was not over. If any planes needed work, the men would head back down to the revetments to labor on the Lightnings again, this time under portable lights run from a generator. Whenever an air attack occurred, which was frequent during those long spring nights in 1943, the lights would be doused and the men would run for cover.

Despite the dirt and dust which seemed to clog everything, despite the air attacks, the battle damage, the landing accidents, the spare parts situation, the weather and the primitive facilities at Dobo, the Flying

Knights maintained a serviceability rate of almost 85 percent. Harley Yates, the squadron's staff sergeant, recalled that the biggest problem the ground crew faced came from battle damage and accidents. For a squadron at war in the middle of a jungle 6,000 miles from home, keeping 85 percent of the birds up and running was nothing short of extraordinary.

Life at Dobo kaleidoscoped into a mix of long patches of boredom dotted with even longer stretches of back-breaking work, punctuated by moments of horror when one pilot or another crashed and burned on takeoff or landing. Seeing a friend, either from the 49th or from a neighboring unit, die in such a manner was never easy to take, but it was a part of the daily life of the squadron. The Japanese threw nighttime nuisance raids into the equation, just to add a little spice of terror into the lives of the Americans at Dobo. When darkness came and the pilots had retired to camp for the night, the Washing Machine Charlies would sneak out from their bases at Lae or Madang or Gasmata. They would drone back and forth over Dobo for hours, dropping a bomb or two at a time at whatever targets that they could find. Though the raids did little actual damage, they gave the Flying Knights many sleepless nights in the muddy, bug-infested slit trenches scattered about the living area. To compound matters, the flak gunners nearby would bang away liberally throughout the night, making at least as much noise as the falling bombs. Though the gunners tried, and the squadron later attempted night intercepts, bringing down one of these nocturnal pests remained an elusive prospect at best.

All of that could be dealt with, had it not been for the microbes and bacteria that attacked the Flying Knights as ferociously as the Japanese did. Disease remained a constant problem for the squadron, with dysentery being the most common. Between the poor food and the unhygienic conditions, diarrhea became nearly a daily fact of life. It debilitated the men, broke down their resistance, and dehydrated them under the burning New Guinea sun. Most of the men, slim and in their prime to begin with, saw their weight plummet in New Guinea. Some lost 20 percent of their body weight, turning their lean, muscled frames into emaciated shadows. For some, the return home, as anticipated as it was, turned into a trial as their medical examination turned up all sorts of problems that required extensive hospital stays. As Blev Lewelling, one of the 9th's great characters, recalled in 1992, "I came home with every jungle disease known to man, and then some."

❧

The next three months were hell on Jerry. It was not the hot, humid days that caused sweat to seep from every pore, or the terrible food, or the bouts with dysentery, or even the mud-spattered, squalid little tent that he called home. Instead, it was lack of action. Although he flew nearly every other day, sat in the Alert Tent with the other pilots and flew whenever a plot was called in, he missed every big fight that spring. Determined to see the Japanese, he volunteered for every mission that the squadron commanding officer, Major Sid Woods, would let him fly. Still, no joy—the bad luck dogged him, taunted him. At one point in mid-May, he flew three missions on the 13th, and three more on the 15th, all without sighting an enemy plane. On the 14th, his day off, the 9th ran into a host of Betties and Zeroes thirty miles northeast of Buna. The squadron claimed four kills that day, including a recon plane winged by Lt. Martin Alger.

Jerry was a victim of circumstance, a fact that caused him deep frustration during those early weeks at Dobo. Despite the dozens of missions flown by the squadron during May 1943, the enemy was rarely seen. The hours spent on alert duty usually brought forth an interception that bore no fruit. Once airborne, the P-38s would quickly run down the incoming bogey, only to discover that the target was a meandering PBY or a B-24 with its IFF shot out. In the squadron's Weekly Status Report, the phrase, "Nil Enemy Sightings" fills entire pages, giving mute testimony to the frustration the entire squadron must have felt. Between May 1 and June 11, the squadron engaged the Japanese only on May 14th.

The 9th's infrequent brushes with the enemy during daylight hours were not uncommon in New Guinea. Some of the pilots assigned to the Fifth Air Force never once caught sight of the Japanese, let alone managed to get a Zero in their sights. Aces are made by opportunity, and in New Guinea, it was either feast or famine, and if a pilot happened to arrive during a lull, he could conceivable return home empty-handed, though with a full retinue of missions to his credit.

For Jerry, Wally, and Tommy McGuire, though, the famine of spring would soon give way to a wild and busy summer, one that would establish all three pilots as among the best in the 5th Fighter Command, while at the same time securing their place in the history of General Kenney's air force.

June came, and for Jerry it did not seem to bring with it a change of his luck. He missed a big fight on June 12th, when the squadron flew over to Jackson Drome at Port Moresby to escort a dozen C-47s to Bena Bena. Usually, covering a transport mission was dull duty with little chance of action. This time was different, however, as the squadron ran head-on into a flight of Nakajima Ki-43 Oscars right near the target area. Dick Bong, who was an element leader on this day, nailed a pair of Oscars, getting credit for one damaged and one confirmed. Lieutenant Clayton Barnes, a lanky native of Washington, picked off another Oscar and claimed a fourth as probable.

Jerry missed the fight when his P-38F suffered mechanical failure at Jackson Drome. Though he wanted to catch up to the squadron after repairs were made, the problem could not be fixed in time. He stewed on the ground, watching as his comrades disappeared into the scattered clouds as he waited for the ground crews to repair his plane. When they finally did, the squadron was long gone, so he returned to Dobo, disappointment bitter on his tongue.

As disappointed as he was, the constant flying started to take a toll on Jerry. He continued to volunteer for every flight that came along, and while he had yet to scrap with the enemy, each mission was full of tension—and sometimes flak. He let his parents know just how frantic the pace was in his new home in a letter dated June 18, 1943. He wrote:

> Remember the tales I told of my flying experiences back on North America last September? Seem like training flights. Now I am certainly profiting from that training.

Fortunately for Jerry, shortly after the June 12 mission, he and Wally Jordan were sent on their first leave since arriving in April. The squadron kept a flat at a four-story apartment building in Sydney, Australia, that had gained the nickname, "The Buckingham." With seven bedrooms and a full kitchen, the pilots used the Buckingham to unwind, feast on steaks and beer, and womanize during their seven-day leaves. Each floor was rented by a different squadron from the Fifth Air Force, so on any given week the place was fairly overflowing with randy, emaciated pilots looking to blow off steam. Wally Jordan quickly fell for a beautiful Aussie woman named Ruby. After their first leave together, the two of them shacked up whenever Wally came back down, which was every three or four months. He recalled later, "I'd give her a call and it would be just like coming home."

The wild nights at the Buckingham appealed to Jerry for the first few days of his leave, but as time went on, he began chafing at the bit, eager to get back to the squadron. So far, he had flown dozens of missions without a single sight of a Japanese plane. That was a big difference from his Aleutian experience, where on all three of his fights he had at least seen the enemy. He spent the remainder of his leave, ill at ease and full of frustrated energy. To help work some of it off, he hiked around Sydney, made forays into the countryside, and ate steaks at night with the rest of the guys.

When Jerry returned to New Guinea, he was now assigned as a flight leader. With two scalps on his belt from his Aleutian tour, plus the dozens of missions he had flown since joining the 9th, he was more than ready for the task. The new job also brought with it new responsibility—he would be in charge of three other pilots in the air, a task he took very seriously. In fact, in three years of combat, he would never lose a wingman, a feat that he remained extremely proud of long after his shooting war had ended.

Seven new replacement pilots blew into camp in mid-July. Jerry and the other flight leaders would need to keep an eye on these new arrivals until they had gained enough experience to survive. Among the seven were Bill Williams and Bob Wood, two buddies who had linked up at advanced training just a few months before. Bill was a Texan by birth, having been born on a farm sixteen miles outside of San Angelo. By the time he left for the service in 1942, his folks had moved to Macamey, where his father had found work in the nearby oil fields. In 1940, Bill started school at Baylor University, where at age nineteen he took his first plane ride at a nearby airport. In the fall of 1941, Bill left Baylor and put all of his money into flight lessons and part-ownership in a two-seat Portfield. Before he went into the service in March 1942, Bill had already learned to fly and had almost 90 hours in the air.

Bob Wood, Bill's friend from training, was a transplanted New Englander from Massachusetts who had gone west with his family in the late 1920s, settling in Yuba City, California. Bob was always interested in flying as a kid; he loved the pulp magazines, studied the Great War aces and their careers, and hoped to find his own career in the air someday. When the war broke out, Bob was working in the Sacramento Air Depot. After his roommate passed the Air Corps entrance exams, he decided to give them a try as well. He passed and went to cadet training, while his roommate washed out when the Army discovered he was color-blind. After training in Arizona and Texas, the Air Corps sent Bob to California for P-38 training at Murock Field, then later at Santa Ana. Along with Bill Williams, Bob finished his P-38 training and then shipped out for the Pacific aboard a converted B-24 Liberator. It took them four days to get to Australia, finally ending up near Brisbane.

While waiting for their assignments at Amberly Field, Bill and Bob discovered that they were to be sent to the 9th, along with four other pilots: John McClean, Glade Hill, Richard Dotson, and Stanley Johnson. The others in the group that went over together in the B-24 were slated as replacements for the 475th Fighter Group.

In July 1943, Jerry and Wally Jordan went on leave and passed through Amberly on their way to the Buckingham. When the two veterans learned through Tommy McGuire, now with the 475th, that there were new six pilots waiting to go up to the 9th, they made a point of introducing themselves. Meeting Jerry and Wally helped ease the newcomers' fears over their assignment, as the two men really talked up the 9th. As Williams remembered later, "By the time we got to the 9th, we felt like we already knew quite a bit about it."

Just before heading up to New Guinea, however, disaster claimed Richard Dotson. While on a routine flight, he lost an engine, then hit a tree and exploded while he tried to crash-land. Much sobered, Hill, Williams, Wood, Johnson, and McClean left for Dobodura a few days later. Of the five, only Wood and Williams would survive the ensuing months.

NINE

The Long Hard Summer

Dear Barbara,

I sit here writing, surrounded by the pitch blackness of the jungle night. My chair is an army cot and my desk is a shaving kit propped on my knee. A single, dull electric bulb serves as light, and my face and hands are covered with perspiration due to both the heat and humidity. Outside above the steady noisiness of the stream, one can hear night birds chattering. And over across the camp are faint noises of a harmonica.

So wrote Jerry to Barbara about the nights around Dobo when the enemy left the scene unharried. He spent many nights that early part of the summer writing home to his family, telling them what little he could, given the censors. Though he wanted to, wartime restrictions kept him from writing about the first real fight he waded into in New Guinea. It would be fifty years before his family learned what happened.

8:00 A.M., July 23, 1943. Jerry sat in the cockpit of #83, a Lightning he inherited with the name *Sooner* written in white block lettering on its olive-drab nose. Both engines were purring beautifully as he waited on the taxiway to take off for the day's mission. Ahead of him, the eight Lightnings from Green and Yellow flights had just begun their takeoff rolls. Today he would lead Blue Flight into the skies over Lae, acting as close escort for 22nd Bomb Group as they went in to hit Malahang. The 22nd, a tough-as-nails outfit that had been through the worst of it back in '42, flew the theater's only B-26 Marauders—the skinny, snub-winged creation of the Martin Aircraft Company. The pilots called it "The Flying Prostitute," since the wings appeared so small it had "no visible means of support."

In addition to Johnson's Blue Flight, the 9th planned to put another eight planes up over Lae to cover several different sorties. Green Flight, led by Lt. Bill Bleecker, was assigned high cover duty, while Yellow Flight was to cover some C-47s making a transport run into Wau, just inland from the Japanese-held bastion around Lae. While all this activity was going on, some B-25 strafers were to hit the Japanese in a low-level run over Salamaua.

Green and Yellow Flights took off first, leaving Jerry and his three pilots, Bob Wood, Charles Ralph, and John McClean, on the ground waiting their turn. When Jerry led them into the air, the B-26s they were to escort were just beginning to form up over the field. For several minutes, the twelve P-38s circled above the B-26s, impatient to get going since every minute above Dobo was one less they would have fuel for in combat. About this time, the 9th's mission leader, Captain Blachly, suffered radio failure. He turned his job over to Capt. Harry Lidstrom, Yellow Flight's element leader. Harry continued to circle over the Marauders until he spotted the Gooney Birds plodding on up to Wau and their drop zones. Not wanting to leave the vulnerable Douglas transports unprotected, Lidstrom chased after them, then pulled in front to sweep Salamaua clear before their arrival.

Meanwhile, Green Flight also began working its way north, flying high cover for Yellow Flight and the C-47s, who by now had some B-25s as neighbors, bent on attacking Salamaua. That left Jerry and his relatively inexperienced members of Blue Flight behind over Dobo, circling with the B-26s. Bob Wood, who had just joined the squadron and had yet to see the enemy, flew on Jerry's wing. Charles Ralph was an experienced first lieutenant, but his wingman, John McClean, was a brand-new replacement pilot just like Bob Wood.

It took forty-five minutes for the Marauders to form up and head northward towards Lae. The bombers soon dipped under the cloud cover and disappeared from Jerry's sight. He waited ten minutes, giving the B-26s a head start, then put his flight on a northern course, assuming the bombers were still below. A short time later, Blue Flight arrived at Lae, where they began patrolling between 10,000 and 16,000 feet. Green Flight hovered above them south and west of Lae, watching the many formations of Allied planes go about their assigned duties. Yellow Flight, after providing close cover for the Gooney Birds, popped up to 10,000 feet and began patrolling nearby Salamaua.

Unbeknownst to the men of the 9th, off to the northeast, the 39th Fighter Squadron ran into the 68th Sentai, a new Japanese fighter outfit equipped with Oscars and the brand-new Kawasaki Ki 61 Tony. At 9:50, the 39th engaged the enemy, and soon a whirling dogfight broke out over the coast east of Lae.

Ten minutes later, the fight spilled into the 9th's patrol zone. High above the other flights, Bill Williams, the number two man in Green Flight, heard his leader, Bill Bleecker, call out aircraft. The flight, still west of Lae and slightly to the south, had just been coming around on a northern heading when Bleecker spotted a distant series of specks coming down east of Lae. At first, Williams's flight mates thought the planes might be P-39s or P-40s, which had been sighted earlier around Wau to the south. But as the range diminished, everyone saw they were radial-engined—that made them Japanese.

About this time Yellow Flight, which was to the south, spotted the same formation above them. Captain Blachly, who had given up command of the flight when his radio had gone out, immediately dived in front of his men and took the lead again. Hoping to get up-sun from the enemy planes, he led his flight into a wide, climbing turn to the right.

At this point, Green Flight engaged the Oscars, diving down on them as they passed below. Bill Williams, who had never seen the enemy before, noted that they were flying in four groups of four, with each flight stack above the other in the same way American squadrons deployed. Flying in the fourth slot in Green Flight, Ralph Wandrey started diving down with his element leader when his left engine sputtered just after he punched his tanks. He had forgotten to switch over to his main tanks, and while he did so, he fell out of formation and landed right in the middle of a bunch of Oscars.

The same thing happened to Bill Williams, who had just dropped his tanks as he began his dive on the Japanese. He picked out an Oscar that was scooting along about 1,000 feet below him and had just got him in his sights when both his engines quit. He fired a short burst, then put his nose down in a steep dive to escape his predicament. At first he thought he had blown both manifold gaskets, but later realized that he had made the same mistake as Wandrey—he had forgotten to switch to internal fuel after punching his belly tanks.

As this fight developed, Blachly and his flight continued their end-around so they could get up-sun of the brewing fight. Suddenly, a single brave 68th Sentai Tony appeared behind George Alber, Blachly's wingman. The Tony began firing, forcing both Alber and Blachly to dive away and let their other element pick the straggler off. Harry Lidstrom, along with Frank Wunder, bulldogged the Tony, hitting it repeatedly, until it finally dove through the scud layer a few thousand feet below. Still, the lone Japanese had completely broken up Yellow Flight's attack.

While all this was going on, Jerry and Blue Flight were patrolling north of Salamaua. Shortly after 10:00, Jerry's element leader, Lt. Charles Ralph called out, "Boogies, two o'clock high!" Dispensing with clever tactics, Jerry climbed straight at the enemy, determined to engage despite their poor position. As they climbed through 15,000 feet, Ralph again spotted a bunch of aircraft, this time below them just over the Markham Bay. Jerry looked down and spotted several radial engined fighters busily looping and slow-rolling just above the scud layer. Forgetting about the planes above him, which may have been Yellow Flight engaged with the Tony anyway, Jerry dove down after the quarry below.

About this time, Jerry's wingman, Bob Wood, ran low on fuel. His belly tanks had refused to feed, so early on in the mission he had switched over to internal fuel. Forty-five minutes later, just as they were poised to engage, Bob's P-38 was critically short on gas. He broke off and returned to Dobo, leaving Jerry with only Ralph and John McClean to enter the battle.

Jerry soon picked out a prime target, which he thought was a Zero but was actually an Oscar. It had slid behind another P-38, probably Ralph Wandrey from Green Flight, who already had another Oscar on his tail and was trying to shake him by going into a steep climb. As Jerry approached and tried to get into a firing position, the Japanese pilot spotted him and chandelled into his attack. Now, they were coming at each other head-on, both pilots snapping out short bursts.

In such attacks, an Oscar was always at a disadvantage since it possessed only a pair of machine guns, compared with the four .50s and the 20mm cannon the P-38 carried. The streams of lead zipping around his wings like fireflies must have convinced the Japanese pilot that this was not where he wanted to be—in the middle of his attack, he rolled his Oscar inverted, then pulled through into a split-ess. His Oscar passed under Jerry's P-38, and the American lost sight of him.

Jerry did not try to dogfight with the nimble Ki 43, just as he had been taught by the old hands in the squadron. Instead, he leveled off, slammed the throttles to the stops, and waded into the growing scrap in search of another target. He did not have long to wait. Below and in front of him, a cagey Ki 61 Tony picked up Jerry and began a climbing pass at him. Jerry ducked the nose down and went head-to-head with the Tony, opening up at 1,000 yards. The Japanese began firing as well, and the two planes barreled toward each other, flames spitting from their noses and wings as they rapidly closed the range. Out of the corner of his eye, Jerry could see the Tony's tracers slashing past his Lightning, just under the nose; the pilot was firing low. Suddenly, a burst of fire came from behind and went shooting past Jerry's left wing. No time to check that out—the Tony to his front was just too close. Jerry held his ground, squeezing out bursts which the Japanese fighter skidded and dodged, but still his fire hit home. The Japanese broke first—bare yards from a collision, the enemy pilot thrust his stick forward, diving under Jerry's P-38.

With that threat gone, Jerry dealt with the one to his rear. That burst of tracer over his left wing told him all that he needed to know, so rather than chasing the Tony he had just shot at, he watched it blaze past below him, then put his own plane into a steep dive. No Japanese could ever follow a diving P-38, and the maneuver soon cleared his tail. Still itching for a fight, Jerry was not about to leave without hunting for more prey. As he climbed back into the fight, a P-38 roared by with an Oscar latched on its tail. Jerry pulled up after them and loosed a volley of .50-caliber shells at the Ki-43 from long range. The tracers woke the Japanese pilot up to this new danger, and he promptly rolled over into a split-ess and disengaged. That done, Jerry called it a day and headed for home. On his way, he caught sight of an American plane in the water in Nassau Bay. He circled above, watching as some P-40s helped direct a rescue launch to the survivors. When they were picked up, Jerry returned to Dobo and landed at 11:35.

Charles Ralph, Jerry's element leader, had followed him down and into the head-on pass with the first Tony. He had fired at it too, which probably explains the tracers Jerry had seen passing over his left wing. Convinced that he had hit it, he refused to pursue the Ki 61 after it dove beneath Jerry's P-38. After recovering from a dive, Ralph spotted an

Oscar heading east over Salamaua. He crept up behind it and gave it a long burst from dead astern. The plane belched smoke, then fell off into a dive toward the mountains below. Before Ralph could follow it, however, another Oscar bounced him from behind, which forced him to dive away. A few minutes later, he returned to the scene and spotted a burning aircraft on the side of the mountain that his crippled Oscar had been diving toward. Based on that, he claimed the Ki 43 as a definite. Although he was attacked on the way home, Ralph made it back to Dobo and landed safely, wondering what Jerry and his own wingman, John McClean, had been doing.

McClean, being a young and inexperienced pilot, got himself in real trouble. At the beginning of the fight, he dived down after the Japanese just like Ralph and Jerry, but his angle of descent was so great his P-38 began buffeting as it entered compressibility, a plague on the early model P-38s. He tore through 10,000 feet, the controls feeling like they were stuck in concrete. Finally, in the heavier air of low altitude, he managed to level out by using the trim tabs. If that was not a close enough brush with disaster, when he swiveled his head around to clear his tail, he discovered three Oscars sitting there. Trapped, alone, and unable to dive away, McClean skidded and jinked, hoping to lose the Japanese fighters.

Enter Ralph Wandrey. Wandrey had been busy in a dogfight of his own when he spotted McClean several thousand feet below him. Wanting to join up with him, he dived down and discovered the three Oscars hounding his comrade. He lined up on the trailing Oscar, leading him by almost four plane lengths since the deflection was so great, and opened up at long range. The Oscar caught fire and fell away on its right wing, which alerted the other two to Wandrey's presence. Meanwhile, McClean used this opportunity to escape, and he returned home safely. Wandrey, however, got bounced from behind, and a cannon round hit his left wing and blew a huge hole in it. After evading several more attacks, he finally managed to return to Dobodura, shot-up but unharmed.

Outnumbered and caught at a tactical disadvantage, the 9th struggled that day in the air over Lae. Ralph Wandrey and Charles Ralph both got credit for kills, while Jerry's Tony went down in the books as a probable. Fortunately, nobody was lost, but it was a hairy battle for all, especially the new replacement pilots.

It was to get worse. A lot worse.

❧

"Bandits! Twelve O'Clock low!" Dick Bong called out over the radio. All eyes in the squadron focused on that patch of sky in front of and below the ten P-38s arrayed in three flights. Dick Bong, leading Blue Flight, arrowed down after the dozen or so Oscars and Tonys they had caught racing down the Markham Valley just northwest of Lae. Red Flight, the lead trio of P-38s, started to engage but broke off. The mission leader, Captain Smith, couldn't punch his tanks, so he headed for high ground with his flight in tow.

Just as Bong and his men engaged, Captain Jim "Duckbutt" Watkins spotted another flight of Japanese planes. This group, well-separated from the others across the valley, was trying to sneak around the Americans and bounce them from behind. It was a trap, and the flanking enemy fighters were just about to spring it.

Watkins refused to let that happen. He punched his tanks, and even as they slipped free of his P-38's belly, he lifted the right wing up and banked hard into the second Japanese formation. Behind him, Jerry's left hand slipped off the throttles and found the belly tank release button just under the switch box. He hit it once, feeling a quick spasm of relief as both tanks broke loose and fell towards the Markham River below. Then he too had broke hard right, chasing after Duckbutt, with Stanley Johnson right behind, guarding his tail.

With Blue Flight's three Lightnings engaged against at least twelve Japanese Tonys and Oscars a little way up the valley, Green Flight would be on its own, fighting against two-to-one odds. Red Flight was totally out of the scene and would not be able to help either Duckbutt's men or Bong's. One way or another, with the Japanese bookending the squadron, this would be one hell of a brawl.

Watkins engaged the flankers first, barreling towards a trio of Ki 61s in a manic head-on pass. Both sides closed at full throttle, closing the distance between them in mere seconds. Jim held his P-38 steady, putting the pipper right on the nose of the third silver fighter. He fired and watched with satisfaction as the Tony's canopy came flying off. The crippled fighter rolled on its back, and Jim saw that the Japanese pilot had jumped free of his doomed mount. One down, a sky full to go.

Behind Duckbutt, Jerry saw his leader take out the first Ki 61, but now they were through the first formation of Tonys, and the fight had spread out all over the place. Jerry stuck with Watkins through all of his wild maneuvering. His tenacity paid off when a lone Oscar arced down behind Duckbutt's P-38, ready to exact revenge. Jerry pulled his nose into the attacking Ki 43, which had already avoided an attack by Stanley Johnson and had still managed to swing behind Jim's lead ship. The Japanese pilot spotted the threat posed by Jerry's Lightning, and quickly decided that discretion was the better part of valor. He broke hard right and began diving away about the time Watkins pulled up sharply and climbed straight into a layer of overcast.

Jerry passed under Jim and over the Oscar before rolling his P-38 inverted and tucking the yoke into his stomach. The Gs made his head swim for a minute as his plane pulled through in a Split-S, but he soon caught sight of the Oscar again, trying desperately to run away. It was no use; Jerry closed the distance in a heartbeat, firing away as the range shrank. His .50s chewed into the Oscar's wings and engine, and Jerry could see the flashes his bullets made as they struck home. Finally, he quit firing as he sped past the Ki 43, overshooting the Japanese fighter. He pulled back on the yoke, sending his Lightning into a zoom climb to avoid any fight the Oscar pilot may have had left in him. While prudent, it was unnecessary, for the Ki 43's engine had been savaged by Jerry's fusillade of cannon and machine gun shells. It fell off into a steep dive, flames licking along the fuselage and gradually consuming the wings as it plummeted to the jungle below. Stanley Johnson, who had stayed in the fight, covering Jerry's tail, watched the scene unfold and confirmed the kill.

But the fight had only just begun. Jerry clawed for altitude, for by now he had lost both Stanley Johnson, whose left supercharger had failed, forcing him to disengage, and Watkins, who was still up in the scud layer somewhere. He looked around, hoping to find a friendly whose wing he could join, until he caught sight of a pair of Lightnings cruising several thousand feet above him. He headed for them and the safety they offered.

Just then, Watkins popped out of his cloud and saw Jerry below him, nose high as he tried to join up with the other Lightnings. Before he could move toward his wingman, two silver dots streaked across his peripheral vision. He focused his eyes and saw two Ki 61s just under and ahead of him, diving down on Jerry's lone P-38. Watkins worked hard on the controls and arched down after the two, hoping he would not be too late.

Jerry saw only one of the Tonys coming, but he instantly stuck his Lightning's nose in the Japanese pilot's face. Throttles to the stops, he came at the Tony, challenging the courage of the enemy pilot. Neither man broke off, and when the range was right, both pilots squeezed their triggers almost simultaneously. Suddenly, the air seemed filled with fireflies as their tracers studded the sky. Jerry held steady, keeping the Tony in his gunsight, watching as its wingspan filled each mil as the two planes rushed toward each other like runaway freight trains on a single, narrow track. As brave as the Japanese pilot was, though, his marksmanship could not match Jerry's. His fire fell low and passed under the P-38's right wing, cleanly missing the American. Jerry kept firing, noting his shots and rocking his nose up and down slightly, hosing the sky around the Tony with a concentrated stream of fire.

The Ki 61 flew right into that stream, and staggered as the bullets tore into its nose and left wing root. Instantly, ugly black smoke belched from the engine housing and left an ever-growing tail behind the Japanese plane. Still, the Ki 61 held its course, snapping out desperate bursts at Jerry's oncoming P-38. Jerry held the trigger down, throwing caution to the wind as the Tony filled first his sight, then his windscreen as the range came down to mere scores of yards. If neither budged now, they would surely collide.

Suddenly, the Tony came apart in midair. Jerry's firepower had paid off, tearing into the fragile enemy fighter's wing root and touching off one of the fuel tanks. The left wing blew off with a great yellow-red explosion, just as the engine brewed up and spewed hunks of the cowling into the air. Instantly, the Tony was transformed from graceful nimble fighter to a crazy dying bird, spinning wildly as its unbalanced frame tore itself apart.

By now the two planes were mere feet apart—Jerry hauled back on the yoke and got his nose up just as the Tony spun under him. He was quick, but not quick enough. Debris from the Japanese plane tore into his P-38, knifing open the underside of Jerry's left tail boom and tearing off the end of his vertical stabilizer. The impact jolted Jerry around in the cockpit, and he strained around to see what had happened, but all he could see was the remains of the Japanese fighter, falling in thousands of glittering pieces towards the valley floor, a greasy streak of smoke and flame marking the place where it had exploded.

Unaware of the damage inflicted on his P-38 by the dying Tony, Jerry began looking for someone to join up with, not knowing that the dead Tony pilot's wingman was still closing on him. That's when Watkins saved Jerry's life. From his perch high above the fight, he watched his wingman claw down the first Ki 61 just as he lined up on the second one. Down he went, making a 45-degree head-on pass at the Tony from above. The Japanese pilot realized the danger, but a split second too late. He tried to escape, but Jim's marksmanship sealed his fate. As the Tony broke into his attack, Jim's shells obliterated its engine. Fire broke out, and as the flames grew along the side of the cowling, the Tony rolled inverted and plunged nearly vertical for 9,000 feet before meeting its end in the rain forest below.

The demise of the second Tony passed without Jerry realizing it. Instead, he was totally focused on joining up with a trio of P-38s, which turned out to be from the 39th Fighter Squadron. They were ready to wade into the melee below, but when Jerry prepared to reengage, he discovered the damage to his left boom. Throttling back, he turned for home and nursed his damaged Lightning down the coast away from Lae, leaving the dogfight far behind.

He struggled back to Dobodura in his mangled aircraft, unable to push it over 200 mph since the twisted metal on the left boom caused so much extra drag. He finally reached the airstrip and set the damaged bird down safely, crabbing to one side as he made his final approach. After taxiing to his parking spot, he cut the engines, shut the systems down, and climbed out of the cockpit to discover a small crowd of onlookers gawking at the damaged boom. He stood there a moment, taking the scene in before running off to get a camera. He spent the next few minutes snapping shots of his ground crew posing under the boom, capturing the tangle of torn aluminum and broken cables on film so he could show his family when he got back home. As it turned out, not only had the horizontal stabilizer been clipped, the bottom of his left rudder had been sheered off as well. Had he been just a microsecond slower at the yoke, he and his plane would have been a charred crater in the Markham Valley. To most, it would have been a sobering thought; Jerry just took it in stride.

As it turned out, this scramble mission to Lae proved to be a red-letter day for the 9th Fighter Squadron. After Jerry left the fight, Watkins stuck around long enough to down two more Ki 61s, giving him four confirmed. Dick Bong also had quite an afternoon on the far side of the valley, where he destroyed a pair of Oscars and a pair of Tonies, bringing his total to fifteen. For the day, along with the ten claimed by Bong, Watkins, and Jerry, Ralph Hays and James Harris gained probables, and the 39th got another, without a single man lost. Ten to nothing in a uneven fight was more than good work—it was cause to celebrate. July 26, 1943 would be remembered for a long, long time.

Three days after their first fight with the 68th Sentai, the 9th battled with it again. Both times the Americans inflicted grave losses on the inexperienced Japanese. It was a rough introduction to New Guinea, and it hinted of worse things to come. By the end of the year, the 68th would be a shattered, desperate unit, down to its final aircraft in a hopeless struggle against the might of the Fifth Air Force.

TEN

On the Deck

July 26, 1943

Hello Dad,

Writing to you is not writing at all, for it seems as I am talking to you right here. Your exceptional letter mailed on June 24th and written on my 23rd birthday reached me today. You remember the strength and vision of purpose you gained from the wisdom of your Dad and Mother about twenty-five years ago, then you understand my response to your words.

I listen to you so closely, Dad, because you do not see man's contest with each other as an evil which we as Americans or Allied powers must stop. To you, the future is not the ending of this puny war or a depression which may follow. Your future is the enlightenment of mankind. Time is not measured by the clocks or calendars of our civilization, but by the growth of spiritual wisdom. To me, there can be no greater man than my Dad, you have been unselfish in your wants and generous in your efforts. Yes, we have seen the seasons come and pass, we have worked side-by-side in the fields and dozed before the same log fire. Our lives and our minds have been nurtured by communion with God and nature.

Whether the physical life we lead shall progress as we plan or not, I have done as Paul did—"Fought the good fight." We have a service to render among men, and it certainly doesn't help to worry about things that may never happen. . .

Well, I've been busy as usual. Repeated my accomplishment of last September—SO!!!—

Your Loving Son,
Jerry

For five days after the July 26th fight, Jerry stayed out of his P-38's cockpit. To his regret, he missed a big scrap on the 28th, another big day in which the squadron brought home seven more scalps, one of which went to Dick Bong and three to Duckbutt Watkins.

Watkins and Jerry became fast friends after saving each other's lives over the Markham Valley. A wild man from Texas, Watkins had a soft southern accent and a voice so smooth and polite that it hid a natural aggressiveness in the air. Jim was a short man, full of energy, who, when equipped with a parachute, tended to waddle when he walked. Someone noticed this and started calling him "Duckbutt," and of course, the name stuck. Back in the early days of the squadron, Watkins flew P-40s out of Darwin, so he had been flying for about a year in the theater when he scored his four Ki 61s that day with Jerry. His three on the 28th brought his personal score to seven, and eventually he received credit for eleven confirmed. Back home, Barbara and Jim's wife, Charlcie Jean, began writing to one another as their loved ones grew close on the far side of the Pacific. The two women would remain friends throughout the war, and even saw each other occasionally after it.

Jerry was among friends there at Dobo, no doubt about it. Gone were his days of isolation amongst his peers, his feelings of estrangement. He had loosened up, discarding his earlier awkward view of the world and gaining, in return, invaluable comradeship. In Watkins and Dick Bong, he had two close friends that he hoped to keep long after the war ended. Of course, Wally Jordan was as tight with him as ever, as was Tommy McGuire, even though he now flew with the 475th Fighter Group. Earlier that summer, Jerry had returned from a mission and was getting ready to go for a swim in the stream behind his tent when Don Good walked in and said hello.

Don had been an upper classman at Eugene High when Jerry started there back in 1936, and the two shared a strong mutual respect. Don looked up to Jerry, since he came from a relatively wealthy family and seemed to make friends easily. Shy and sometimes awkward, Don stood in awe of his younger friend's natural charisma. As it turned out, before Jerry and Barbara met, Don dated Barbara briefly in 1938. Don lived in a small house near downtown Eugene, and his family struggled to make ends meet through the Depression. Like many of the kids from the high school, Don delivered papers for the *Register-Guard* to earn a little spending money. Part of his route included Barbara's house, and through his deliveries, had made friends with the Hall family. He looked up to Barbara, since she was both popular and from a family that did not have to scratch for every dime. He was quite surprised when she accepted his invitation to the dance, and they had a wonderful time. They shared only that one date, but Don remembered it fondly for the rest of his life.

Later, at the University of Oregon, Don began dating Hope Carlton, with whom he had fallen deeply in love by the time Jerry and Barbara began getting serious a few years later. Together, the foursome went to dances at the school and saw each other frequently at other social events. Hope later joined a sorority and gradually drifted away from Don, who did his best to keep her. He went so far as to drop out of school for one term so he could earn enough money to pledge a fraternity, thinking that would help save their relationship. It did not, and when Don left town in 1940 to join the Air Corps, he was a single man.

When he and Jerry met in that squalid little tent in the middle of New Guinea's jungle, Don had been in the theater for a little over a year with the 3rd Attack Group, one of the Fifth Air Force's hard-charging outfits. Flying a combination of B-25s and A-20s, the 3rd Attack had taken the war to the Japanese at a time when Allied fortunes were on the decline everywhere across the Pacific—and had paid for their efforts in blood.

On his first mission in New Guinea in August, 1942, Don's A-20 had been only one of two bombers to survive an interception by the Tainan Air Group over Lae. Six of his comrades were shot down, and only the good fortune of finding a convenient cloud to duck into had saved his life. His A-20 full of holes, Don and his wingman had limped back to Australia, where their commanding officer immediately sent them on an extended leave.

Now in the summer of 1943, Don was a major who held the respect of his unit and of his old buddy Gerald Johnson. As the two friends began talking shop, they discovered that they had flown several missions together. Since their squadrons now shared the same airfield, they also knew they would be flying many more missions with Jerry as the shield, Don as the sword.

The two Oregonians stayed in touch for the rest of the summer, seeing each other whenever their schedules permitted. Don sometimes joined Jerry for a drink at the 9th's Officers' Club, which had been built entirely by the outfit's officers and even had a long, heavy mirror behind the bar that Wally Jordan had dragged back from Sydney after one leave. In return, Don hosted Jerry at the 3rd's club, which was a true piece of work that even sported a twelve foot neon sign out front spelling the words, "Tropical Paradise" in several colors. One of the group's true characters, John "Jock" Henebry, had hand-carried the sign from Australia up to Dobodura earlier that spring.

Later that summer, Don would endure one of the most painful events of his life, one which would stay with him for years afterwards as his mind refused to shake free the memory of that day. On a mission to Lae, Don stayed low over the water of the Markham Bay as he made his approach on what he thought was a merchant ship. As he closed on the target, he discovered that it was actually a sunken old hulk. Already committed, he stayed on his attack run, the sky around his A-20 alive with waspish red fireballs as Lae's anti-aircraft gunners blazed away at him. The Havoc took many hits, and soon one engine caught fire, but Don held true until he reached his release point and cut his bombs loose. They skipped across the water and into the hulk just as he broke away to make a run down the coast for friendly territory. Then the other engine took a hit and began streaming smoke. Convinced that his aircraft was doomed, he ordered his two crewmen to bail out. Just off the beach, they jumped while Don held the plane steady until they escaped the burning craft. Neither man survived, and to this day their exact fates are unknown. Don, however, decided to stay with the stricken bomber, coaxing it southeastward as flames ate away at the engine. Fifty miles from Buna Mission, the A-20 finally surrendered to the flames and flak damage. With one engine already feathered, the other gave up the ghost. Don ditched in the surf and waded ashore. The next morning, with Japanese troops nearby, a PT boat picked him up. Though he had survived, and though he earned a Distinguished Flying Cross for his steadiness over Lae, he had lost two dear friends. For the rest of his life, he would always feel responsible for their deaths.

☙

The OD shined a flashlight into Jerry's tent and called out quietly to him. Unlike other ODs, this one at least made an attempt to let the other men in the tent sleep. Jerry rose, went through his early morning routine, shaking his boots out and throwing his clothes on, before heading off to breakfast and the morning briefing.

Today's mission would be a low-level escort of a B-25 group that would be barge-hunting along the northern New Guinea coast. Ever since their last convoy was annihilated by the B-25 strafers at the Battle of Bismarck Sea in March, the Japanese had been forced to supply Lae via "ant transport"—ungainly flat-bottomed barges that hugged the coast by day, camouflaged with netting and tree branches. At night, these tiny craft would creep out just past the surf and inch along the shoreline, keeping vigilant for marauding American PT boats that now prowled the waters of Huon Gulf.

The B-25s were to scour the coast from Lae up to Saidor for anything that floated. Armed with bombs and eight to twelve forward-firing machine guns, the B-25s could kill anything smaller than a cruiser with their savage firepower. They would fly on the deck, with the 9th and 80th Squadrons covering them from about 8,000 feet.

At the same moment that Jerry was briefing his pilots, for he would lead the squadron that day, the Japanese were going over their operations for the day at Wewak. For them, their assignment was of extreme importance. The Eighteenth Army's commander, Lieutenant General Hatazo Adachi, wanted to make an inspection trip to Lae, since he realized that the vital base would soon come under land attack. Flying in the middle seat of a Ki 36 Sonia, a fixed-gear reconnaissance and light attack aircraft, Adachi would fly down the coast at low altitude and land at Lae, his plane covered by an entire sentai of Ki 43 Oscars. Given the deadly effectiveness of the Fifth Air Force and its recent penetrations by fighter aircraft deep into Japanese territory, Adachi was taking an enormous risk.

The Japanese formation assembled over Wewak and began their flight down the coast to Lae, a few hundred miles away. Simultaneously, Jerry led the 9th into the air over Dobo, rendezvoused with the 80th's P-38s, then linked up with the bombers as they skimmed the waters of Huon Gulf, noses pointed due north as they searched for targets.

Thirty minutes into the mission the 9th's ranks thinned out a bit. First, Bob Wood, flying on Duckbutt Watkins' wing, had his left throttle stick at 25 inches of mercury; he could not free it, so he aborted and returned to Kalamazoo. A few minutes later, as the squadron approached

Gona, just up the coast from Buna, Wilbert Arthur's P-38 suffered radio failure and lost its left propeller controls. He banked away from the squadron and returned safely to Dobodura. The squadron was now down to fourteen Lightnings, and would lose one more before the formation passed Lae. Lt. Gilbert Milliff's P-38 had behaved up to this point, but just off Lae, as the B-25s went into action, his hydraulic system failed. He limped home to Dobo and crash-landed; he escaped the wreck without injury.

Off Lae, Jerry, leading Red Flight ahead of the B-25s, spotted a couple of small boats in Markham Bay. He called them out to the bombers, who promptly set both afire with bombs and gunfire. The firepower these strafers possessed was awe-inspiring, and the damage they inflicted upon these vessels prompted Jerry to write later, "There could not have been any survivors."

The formation continued up the coast, hitting Finschhafen after shooting up several more boats and barges. The B-25s left a trail of smoke columns rising into the noontime air, marking the locations of their luckless victims. At 1:10, just east of Saidor, the 9th made contact with the enemy.

General Adachi and his retinue of about twenty Ki 43 Oscars had made it down the coast to Saidor thus far unharried by any Allied fighters. That luck did not hold as they ran smack into the 9th at low altitude. The Oscars seemed to be spread out all over the sky when they first came into view. The seven Ki 43s in the high cover flight stumbled straight into Wally Jordan's Blue Flight at 6,000 feet. Below Wally, Jerry's Red Flight was tucked in at 4,000 feet, and the high-cover Oscars began diving on them. Wally watched as one Oscar split-essed and began a run on the Red Flight Lightnings. Wally instantly dropped his tanks and peeled off to the left, pursuing the Ki 43 and firing a long burst at him. Jordan's wingman, Grover Fanning, followed him through this initial maneuver, despite the fact that his tanks had hung up and he could not release them. As the two P-38s dived on the lone Oscar, who by now had gone into a tight turn which Wally began to mirror, another Oscar from the high-cover flight dived down behind them both. Fanning saw the threat just as the Ki 43 began a pass from astern and off to the right. He pulled up, broke hard right, and met the threat head on. The Oscar pilot refused to break off his attack, and the two planes hurtled towards each other, spitting out deadly tongues of flame until Fanning's guns finally tore apart the Japanese plane's cowling and cockpit. The Oscar rolled on its back and plunged into the ocean, flames streaking out behind it like a red-orange streamer.

With his back clear, Jordan stuck with his quarry, following through a 180 degree turn, snapping out long bursts all the while. Finally, the Oscar flipped inverted and went into a shallow, lazy split-ess. Jordan followed it through until it began to burn. Below Blue Flight, Jerry, his wingman Stanley Johnson, and James "Jump" O'Neil watched the dogfight Wally and Grover Fanning precipitated unfold as they climbed to engage the other Oscars of the high-cover flight.

There was no time to be a spectator, for the remnants of the high-cover flight descended on them. Jerry pulled up and rolled into one Oscar, taking a 90-degree deflection shot on the dirty gray fighter. He gauged the lead, then pressed the trigger. Nothing—no familiar vibration as the guns cut loose, no muzzle flashes as the cannon churned out one explosive shell after another.

By now, Jerry was upon the Oscar, so close he could clearly make out the features of the pilot, who, according to some accounts, waved at him. As Jerry sped past him, the Japanese pilot broke away, putting his agile fighter into a hard left turn. Jerry came back around, charged his gun and prayed that they would fire. They both lined up for a head-on pass—the Japanese opened fire, but Jerry's guns remained silent. Once again, he whipped by the Oscar, but before the Japanese could capitalize on his predicament, Stanley Johnson swung in behind and cut loose with a barrage of fire. It was a perfect 45-degree deflection shot, and Stanley's shells tore apart the Oscar in just a few seconds. The doomed Japanese fighter tumbled into the sea, where it left on a few pieces of debris and a thick smudge of oil on the surface to mark the pilot's grave.

Behind Jerry, Jump O'Neil was in trouble. Like Fanning, he couldn't shake his tanks loose either, but he tried to stay with his flight mates as they waded into the Oscars. He immediately attracted unwanted attention as a Ki 43 slid behind him and gave chase. Jump put the nose down and firewalled the throttles, running flat-out away from the menace on his tail. Finally, after several minutes of this race, the Oscar fell behind and broke off the chase, giving Jump a chance to work on getting rid of his tanks. He finally got one loose, then ripped the other off in a dive, so he turned back toward the fight, climbing to 10,000 feet. After patrolling for several minutes without sighting the enemy, Jump called it a day and headed for home.

Meanwhile, well away from where Jump was running for his life, Jerry had cleared his tail for the moment and was taking stock of the scene. His scanned his gauges, noting that his altimeter read 4,500 feet. Above him, he caught sight of two burning Ki 43s. They fell past him and plunged into the water below. They were Wally's and Grover Fanning's kills, and later that day he and Stanley Johnson confirmed both of them for their friends. Then a third Oscar tumbled on by, seemingly in a death spiral. But at the last possible second, it leveled out right above the whitecaps and sped westward out of the fight.

Seconds later, the rest of the squadron, Green and Yellow flights, waded into the scrap, and the air around Jerry's defanged Lightning was a chaotic melee of fleeing Oscars, prowling Lightnings, and falling, flaming aircraft. Without guns, he knew he was worse than useless, so he disengaged. Too low to the water to dive out of the fight, he poured on the coals and climbed away, leaving Stanley to join up with Frank Wunder, the third man in Blue Flight.

As he headed back to Dobo, he picked up a stray P-38 which turned out to be 2nd Lt. Glade Hill. Glade had entered the scrap, but had dropped his tanks without switching to his internal fuel. Thus, just as the squadron engaged, he lost power in both engines. Diving away, he managed to restart both engines and climbed back into the fight when he ran across Jerry, who ordered him home. Glade escorted him back to Dobodura, where they landed about ninety minutes later.

Behind them, the rest of the squadron was really cleaning house. Yellow Flight, flying top cover for the rest of the squadron, got into the scrap in time to get some of the choicest opportunities, and Jim Watkins took full advantage of this. In just a matter of minutes, he had knocked down three more Oscars, giving him eleven kills in eight days. Larry Smith, Francis Nutter, and James Harris all claimed an Oscar as well, and the day's total came to eleven confirmed and one probable, scored by Charles Ralph. Toward the end of the fight, with the Oscars desperately trying to escape on the deck, the Flying Knights came across one of the best Japanese pilots they had ever seen.

Flying his Oscar with his canopy open, the canny Japanese evaded every attack that came his way. His efforts soon attracted nearly half the 9th Squadron, but even such improbable odds failed to spook this brave young man. He carefully broke into every attack, bobbing and weaving while hugging the wave tops and moving steadily towards Wewak. Unlike some of the other pilots, he steadfastly refused to meet the Lightnings head-on, obviously aware that his two 12.7m machine guns were no match for the American's four .50s and 20mm cannon. For fifteen minutes he played cat and mouse with the Flying Knights, artfully dodging every pass the P-38s made on his nimble Ki 43. His efforts paid off. Eventually, the Americans tired of the game and disengaged; the phenomenal Japanese pilot would live to fight another day.

Though that one extraordinary JAAF pilot survived, when the Knights turned for Dobo at the end of the fight that day, they left in their wake a scene of unmitigated disaster. Below the battle site, bits of metal and fabric bobbed in the waves amid ugly smears of avgas and oil that marked the graves of the many Oscars lost that day. When heads were later counted at Wewak as the survivors straggled home, it was discovered that the sentai leader had been killed, and that General Adachi's Sonia was missing. Only hours later did word reach the Japanese at Wewak that Adachi was safe. His pilot had managed to skirt the deadly melee and divert to Rabaul, probably via Cape Gloucester. Though safe, Adachi could no longer harbor any illusions about just how strong the Allied Fifth Air Force had become during that summer of 1943.

He would get another lesson two weeks later.

ELEVEN

Wewak Slaughterhouse

Don Good was going back to Lae, and it terrified him. He had very bad memories of that place, starting with his very first mission, when his squadron had been annihilated by the crack Zero pilots of the Tainan Air Group. Now, with the weather closing in, it looked like the 3rd Attack would be going back unescorted. Towering cumulous clouds surrounded his formation of A-20s, blotting out the sun and much of the ground below as well. Without sophisticated navigational aids, the fighters would be hard pressed to fly through such stuff and, one by one, Don saw the assigned fighter squadrons peel off and head for home.

Now Good and his men were alone—or so they thought. There was a small break in the clouds up ahead, and as they approached it a formation of twin-boom fighters appeared out of the murk. A wave of relief swept over Don as he realized that one of the P-38 outfits was braving the weather to stick with his vulnerable attack planes. Together they went in to Lae, but unlike past missions there, this one was a milk run. Flak was light, and not a single Oscar or Tony made an appearance.

When he returned to Dobodura, Don waited down on the flight line until all the P-38s were down, then he wandered over to the 9th Squadron's area looking for Jerry.

"Hey, Jerry!" he called out to his old high school friend after finally tracking him down.

"Hiya, Don!" came his reply.

"Say, was that you this morning covering us?"

"Yup, I figured you guys could use the help," said Jerry, a wide grin stretching across his face, showing no hint of the danger he had placed himself and his squadron in to stay with Don's men.

Don laughed, clapped Jerry on the back and thanked him. With an old friend like Jerry Johnson covering his back, Don felt he just might make it through the war yet.

Lae was doomed, and the Japanese knew it. With the Australians pressing them from the south out of Wau, and the Fifth Air Force cutting off its only source of supply—ant transport—the Japanese were isolated and running short on everything. Adachi and the rest of the Eighteenth Army knew it was futile to commit any more troops into the area, and sending aircraft that far south was now a death sentence. Still, they could not afford to lose any more territory in New Guinea, and to stem the tide the Japanese Army Air Force had been building up its strength further up the coast at Wewak. Apparently out of range of American fighters, Wewak and its complex of airdromes seemed like the perfect place to use as a launch pad for a new bid at air superiority.

Not that getting reinforcement sentais into Wewak was an easy thing. The Japanese fighter and bomber regiments had to fly in from all over the Empire—Java, Malaya, China, even the Home Islands themselves. Not as well trained as their Navy counterparts, the Army pilots had little experience in transoceanic navigation. Consequently, every unit suffered serious attrition en route to their new base. This tended to be especially true of the Ki 61 sentais, whose new in-line engined fighters had many teething troubles that at times caused catastrophic failures.

By the end of July 1943, however, the Japanese had assembled quite an impressive force at Wewak. As part of the Fourth Air Army, the 14th Air Brigade and 7th Air Division constituted the bulk of the fighter and bomber strength at Wewak. In mid-July, the 14th Air Brigade was combined with the 7th Air Division. Included in this new arrangement were the first two Kawasaki Ki 61 Hien (Tony) units to be deployed into the theater, the 78th Sentai, and the 9th Squadron's old foe, the 68th.

Initially under the command of the 12th Air Brigade at Rabaul, the 68th Sentai began flying missions in mid-May 1943. At first, they flew cover for the bomber sentais attacking Wau, an airfield used by the Fifth Air Force to supply the Australians fighting in the jungle. A month later, the 68th moved to Wewak, where it could be better employed against targets in New Guinea. On July 20th, the unit claimed its first kill, a B-24 Liberator that Captain Takeuchi and his flight of four other Ki 61s shot down over Bena Bena. Three days later, while flying in company

Japanese Aichi D3A Vals in formation en route to target. By 1943 the fixed-gear Val was easy meat for sleek American P-38s.

Imposing and austere, H. V. Johnson cut an impressive figure. H. V. became an attorney but never lost his love for the soil. He owned a farm in Oregon for much of his life.

Jerry, in high school, loved being a dare-devil. Here he scales a flag pole on a dare.

All of the Johnson boys loved to hunt. After Jerry went into the service, he gave his beloved 30-30 to Art. Art treasured the gun and still has it today.

Barbara and Jerry (at right) at the base of old Baldy, probably 1939. Eugene's kids were very outdoorsy and spent much of their free time roaming the hills or climbing in the Cascades. Barbara's sister is standing to her left.

Early days at the Cal Aero Academy. Some of the cadets were housed at a local high school, where they had no hot water. It would be some time before on-base facilities would be available for every would-be pilot.

Jerry over California's Central Valley at the controls of a Vultee BT-13.

Harry Huffman poses next to a Vultee BT-13 at Bakersfield, summer 1941.

Jerry Johnson's graduation from cadet training. After graduation, he was one of only a handful of his class to be assigned straight to a fighter unit. Many of his classmates were sent directly to Hawaii, where they arrived only days before Pearl Harbor.

The Green Death Squadron's logo, as seen on the fuselage of a P-39.

Men of the 57th Pursuit Squadron pose next to a P-40 at Harding Field. *Standing:* Stetson, Zetterquist, Nollmeyer, Johnson. *Kneeling:* Burns, Beagle, Jordan, Wilson.

In the spring of 1942 Jerry and Harry Huffman were sent to San Antonio, where they spent a few joyous days terrorizing a squadron of Piper L-4 pilots.

Harry Huffman poses with the boy who saved his life after his mid-air collision. Harry remained in the service even after his amputation, working in a West Coast fighter control center. After the war, he returned to Long Lake Dam, where he worked until retirement.

Jerry in his P-39 en route to Alaska. Later, he named his '39 "Scrap Iron" in honor of Barbara's brother, Howard. Howard earned this nickname before the war after he hauled on his back an iron stove up to a mountain cabin the Pack Rats used as a base camp in the Cascades.

Living conditions at Adak were downright primitive. The 54th's camp area, seen here, was buried in snow by late 1942.

Frank Beagle Collection.

Jerry with Art Rice, one of the few pilots who actually hit an airborne aircraft with the P-39's massive 37mm cannon. Art received a DFC for the feat.

After returning to Eugene, Jerry gave talks around town, describing the war in the Aleutians. The weather, he always said, was their worst enemy. Here, Adak's runway and dispersal area lies under several feet of water. Note the variety of aircraft, including a B-18, 54th P-39, B-24s, and a B-17.

Frank Beagle Collection.

Though McGuire left the 49th soon after arriving in New Guinea, he remained close to his fellow Eskimos Wally Jordan and Jerry Johnson. This photo was taken in the fall of 1944, probably at Biak.

Jerry with Bill White and Joe Jenkins at the 9th's
flight line at Dobodura, summer 1943. Bill and
Joe were two of the overworked but very
dedicated ground crewmen who kept the
Flying Knights in business.

The Flying Knights, late summer of 1943, probably just after
Jerry took command of the outfit. Standing (left to right): Capt.
Johnson, Lt. Johnson, Arthur, Love, Wood, Markey, O'Neill,
Bong, Wire, Stowe (rear), "Doc" Peggs (front), Wally Jordan,
Fanning, Lidstrom, Hays, Wandrey, Nutter, Price, and Alger.
Kneeling (left to right): Mclain, Williams, Hill, Donnell, Barnes,
and Wunder.

James "Duckbutt" Watkins and his P-38. His wife, Charlcie Jeanne, became friends with Barbara. They sometimes saw each other after the war as their husbands went career Air Force. Watkins himself was a wild one, whom his friends nicknamed "Duckbutt" due to the waddling way he walked with a parachute seat pack on. He was also one of the shortest pilots in the squadron.

The wreck of a Ki-61 "Tony," captured at Aitape in the spring of 1944. When they first arrived in New Guinea, the Americans thought they were Messerschmitt-109s.

National Archives.

The damage to *Sooner*'s tail section after Jerry's collision of July 26, 1943.

Colonel Cooper with Jerry and John "Jock" Henebry. Henebry played football for Notre Dame before the war after growing up in Chicago, where his Dad had been an elevator operator.

Jerry always led from the front. Here he is at Dobodura, just back from a mission. The photo was probably taken in the early fall of 1943.

The twin-engined mystery plane, the 9th encountered over Cape Glouster was actually this plane here. The Kawasaki Ki-45 Toryu ("Nick") was more maneuverable than the P-38 but lacked power and speed. The JAAF soon relegated it to night fighter and anti-shipping roles. The antiship version had a 37mm cannon.
Hoover Institute.

Dick Ellis stands beside the slowest B-25 in the SWPA, *Seabiscuit.* Ellis later rose through the ranks to become the Vice-Commander of the Air Force before he died in the mid-1990s.

An extremely rare photo of the November 2 raid, showing a 3rd Attack B-25 running on the deck through Simpson Harbor.

John Henebry's targets in Simpson Harbor, as seen from the tail gunner's position of a 3rd Attack B-25.

Henebry's nemesis: the *Haguro* at anchor during the November 2 raid.

Escape! Leaving the harbor sheathed in smoke, the 3rd Attack's Mitchells run for home.

Back home after the November 2 raid. Jerry poses on the left, showing two fingers for the kills he gained over Simpson Harbor. Next to him stands Lee Van Atta, the war correspondent. At the far right is a relieved Dick Ellis.

Jerry Johnson, fresh from a mission, poses with his
beloved P-38 in November of 1943.

Opposites attract. Quiet and reserved Dick Bong became fast friends with the outgoing and puckish Jerry Johnson. They had planned to do some fishing in Oregon together after the war ended, but Dick died in a Stateside P-80 crash the same day Hiroshima was A-bombed.

Cool as a cucumber. Bill Runey returns with a damaged P-40 after scoring some of his first victories. Bill went into the logging business after the war and returned to his native Oregon.

William Runey.

Jerry's much hated P-47, probably taken in late January or early February of 1944 at Gusap.

The world's only feathered air combat veteran. Huckleberry had the great misfortune to be in Ralph Wandrey's cockpit over Gusap on December 10, 1943. He later had even worse luck, when another 9th squadron mascot had him for dinner.

The newlyweds. Jerry and Barbara outside the
St. Francis Hotel in San Francisco. It was at the
hotel that Barbara discovered she was pregnant.

Jerry in faithful #83 at Biak, October 1944.

High scorers. The Flying Knights celebrate their victories over
Balikpapan, October 14, 1944.

First into Tacloban. The pilots Ged brought into Leyte pose with a 7th Squadron P-38. Top of plane: Krankowitz, Kirkland, Curl, Swift, Heltaline, Curton, Fisher, Curley, Boyd, Campbell, Norton, Nelson, Mathre. On ground: Morrissey, Walker, DeHaven, Drier, Smerchek, Estes, Jordan, Bong, Johnson, Lewelling, McElroy, Wood, Williams, Forgey, Smith, Gupton.

Carl Estes

Jerry with his faithful crew chiefs, Jack Hedgepeth (left) and Doug Harcleroad (right). Jerry had profound respect for both men and grieved over Jack's loss at Tacloban.

While visiting Jock Henebry at Nadzab on R&R during the Philippines campaign, Jerry met Irving Berlin. The two shared a small house together one weekend there at Nadzab and explored the New Guinea countryside with Jock. After Berlin returned to the States, he wrote Barbara and told her he'd had a wonderful time with her husband.

Jerry as Deputy Group Commander in early 1945. This was one of his first P-38s he named "Barbara," after his pregnant bride.

Harold Johnson, left, joined Jerry on Luzon as a
replacement pilot for the 348th Fighter Group.
Here the Oregon twins entertain Joe E. Brown.
Jene McNeese.

In May of 1945, Jerry took Joe E. Brown up on a dive-bombing mission. Brown sat behind Jerry where the radios were normally located. Note the single Australian kill flag, a feature that graced Jerry's P-38s for only a short time in the late spring and early summer of 1945.

Jim Gallagher

Barbara in the hospital after delivering Jerry. It was days before Jerry Sr. learned of the birth.

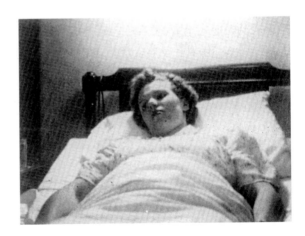

After the news of his son's birth reached him, Jerry had his P-38 repainted. His son's name replaced Barbara's, and a painting of a baby boy graced his Lightning's nose. Some historians have thought he named the plane after himself and the painting was of his wife. Neither is true. Jerry always referred to himself as "Gerald" or "Ged"—a family nickname. The painting is clearly a smiling baby.

Pictured: standing: Laven, Johnson, Tice
Sitting: DeHaven, Jordan, Watkins

Jerry and Barbara back home in the States during the summer of 1944. After getting married in Eugene, they spent the next two months in Kansas while Jerry attended Command and Staff School at Ft. Leavenworth.

First official word of Jerry's disappearance came over a week after Barbara learned of the news over the radio.

One of the survivors of Jerry's B-25, Sgt. Patrick Chilsen (third from left), stands in the cargo door of a transport plane. Chilsen had been part of the B-25's crew and had his chute. The B-25 had been part of an Air Commando outfit commanded by ETO ace Colonel Walker Maharin.

Phyllis Chilsen.

Jerry's P-38 from April of 1945.

with the 78th Sentai, they ran into the 9th Squadron's buzzsaw over Lae. Three days after that, they ran afoul of the 9th again, suffering high losses at the hands of the veteran Americans. Flying new and relatively untested aircraft, the inexperienced sentai paid for its lack of seasoning with the blood of its own pilots.

More bad news awaited the 68th and 78th at Wewak. With forty-two pilots and twenty-six planes at the beginning of June, the 68th formed one of the key units in the build-up at Wewak, along with the 78th, which had similar strength on hand. But these numbers dwindled as combat losses mounted and the men began suffering from a variety of jungle diseases. Conditions at Wewak were grim, and many of the fliers contracted dysentery and malaria, reducing both morale and operational strength. Supplies were getting harder and harder to come by, and food became scarce. As conditions restricted their diet, the pilots began to display the first signs of malnutrition.

Nevertheless, the build-up at Wewak continued. Along with the 68th and 78th Sentais, the 1st Hiko Sentai and its Oscars helped provide fighter support for the Lilly and Sally bomber regiments stationed nearby. The 24th and 59th Sentais and their Ki 43s also called Wewak home. Altogether, the aerodromes at Wewak held several hundred Japanese aircraft, a major threat to General Kenney's Fifth Air Force. MacArthur was planning to launch an amphibious assault against Lae later in the summer and, should the Japanese strength at Wewak remain unchecked, the landing would be in grave jeopardy from air attack.

So Kenney prepared one of the most devastating series of raids in the history of the Pacific War. It began just after midnight on the night of August 16–17, 1943, when the 43rd Bomb Group's B-17s and the 90th Bomb Group's B-24s pounded three of Wewak's airstrips. Flak was heavy and searchlight beams lanced upward, searching for the bomber formations. A few primitive Japanese night fighters lurked in the darkness, looking for stragglers to pick off. Three of the heavy bombers were sent earthward by Wewak's defenses. At the cost of those three heavies, the Fifth Air Force inflicted massive damage on their targets.

The Japanese Army Air Force's 7th Air Division and its fighter regiments suffered grievously from the attack—nearly all of its aircraft were either damaged or destroyed. Only ten aircraft remained serviceable when dawn broke on the 17th. The 68th Sentai, battered and nearly broken by the events of the summer, was hit hardest by the raiders and had only six Tonys left by daybreak.

Determined to retaliate, the Japanese prepared for a large-scale morning strike against Marilinan, an airfield south of Lae that housed, among other units, the "Black Sheep" of the 8th Fighter Squadron, the Flying Knights' sister unit. When dawn came, the airfields around Wewak bustled with activity. At the strips hit early in the night, the bomb craters were quickly filled and the damaged planes were attended to by the ground crews. At the other fields that had not come under attack, pilots and crewmen manned their aircraft in preparation for the day's missions. All along the flight lines, twin-engined Lilly and Sally bombers were manned and ready to go, their engines just beginning to turn over. Nearby, the fighter units slated to escort them were also warming their engines.

Kenney's second surprise came over the horizon. Hugging the treetops, thirty-three B-25s from the 3rd Attack and the 38th Bomb Group appeared over Borum, Wewak, and Dagua aerodromes, flames spitting from the barrels of their dozen .50-caliber machine guns. With the Japanese on the ground lined up for take-off, the targets were ripe and plentiful. When the 3rd Attack Group's commander, Colonel D. P. Hall, led his men over Borum, the first of the Japanese planes was actually making its take-off run. The Mitchells spread out, shooting up everything that moved, while from their bellies blossomed thousands of tiny parachute fragmentation bombs. The parafrags exploded on contact with the ground, showering the airstrip with millions of metal slivers that shredded men, trucks, gun positions, and aircraft with deadly efficiency.

The scene became a slaughterhouse. So powerful were the strafers that one touch on the trigger was enough to reduce any grounded Japanese plane to junk. With the long, straight lines of Lillies and Oscars and Tonys stretched before them, the attackers could not help but precipitate a massacre. They left in their wake the charred remains of Japan's Army Air Force. Ground crews, pilots, gunners, navigators, and bombardiers—all died together in that maelstrom of machine-gun fire and parafrags. Supplies, gasoline stores, ammunition depots, anti-aircraft positions, and storage facilities burned furiously, and in their funeral pyres months of tedious and dangerous resupply efforts went up in smoke.

Over one hundred and fifty aircraft were destroyed—and it was not yet over.

The Fifth Air Force struck again the next day. This time, Jerry brought the 9th along to provide cover for the bombers. Again, the fields were raked by gunfire and savaged with bombs. Again, the Japanese offered nearly no resistance. The 9th did not even see any enemy aircraft in the air, since most of the fighter units had been smashed on the ground the day before.

Writing years later about the attacks, General Kenney commented, "During two days of operations, we had destroyed on the ground and in the air practically the entire Japanese air force in the Wewak area. . . . It was doubtful if the Nips could have put over a half dozen aircraft in the air from all four airdromes combined."

He was not far off the mark. The 1st Hiko Sentai, veterans of the Malayan and Burma campaigns, had been devastated by the attacks. Its few remaining Oscars were withdrawn from Wewak and sent back to Japan, where the regiment was eventually reequipped with the new Naka-jima Ki 84 Hayate. The 78th Sentai also took a beating in those two bloody days at Wewak. After losing most of its Ki 61s on the ground, the unit was sent back to the Phillippines to rest, regroup, and return to full strength. Like the 1st and 78th Sentais, the 68th Sentai suffered almost complete destruction, forcing its new commanding officer, Major Kiyoshi Kimura, to send his pilots back to Manila by heavy bomber to await reinforcements. With no aircraft to fly, they were of no use for the time being.

TWELVE

First Command

As the Japanese Army Air Force's fortunes waned in eastern New Guinea, Jerry's fortunes rose spectacularly. He started the summer as a first lieutenant, and he ended it as a squadron commander, a job that he thought was months away. He got the 9th Squadron after the last of the Darwin veterans were finally sent home. That contingent included Sid Woods, the squadron commander through the summer, and Duckbutt Watkins. Bidding farewell to his Texas friend was difficult for Jerry, but he and Jim would link up later in the Philippines.

With new responsibilities, Jerry found that he had to distance himself somewhat from the other pilots. He was no longer "one of the guys"; now he was "the man." Jerry discovered that the gulf between second lieutenants and captains who were on the cusp of promotion to major was quite wide. Though he fraternized less, he treated his men with a fairness that they grew to appreciate, as well as a sense of loyalty that they knew they could count on. In a pinch, his men knew if they were in trouble, they could count on Jerry to support them to the hilt.

Even more important, Jerry led from the point of the spear, putting himself in as much danger as his men would have to endure. Though administrative duties curtailed some of his combat flying, he was still in the air several times a week, fighting beside the men who counted on his leadership. For that, they loved him.

The pilots soon discovered that their new commander had not lost touch with his cheerleader roots. He would usually gather the squadron together before tough missions, and give rousing and unabashedly patriotic pep talks. He had a knack for these locker-room style go-get 'em speeches, and his enthusiasm was usually infectious. Some of the pilots, however, confessed later that Jerry would sometimes get so wound up while delivering the words that they grew embarrassed for him. Even so, for most of the men, the pep talks endeared Jerry to them, and even a half-century later they had not forgotten the words of some of his more inspiring orations.

At the same time, Jerry could be tough when the situation demanded it. One character in the squadron refused to follow orders in the air; several times, Jerry caught him glory-hunting at the expense of his flight's integrity. Instead of focusing on teamwork, which Jerry preached throughout his tenure as squadron leader, this pilot had a habit of leaving his wingman to go stir up trouble on his own. Covetous for kills and acclaim, the man became a danger to his fellow pilots. Jerry evaluated the situation, and then grounded the pilot. Embittered by Jerry's actions, his attitude turned sour, which isolated him from the rest of the squadron. For quite some time after the incident, he would slip into the O Club at night to drink beer. The other pilots would leave him alone as he sat close to the Philco radio, listening to Australian broadcasts. He cut a lonely figure, far from home and ostracized by his peers. Yet, Wally Jordan for one felt no sympathy for him—he had made his own bed when he refused to follow orders.

❧

September 2nd: the Flying Knights would be Gloucesterizing again today. The Fifth Air Force bombed the Japanese installations and airfield at Cape Gloucester, New Britain, so often that General Kenney's men had added a new word to their lexicon: anything that was going to get pounded was Gloucesterized. That day, twelve aging B-17 Flying Fortresses from the 43rd Bomb Group, along with the 19th Bomb Squadron's B-26 Marauders, were to strike the Cape's dirt airstrip that had been built right on the water's edge.

At 9:00 A.M., Jerry led sixteen P-38s off Horanda Strip at Dobo, turned north and linked up with the bombers thirty miles out over the Solomon Sea. As they proceeded to target, the 8th Fighter Group and a B-25 outfit hit Wewak again, right at 10:00. Over Wewak, and then later down the coast at Madang, the 8th ran into a mix of what they thought were Zeroes and reconnaissance planes, code-named Dinahs. In all probability, however, the Japanese aircraft were Ki 43 Oscars and the twin-engined Ki 45 Toryu, which was a twin-engined heavy fighter that had been deployed to Rabaul with the 5th and 13th Sentais earlier that summer. Very probably, this was one of the first encounters the Fifth's fighter groups had with the new plane, causing it to be misidentified as a Dinah, or just as a TE (twin-engined) fighter.

While the 8th fought its battle over New Guinea, the Marauders and Flying Forts arrived over Cape Gloucester, to be greeted by heavy anti-aircraft fire whose ugly black puffs stood out starkly against the huge white clouds that stretched from 3,000 feet on up over 10,000. The "Silver Fleet" (the 19th Squadron's B-26s so named for their unpainted finishes) went in low, dodging the flak and clouds as they laid their bombs on the target. By 10:30, they had finished their runs and were egressing south; a flight from the 9th stayed close as they scampered back towards the New Guinea coast.

Above the Marauders, the B-17s were having trouble. Pitched and rocked by the intense flak, they made pass after pass over the target area, finally breaking up into single flights as the pilots tried to find holes in the cloud cover that they could use. Before long, the 43rd's dozen Forts were scattered all over the sky as each crew sought its way through the weather.

Jerry led Blue Flight, circled overhead, watching the bombers straggle over the airstrip, occasionally loosing a volley of bombs that would explode brilliantly upon impact. From 12,000 feet, the shock wave from each bomb could be seen roiling out from detonation point in an ever-widening circle, engulfing trees and other objects.

The bomb runs continued for almost another hour, until, at 11:10, Jerry had his flight slightly northwest of Cape Gloucester, still keeping an eye on the bombers. Above him, Yellow Flight hovered protectively at 15,000. That's about when the Japanese showed up. With his 20-15 vision, Jerry sighted them first. There were only five or so that he could see, twin-engined types running along at 8,000 feet and heading towards a B-17. These were possibly the survivors of the scrap over Wewak and Madang, coming east towards Cape Gloucester and their home field at Rabaul. Both Toryu outfits were stationed around Simpson Harbor on the east end of New Britain, so they could have been using Cape Gloucester as a refueling stop between New Guinea and their base. The 49th Group records do mention that along with these twin-engined fighters (identified as Dinahs, incidentally), there were some single-engined ones (identified as Zeroes). Though Jerry and the rest of his pilots engaged that day saw only the Toryus, there could very well have been some Ki 43s around as well.

Jerry could not have cared less where the Japanese fighters came from—he just wanted to knock them down and keep them away from the heavies. He called out to his flight to drop their tanks, and they broke down and into the odd-looking Japanese fighters. Jerry picked out one of the enemy planes and lined up on him, noting that the twin-engined craft was overall silver with little green squiggles covering the wings and fuselage. The Toryu pilot must have seen Blue Flight's three P-38s dropping on him like an anvil, but he gamely held his course and finished his attack on a Flying Fort. But then, another P-38 came out of nowhere, and beat Jerry to the Ki 45 and unloaded on it with a quick snap-shot. He missed, but Jerry did not—he struck the Toryu with a knock-out punch from his five guns as he swept in from above and behind. The Toryu stumbled, belched smoke as the Oregonian's fifties turned the plane's engines into useless junk. Jerry's steady stream of fire walked across the wings and into the cockpit, tearing pieces out of the plexiglass canopy and almost certainly hitting the crew.

From eight thousand feet, the Toryu rolled over, both engines afire, and plunged straight into the sea. Grover Fanning, Jerry's wingman that day, saw the remains of the Kawasaki burning on the water.

Jerry had no time to revel in the kill, which in his mind made him an ace with five down. A split second after shredding the first fighter, Jerry spotted another Toryu attacking another Flying Fort. He pulled his P-38 into a hard turn until its nose was fixed on the attacking Toryu, opening the throttles so he could close the range quicker. Suddenly, Theron Price, Jerry's number three, burst in on the scene and dropped the Toryu with a four second burst that raked the plane from bow to stern. With smoking trailing from the left engine, the Japanese fighter fell into a dive and disappeared. Unable to see it crash, Price could only confirm it as a probable.

Another Toryu remained, but its pilot knew he was the hunted now. He dived away from the Flying Forts, hoping to disengage and be rid of the deadly twin-boomed American fighters. If this was the same outfit that had mixed it up with the 8th Group an hour earlier, then this pilot must have been on the edge of exhaustion. He raced for safety, his tail gunner keeping a sharp eye on their vulnerable rear.

Price and Jerry would not let the Japanese escape. They gave chase, speeding eastward over Borgen Bay near the airstrip, taking a couple of deflection shots at the Toryu when the opportunity presented itself. Then Jerry had a clean shot, and he bored in for the kill. The twin-engined craft filled his gunsight, and from point blank range he let him have it. His tracers shot out and plunged into the Toryu's fuselage, but before any crippling damage was done, Jerry had to pull up and over his target to avoid a collision. He looked back to see the Toryu heading for the deck.

The Japanese pilot was in deep trouble, and he knew it. He had been able to evade these first attacks by breaking hard and presenting as poor a target as possible, but now he was running out of airspace, and maneuvering room. He spiraled down, holding his Toryu in a tight, diving right turn until he was just at a thousand feet. In a flash, his wings were level and he was running all out for the safety of the airstrip.

He didn't make it. Theron Price, who had himself little more than a month to live, killed the Toryu and its crew just as it reached Cape Gauffre. Burning and out of control, it cartwheeled into the trees and exploded. For Price, it was his first kill, and while he did not see its actual demise Jerry, coming up behind him, witnessed the whole scene through to the flaming end.

With no more enemy planes nearby, and their fuel gauges sagging towards empty, Jerry and Price called it a day and turned for home. For the fourth time since July 23rd, the 9th Squadron had scored without loss. Jerry and Price each got one, while Grover Fanning claimed two more definites. Francis Love shot another one down, bringing the day's total to four down and one probable. Five Toryus seen, four flamed and one sent home smoking, its left engine destroyed—not a bad day at all.

Back at Dobo, after the pilots had showered, they met with Spence, the squadron's intel officer. A Boston lawyer by profession, Spence was older than most of the other officers in the squadron, and his Yankee accent and non-flying status made him the butt of many jokes and nicknames, among the most charitable of which was "Pebble-Cruncher." He gave as good as he got, however, blasting back with clever one-liners that often would have the men in stitches.

Today's debriefing was laced with confusion at what exactly they had shot down earlier in the morning. A couple of the pilots thought they were Dinahs, though the cockpit canopy seemed much longer, stretching for what seemed like half of the fuselage's length. After some discussion, they came to realize that these were not some fighter version of the recon plane they knew so well. Still, they were at a loss for what to call them. As a result, the four kills were logged under the generic label of "Twin-Engine Fighters."

Later, on the after-action reports, several of the fliers explained the characteristic features of the new aircraft. Martin Alger, Yellow Flight's leader, wrote in his report:

> This enemy plane had the lines of a "Dinah" bomber except that the canopy seemed to extend from the cockpit back to the middle of the fuselage, where there was also an opening for a pair of swivel guns like on the A-20s. The airplane did not seem very fast, but it was very maneuverable.

Francis Love also noticed the differences between this new type and the Dinah, writing:

> The enemy airplane was a twin-engined fighter with a light background and dark green sloshes all over. It had a long glass green house extending from the pilot halfway back to the tail with a gunner's position at the rear, similar to an A-20.

Later, as the Americans became more familiar with this new type of fighter, the code name "Nick" would be assigned to it. Martin Alger described the new Japanese fighter accurately. While the Nick was not fast—its top speed was just over 330 mph—it was highly maneuverable and could turn inside any P-38 or similar-sized aircraft. It would be a dangerous adversary in the future, whatever the Allies decided to call it.

THIRTEEN

October Heartbreak

October 11, 1943

Dear Barbara,

I thank God that I am, in a way, qualified to serve my fellow men as a warrior. I alone am only a tiny speck in the mass of humanity, but the principles I believe in are greater even than humanity itself.

Do I get scared? Certainly. I've had many times a feeling of emptiness in my stomach. But I meditate, remembering men who served their fellows, soldiers, poets, doctors, the greatest and the least. Then, the emptiness vanishes and I am alert, alive, filled with a spirit that my task shall be completed. I ask not for wealth, or fame, or long life, only that I many have strength and courage to get to my objective and hit it, and hit it and hit it.

The enemy wants to take our life, our liberty, our happiness. If these things are not precious enough that we give our lives for them, we do not deserve them.

Always,
Jerry

Tommy McGuire was about to die, and he knew it. Down low, with a wrecked engine and shattered cockpit, he was a crippled duck just waiting for the hounds. The hounds soon appeared, eager to swat down one who could not fight back. Unless a miracle blessed him, Oro Bay would be Tommy's final resting place, and his battered Lockheed would be his tomb.

Tommy checked his tail, noticing as he twisted to look over his shoulder that his left engine was trailing smoke. Worse news lay behind, for between his booms he could see a Zero, less than a hundred feet behind, its nose and leading edges sparkling at him as the pilot snapped out a burst. The Lightning shuddered, great gouging holes opened in the wings and nacelles in long, ragged lines. A tremendous *whump* shook him violently when a 20mm cannon round buried itself in the radio equipment right behind his back and exploded.

Tommy began to dive, praying that he might be able to shake his attacker, but without much altitude left, he did not have enough room to run, and the Japanese pilot had the range. The cockpit suddenly erupted in a whirlwind of bullets, shrapnel, and broken glass. A machine gun round clipped Tommy's wrist, then slammed into the instrument panel. Another cannon round exploded nearby, peppering his right hip and arm with bits of stinging hot metal. The fusillade continued; bullets thumped into the cockpit floor, crashed through the control column and severed the elevator cables. In desperation, Tommy tried to pull out of his dive. No use; the controls were totally shot away. With the engine now bathed in fire, only seconds remained before the P-38 would mushroom into a huge fireball and plummet into the bay like some crazed banshee.

With rounds still slicing through the cockpit, Tommy reached up and yanked the hatch release. The slipstream caught it, and spun it away wildly, until it disappeared well behind his doomed fighter. Though in pain from his many wounds, Tommy was able to release all the safety straps and pull himself out of the cockpit. He jumped clear, missing the horizontal stabilizer as the P-38 went into its final, fatal spin.

Then he realized he had made a mistake. As he left the cockpit, he forgot to ditch his oxygen mask. Now, as he tumbled towards the bay, far too close now for safety's sake, the screaming wind slapped his mask up into his nose and eyes with a boxer's ferocity. The sudden pain and loss of sight must have caused him both panic and confusion, but his instincts proved sound. His hand found the O-ring and pulled, releasing his chute. It blossomed out above him, opening with such a sudden jerk that Tommy's body was flung about as if he had just been in a car wreck.

Dazed, blinded, and bleeding from many wounds, Tommy splashed into the bay about twenty-five miles from shore, where he discovered his Mae West had been shredded from all the shrapnel zinging around in the cockpit. It would not inflate, so Tommy treaded water, gritting it out and metering his energy so that he could keep his head above the waves and live through this horrible ordeal. Thirty minutes later, *PT-152* fished him out and took him back to Buna. Though alive, Thomas McGuire Jr., late of the 431st Fighter Squadron and the killer of thirteen Japanese planes since August, was out of the war for almost the rest of the year. He was air evacuated from New Guinea aboard a Fifth Air Force transport to a hospital in Australia. Though he had taken out three Zeroes and riddled two more, the odds had caught up with him and nearly left him for dead. It would not be the last time, though, especially since Tommy played the game the hard way—all raw, bull-headed aggression, where caution and a measuring of the odds were never options. Despite his close brush with death that morning, October 17th, McGuire never changed his ways.

❧

Clayton Barnes, the gentle and deeply introspective native of Washington state, who sometimes flew on Dick Bong's wing, was burning alive. He'd lost an engine on take-off and belly-flopped into the ground at the end of the runway. He was trapped in the cockpit while his fuel tanks detonated around him. Soon, the cockpit was encased by a sheath of flames, and even as he fumbled at the safety straps, liquid fire began seeping in around his feet. He worked frantically to free himself, smoke boiling around him as the fire consumed everything. His clothes caught fire, and wickedly quick tongues of flame flicked up around his face, searing his cheeks and nose, hands, and arms. Only his goggles protected his eyes from the same fate. He released the hatch; the roar of the fire welled in his ears as he struggled to free himself from the inferno's deadly embrace.

Barnes made it—barely. His face was blackened and torn, with raw, angry-looking burns from his jaw to his cheeks, and when his goggles were removed, he looked like a horribly disfigured raccoon. Gingerly, the field's medical staff tended to him, trying to make him as comfortable as possible with morphine and salves for his burns. A short time later, he was sent down to Australia, where he was treated in the same hospital where Tommy McGuire convalesced.

Gradually, as Clayton recovered, he would take short walks through the hospital's sterile halls. Each day he met Tommy McGuire, who, while still blinded, insisted on feeling his way out of his room and into the corridors for some exercise. That image of the brave and wild Tommy McGuire, tentatively creeping along, hands stretched out before him or pressed searchingly against the walls, stayed with Clayton for the rest of his life.

Though McGuire's war was far from over, Clayton's was. He was shipped home later that year, and would make a complete recovery. He had been in New Guinea since late 1942, growing as close as brothers-in-arms can only be with the other guys in the squadron. Yet, when he left Sydney still suffering from his many burns, he closed that chapter of his life for good. Even in the presence of other combat pilots, Clayton would remain tight-jawed about his own battles, his own two confirmed kills, for the rest of his life. Though he ran into one or two of his buddies later in life through pure chance, he never again saw the majority of his Flying Knight buddies.

❧

Jerry was fighting a brutal battle within himself as he struggled to contain his emotions. Though they had not lost a man through the entire summer, October came and saw the 9th's men fall like autumn leaves. On the 12th, Hays, Price, and Wunder were lost—all three promising young lieutenants who had proved themselves in the summer dogfights around Lae. The next loss struck Jerry like a blow to the solar plexus. His second-in-command, Captain Harry Lidstrom, a man whose energy he admired and whose open, happy ways earned him the friendship and respect of much of the squadron, went missing. While returning from a forced landing at Lae (now in Allied hands), Lidstrom radioed Dobo that he had lost an engine somewhere north of Cape Ward Hunt. Nothing further was ever heard, and despite much searching, Lidstrom had just disappeared. It was not until February 1944 that natives stumbled upon the crashed P-38 and brought Harry's body back to Dobodura.

Later that evening, the 9th suffered yet again. A PBY loaded with ground crewmen from the 9th had gone off in search of Harry Lidstrom, only to run into a storm and disappear, just as Harry had done. Seven more men from the squadron went missing, and their remains were not found until October 1944, near the native village of Pongani. All seven died when the PBY crashed into the jungle.

Eleven men from the squadron died in less than a week, after a summer without loss. Even harder to take was the fact that none—not a single one—had been killed by the enemy. All had been killed by the capricious and formidable New Guinea weather. Between these eleven men, Tommy McGuire's near-fatal crash, and Clayton Barnes's disaster, Jerry had to use every ounce of strength he possessed to not give in to his crushing sense of loss and responsibility.

He emerged from his inner struggle a different man, sobered by the experience. First off, he recognized that his priority was not to score kills, but to keep his men alive as they dealt the enemy the hardest blows they could deliver. Whenever he could, he would make sure that his men went into battle with the best possible information, equipment, and plan. If they lost a man, he would spare nothing to try and get him back, especially if he went down at sea. Unfortunately, a few weeks later his men were given a graphic demonstration of that over the Solomon Sea.

As Jerry became tougher internally, he toughened externally as well. He grew devoted to his men, enlisted and officers alike, marveling at their personal dedication to the war effort, to seeing this miserable war through despite all adversity. Jerry felt like he owed them a debt, one that made him ensure that they had every ounce of his own effort, his own loyalty, and his own perseverance. In the midst of that terrible month, he rededicated himself to the war effort and never once, for the rest of the war, did his commitment flag. His determination to see it through to the end, to protect his men as best he could while fighting the Japanese with every bit of skill and strength he possessed, would soon solidify his reputation in the Fifth Air Force as not just one of the best fighter pilots, but one of the best leaders as well.

At the same time, he began to detest slackers. Here he was in the middle of absolutely nowhere, watching some very fine and bright men fling themselves at the enemy and the elements and die with terrifying regularity. Meanwhile, as he discovered through letters from home, some of his friends were still back in the States, contributing nothing to the war effort. He wrote home bitterly,

I get to feel mad as hell about fellows . . . who have no worries and who have given no sacrifice. Some of my men here have fought and worked overseas for over 20 months, all carry on for a hope of seeing America again and living in peace. How can John and his kind know the swish of falling bombs, the chatter of machine guns, the startling wail of a siren announcing the approach of enemy aircraft? How can he know the tightness on a fellow's heart as he dives to attack the enemy? Never fear, darling, I am not tired or discouraged. After all, I have something to fight for. Maybe those fellows do not. If I had to fight here for five years, I'd still carry on because of you and everything you stand for.

For the rest of the war, Jerry's commitment to final victory grew, as did his total disgust for those whom he felt were not pulling their own weight in helping to end the bloodshed. Every piece of news from home that gave even a glint of someone slacking off made him seethe with anger. His wrath spared no one, and later in the war, when his twin brother seemed to be enjoying the high life, care of the Army Air Force in the Midwest, he spared him no criticism either. His most enduring hatred, though, grew from news of strikes back home and of unions demanding higher wages. To Jerry, that was akin to treason, while young Americans died in festering hellholes like New Guinea and got paid a fraction of what the union men back home were earning in what he felt were cushy jobs.

As Jerry came out the other side that October, this newly-exposed raw nerve would remain so for the remainder of the war, and woe be unto anyone whom he felt deserved his wrath. With despair turned into a sense of purpose, a fire alighted in Jerry's belly that spurred him forward, preparing him for his toughest challenge yet: Rabaul.

The aircraft were getting weary, and no replacements were on the horizon. The 9th's complement was now sixteen flyable P-38s—nine short of full strength—and it took every ounce of effort the mechanics and ground crews could muster to keep them serviceable. Between all of the repairs for battle damage, burned-out machine guns, engine changes, and the myriad of other tasks needed to keep the planes flying, aesthetics were ignored. The Lightnings had once been beautiful and elegant in their factory-fresh olive drab and gray paint, but now, after months of combat, dust, and abuse, they were scuffed and chipped, with large portions of the wings and booms marked with natural-metal patches.

It was in this condition that the squadron went to Rabaul on October 23rd. Once again, Jerry and his men were assigned to cover for the 90th and 43rd Bomb Groups, both now flying B-24 Liberators. The 90th Group—the Jolly Rogers—was assigned to bomb Lakunai Aerodrome, while the 43rd—"Ken's Men"—was assigned to hit Vunakanau.

To make it to Rabaul and back, the P-38s would all have to stage out of Kiriwina, an island off the east coast of New Guinea. In the early hours of October 23rd, both Port Moresby and Dobodura came alive with the thundering sounds of Allison engines as the five Lightning squadrons got airborne and headed to their refueling point. By mid-morning, all the units had landed at Kiriwina, where their tanks were topped off and the pilots fed sandwiches. At 11:00 A.M., Jerry took off with fifteen P-38s and linked up with the forty-nine B-24s as they lumbered north to Rabaul at 20,000 feet.

Over the target, things did not go as planned. First in over the target area was the 475th Fighter Group, sweeping ahead of the Liberators to take out any interceptors. Just after noon, they ran into a swarm of fighters and soon became embroiled in a shoot-out, which the Americans figured cost the Japanese about a dozen fighters for the loss of a single Lightning. While this battle developed, the stately Liberator formations approached the target at 20,000 feet, only to discover that both aerodromes were socked in. Thus protected by the weather, the Japanese fields escaped attack that day.

Both bomb groups hesitated as they tried to figure out what to do next. The two B-24 commanders conferred over the radio for several minutes until they decided to strike out at Rapopo, another of the airstrips protecting Rabaul. When the word went out to the rest of the bomber, confusion broke out amid the tightly-packed formations as they turned to make an ad hoc run at their new target. The flights split up, spreading the bombers all over the sky and making the job of covering them much more difficult.

Shortly after 1:00 P.M., the 9th Squadron spotted about ten Japanese fighters poking around on the fringe of the bomber formations, right over Rapopo Aerodrome at 25,000 feet. Jerry dropped his tanks and dived after a dark-green Zero that had just finished a pass at a flight of B-24s. He closed the range so quickly that, as he slid behind the enemy fighter, he had to chop his throttles in order to keep from ramming it. He fired from point-blank range, dead astern. The Zero immediately erupted in flames as bright explosions blew off its tail, throwing bits of metal into the air, which Jerry was forced to fly through. His P-38 shuddered as he collided with several large chunks of debris that dented his propeller hubs and nicked his wings.

The remains of the Zero fell out of the sky, a broken and flaming bird.

Though the Zeroes remained in the area, hovering just on the periphery of the bomber formations, no further attacks were made by the Japanese. Keeping a wary eye on the black-green fighters, Jerry assembled his men and brought them out of the target area, covering the B-24 flights that had completed their bomb runs and headed home.

Later in the week, Jerry had a chance to write home about his most recent experience. Usually, because of rigid censorship rules, he said almost nothing about combat, but on this occasion he mentioned a few details.

Dear Barbara,

I am certainly piling up the combat hours. Have over a hundred and thirty missions now. I've seen every Jap base in this area and fought enemy fighters over most of them. I shot one down the other day from behind. When I fired, he just blew up. They send some of the gun camera pictures to news reels, so you may get some idea of what it looks like to see pieces fly off an enemy plane and watch your cannon shells explode on his wings or fuselage gas tanks.

❧

The next day, October 24th, the 9th went back to Rabaul, this time covering the 3rd Attack Group as it beat up Tobera Aerodrome. In a running fight that spread for over a dozen miles, the squadron claimed seven Zeroes, but Dick Bong lost his young wingman, Second Lieutenant Woodson Woodward. His death dampened the mood at Dobo that night, especially since the men knew that they would be going back to Rabaul again in the morning.

Dawn broke over Dobo on October 25th and revealed a scene of bustling activity. Engines were warmed up in the revetments, the pilots were briefed, and breakfast was served to anyone who could stomach it. Once again, the 9th would be riding shotgun for the Jolly Rogers as they attacked targets around Rabaul. After refueling at Kiriwina, the 9th linked up with the B-24s over the Bismarck Sea, only to run smack into a solid wall of overcast a few minutes past the rendezvous point. After probing the fringes of the weather front, Jerry decided it was too thick to get through. He had learned the hard way two weeks before what would happen if he tried to push the squadron into that sort of mess, so he turned the formation for home and brought the Flying Knights in to Dobo. All the other P-38 squadrons aborted the mission as well, except for Major Charles MacDonald's 431st Fighter Squadron. They stayed with the bombers after climbing above the storm, where they found open blue sky all the way to Rabaul. The risk paid off, for not one of MacDonald's men was lost, and he managed to destroy a Zero that was attempting a pass at the B-24s. For MacDonald, that would be his fourth kill in what became a long and auspicious career.

The weather remained bad for the next four days, giving the Flying Knights a short breather. They returned to Rabaul on October 29th, as bomber escorts yet again, claiming seven without loss. Dick Bong, Jerry's gentle and quiet friend who hailed originally from Minnesota farm country, nailed two Zeroes that day, giving him nineteen planes to his credit. That made him one of the top American aces of the war to date.

Thus closed one of the busiest and most difficult periods in Jerry's life. He had seen his squadron hit the enemy hard, again and again, but his men had suffered in return. Barnes was gone, never to return; Harry Lidstrom had disappeared, as had Theron Price, Ralph Hays, and Frank Wunder. Seven more men from the squadron went down in the PBY that had gone out in search of Harry, and by now everyone had given up hope of finding them alive. Woodson Woodward died over Rabaul at the hands of the Japanese air defenses on the 24th, capping the losses of the month.

As the pilots and planes drained steadily away, the 9th Squadron's operational strength shrank as well. The supply of P-38s from stateside factories had all but dried up, and the birds on hand were getting worn out. Jerry's faithful *Sooner* had survived all sorts of calamities, ranging from the collision with the Tony in July to the shower of debris Jerry flew through after he scored his seventh kill on the 23rd. Now it was scratched and marred, with wide swaths of paint scuffed off, giving it a ratty and almost decrepit appearance. The other planes in the outfit looked about the same.

From the sixteen planes ready to go for the October 23rd mission, one had been lost in combat and four others were out of commission by November 1st. With but eleven P-38s left, the 9th was at less than half-strength. Yet in this condition the men continued to fight, continued to pile up kills, giving always better than they got. They would need that determination in the coming weeks.

PART FOUR

Bloody Tuesday

FOURTEEN

Wavetop Surprise

General Kenney would not give up on Rabaul. He had pounded it all through October, determined to destroy the Japanese air presence there through high and low level attacks, similar to those he had launched against Wewak with so much success back in August. The Japanese fields around Rabaul, however, were better developed, better prepared, and certainly better defended than those at Wewak. There would be no single battle over these critical aerodromes that would tilt the balance against the Japanese. The B-25s and B-24s would have no opportunity to blast hundreds of enemy planes to pieces as they sat on the ground, wingtip to wingtip. Instead, Rabaul became a bloody slugging match, a campaign of attrition that forced the Fifth Air Force to pay dearly for every success they achieved. The well-revetted Japanese planes on the ground had to be hunted out and destroyed one by one in their protective enclosures. In the air, the Japanese fighters that rose to meet the incoming waves of Mitchells and Liberators proved to be manned by excellent pilots, who picked their targets well and were determined to sell their own lives at a very high price.

There was no doubt at Fifth Air Force headquarters that the Japanese were suffering more than the Americans and Australians. They had lost scores of planes over the month, and were in desperate need of reinforcement. The only available planes, however, were the air group on the remaining Japanese aircraft carriers, but the theater commander did not hesitate to throw those into the inferno around Rabaul. In the last days of October, over two hundred fighters, dive bombers, and torpedo bombers flew from Truk to the fields around Simpson Harbor. The Japanese knew that if they lost the air battle over Rabaul, they would surely lose the entire southwest Pacific theater to the advancing Allies.

On November 1, American marines landed at Empress Augusta Bay on the south side of Bouganville, the northernmost island in the Solomon chain. This would give the Allied forces in that area an excellent base from which to pound Rabaul. The Japanese knew they had to throw everything they had against this new beachhead if Rabaul was to be saved. That night, they tried to attack the landing ships with a surface task force of cruisers and destroyers. In what became known as the Battle of Empress Augusta Bay, the Japanese were stopped cold, suffered severe losses, and never did get a crack at the vulnerable amphibious fleet. Battered and dispirited, the Japanese ships returned to Rabaul, seeking the protection of Simpson Harbor's flak and fighters.

General Kenney wanted to knock those ships out cold so they couldn't make another sortie against the beachhead. Promising everything he had to help support Admiral William F. Halsey's attack on Bougainville, he cut orders to the bulk of the Fifth Air Force's available units that Rabaul would be hit again with another maximum effort strike. This time, though, instead of hitting the airfields, the main targets floated in the harbor.

The orders were cut on the evening of November 1, and sent to all of the groups involved in the attack. Jerry received orders to have the 9th Squadron escort the 3rd Attack Group right into Simpson Harbor. Their B-25s would be the main striking force against the cruisers, destroyers, and merchantmen riding at anchor there, while the 38th Bomb Group's Mitchells would lay smoke along the shoreline to mask the anti-aircraft batteries. To surprise the Japanese, the entire strike force would fly east and up past Rabaul and then wheel southward to drop on Rabaul from the north. Everyone would be down low—the 3rd Attack would stay only a few hundred feet off the water, while the 9th kept vigil close overhead at 5,000 feet.

Jerry knew this would be the biggest strike of the war for the Fifth Air Force, and he recognized the importance of executing it well. If they knocked out the shipping, the American beachhead at Empress Augusta Bay would not be challenged again by naval forces. If they failed, the beachhead would be in jeopardy again.

That night, he called his men together to brief them about the attack. The raid had been scheduled for the last four days, but each time weather had scrubbed the mission. This time, it looked like it was a go. To help with the briefing, Jerry enlisted the aid of Ralph Wandrey, one of his most trusted pilots and an ace in his own right, who helped deliver the pre-battle pep talk Jerry loved so much to give. When the men hit the sack well after dark, they realized the morning would bring a tough fight—perhaps the toughest they would face.

But again, when dawn arrived, it looked like the weather would scrub the mission. After breakfast, the pilots gathered at the Ops shack, waiting to hear if the mission was on or not. The ground crews had performed miracles over the past few days, getting eleven P-38s ready to go. It was a polyglot force, a mixture of P-38Fs, Gs, and Hs, but all were fueled, armed, and waiting for their pilots in the squadron's revetments.

Word came that the mission was on hold until a couple of recon planes checked out the weather at Rabaul. Several squadrons of bombers had actually started taking off when the recall order was issued. The bombers wheeled around and landed at their home airfields, their crews anxious to know if today was the day or not.

Tension mounted as the men waited to hear which way things would shake out. Down at the 9th's Ops shack, a couple of the pilots lay on cots, reading tattered issues of *Reader's Digest* that Jerry's folks had sent to the outfit. A few others settled down to play a quiet game of cards, silently going through the motions as a myriad of thoughts passed through their minds. Jerry stayed within arm's reach of the telephone, watching his men and trying to lighten the mood with his humor. Blev Lewelling sat nearby, listening to the scattered conversation around him.

Blev was a relative newcomer to the squadron, and an Oregonian by birth. Born in Albany, midway between Salem and Corvallis, Lewelling was an Oregon State University student who got caught up in the war like so many others. Being from Jerry's arch-rival college gave him and Blev quite a bit to talk about, and as they got to know each other, they discovered that their fathers were acquainted. Blev's dad was a judge, and Jerry's father had argued several cases before him.

Bob Wood, the transplanted, soft-spoken Californian who had nearly been killed over the Markham Valley during the July dogfights, was also scheduled for the day's mission. He would be in Green Flight, flying with Carl Plank and Wally Jordan.

Stanley Johnson, one of the replacement pilots in Wood's group that had arrived in the early summer, would fly Jerry's wing that day. The two Johnsons had flown on several missions together, becoming good friends in the process. Stanley knew that Jerry took care of his wingmen, and to date had never lost one in action, a fact that must have provided some comfort to him, given the mission ahead.

The telephone rang just after 10:00 A.M. Jerry stood up, reached for the handset and picked it up. A few curt words, an unconscious nod, and the handset was dropped into its cradle.

"It's a go. Let's get to the ships."

Eleven pilots clambered aboard three jeeps and rode down to the flight line. The driver slowed at each revetment, and allowed the assigned man to slide off the fender and jog to his P-38. When the last man jumped clear, the drivers parked their jeeps and trotted to their own fighters, where their crew chiefs waited on the wings.

Across the field, Major Jock Henebry and his 3rd Attack Group were going through similar preparations. Born in Plainfield, Illinois, John P. Henebry was a Midwesterner to the core. His father had been a grain-elevator operator and a member of the Chicago Board of Trade. Raised in Plainfield, he graduated from high school there in 1936 before going on to study business administration and accounting at Notre Dame, where he also played right end for the football team during his freshman year. Later, he learned to fly through the school's CPTP, much as Jerry had a few hundred miles west.

While still in school, John's dad died exactly at noon one day in a car wreck. His widowed mother continued to watch over him, keeping him on the right path. When John decided that he wanted to go into the Air Corps, his mom sat him down and talked him out of the idea, convincing him to stay at Notre Dame until he earned his degree. He did and, in retrospect, it was the best advice he was ever given.

In 1940, John graduated from Notre Dame. Degree in hand, he was sworn into the Army Air Corps that summer as a new cadet. He was sent to Tulsa first, where he went through Primary Training. From there, he and his classmates went to Randolph Field, Texas for Basic, then on to nearby Kelly Field for Advanced. Once he graduated as part of Class 41B, John joined the 22nd Bomb Group, one the units that would eventually wind up in Kenney's Fifth Air Force in New Guinea. A short time later, the 22nd was divided up and served as the cadre for two new bomb groups, the 13th and 38th. John went with the 13th to Florida, where he spent the first few months of World War II flying anti-submarine patrols over the Gulf of Mexico.

After Midway, he and six others were detached from the 13th and sent to Australia, where they were assigned to the 3rd Attack Group. He flew with the 3rd through some of the most dangerous missions of the war, including several during the Battle of the Bismarck Sea in March 1943. He'd been in the theater for over a year by the time of the November 2, 1943 Rabaul raid, had seen much combat, and had recently been given command of the group. He would lead it into battle on this day from the left seat of his own B-25, *Notre Dame De Victoire*.

John Henebry and Jerry were two peas in a pod. Both were aggressive, intelligent, and full of beans, and as they got to know each other at Dobo, a mutual respect and admiration grew between them. The bond extended into the air, where Jerry would frequently drop down on Henebry's flight on the way back from escorting the 3rd Attack to a Japanese target. He would fly formation for a while with John and his B-25s, then playfully roll inverted and tack onto his friend's wing—upside down. Today though, there would be no silly antics—just grim determination to make it through this strike in one piece, and to do as much damage as possible.

Flying with John Henebry on this day was his youngest squadron commander, Captain Dick Ellis. At twenty-three, he was Jerry's age and just as cool under fire as his Oregonian friend. Ellis and Jerry knew each other through John and Don Good, through the nights they had passed at each others O Clubs on either side of Horanda Strip at Dobo. With Ellis that day was a war correspondent who later became quite good friends with Jerry. Lee Van Atta had finagled his way aboard Ellis's B-25, *Seabiscuit*, which was reputed to be the slowest Mitchell in the entire Fifth Air Force. Van Atta would have a bird's-eye view of the water-level attack on Simpson Harbor from between Dick Ellis and his copilot. Later on, Lee would be present at the Bikini Atoll A-Bomb tests in 1946, where he would broadcast live the events as they unfolded to an enthralled America.

The B-25s took off first, leaving in their wakes great clouds of reddish dust kicked up by their landing gear and three-bladed props. When the echo of their Wright Cyclone engines died away as the 3rd Attack sped eastward, Dobo became almost eerily silent. Then the Allisons churned to life, sweet sounding and precise, unlike the throaty roar of the bomber's engines. One by one, the P-38s of the 9th Fighter Squadron rolled out of their revetments and taxied to the end of the runway. They took off by flights, four abreast and already in formation as their wheels left the ground. By the time the last one lifted off, nearly every head around the strip had turned to watch their planes go to challenge the enemy. For these ground-bound, dedicated men, this was a proud moment, the culmination of hours of frustrating work. They knew that those P-38s were the way that the squadron collectively struck at the Japanese; it took not just aviators, but mechanics, radiomen, armorers, clerks, and doctors to get those birds in the air day after day. It was a team effort to launch them at Rabaul, a fact overlooked for years by reporters and historians alike.

After a brief refueling stop at Kiriwina, where the men had just enough time to wolf down sandwiches the cooks had prepared for them, the 9th fanned out into battle formation and linked up with the 3rd Attack Group over the Solomon Sea. Trouble developed soon after, when Wally Jordan's P-38 began to act up. He stayed in there for several minutes, fiddling around in the cockpit until his mechanical problems forced him to abort the mission. He broke away from his flight, handed the lead over to Carl Plank, and returned to Kiriwina, thoroughly disgusted with his bad luck.

The others pressed on, staying close to the bombers at about 5,000 feet. Oddly, Henebry, at the spear point of his group's formation, could not see the P-38s above him, but he knew Jerry would be there and trusted his close friend to keep the Zeroes off his back. The B-25s skimmed the wavetops, throwing up froth in their wake as their props sometimes nicked the whitecaps. They went up St. Georges Channel, passing over a couple of small warships which almost certainly reported their position. The element of surprise had been lost—the Japanese would be expecting them.

The lead bombers, all from the 345th Bomb Group, went in first. Past the mouth of Blanche Bay, they wheeled west, then south, hitting the north coast of New Britain four minutes ahead of Jerry's P-38s and Henebry's Mitchells. Practically clipping the treetops, they poured out into the harbor from between two volcanoes, North Daughter and Rabatana Crater, guns blasting away at anything military that lay in their paths. Above them, the P-38s from the 475th, 39th, and 80th Groups ran right into a swarm of Japanese interceptors. Outnumbered and attacked from all directions, the P-38 pilots fought frantically to keep the Zeroes off of the B-25s.

Right on the deck, the 345th swarmed over Rabaul Township, tracers arcing out before them as the pilots cut loose with their forward-firing machine guns. They dropped phosphorous bombs behind them, and soon the coast was filled with dozens of spouting gray-white explosions that flung tendrils of smoke and flames fanning out in dozens of directions.

The first wave had done well, masking the AA guns pointing toward the harbor as they pressed on to hit Lakunai aerodrome. Once over the field, the B-25s discovered all sorts of juicy targets. A Dinah lay right in the path of the oncoming bombers, and the crew bailed out of it, as they saw they stood no chance of taking off with such firepower thundering down on them. The strip was sprayed with thousands of rounds of machine-gun bullets; grounded Japanese planes stood little chance against this onslaught, especially since not all of the new replacement aircraft had their own revetments. Some stood right out in the open, just as at Wewak and they were shredded by the American fusillade.

It took barely five minutes for the first wave to hit their targets and clear out, Zekes chasing them all the way out as they poured on the coals to get away. The P-38s stayed with them, sometimes even after their ammunition was gone, using every trick they had to keep the Zeroes at bay. Here and there a Zero caught fire and plunged into the jungle, leaving an ugly streak of smoke hanging in the air. One observer on the ground watched the dogfight unfold, captivated by the scene until a P-38 roared overhead, fire spurting from its engines as an AA gunner found the range and laced the American plane with explosive shells. It crashed into a mountain just outside of Rabaul Township.

Amidst this chaos, the main blow arrived. John Henebry had led his group around North Daughter, coming in at a slightly different angle of attack than the first wave, hoping that the smoke their comrades had generated would cover their approach. Doing over 230 mph indicated, they tore into the target angle and found the harbor full of ships. There were merchantmen, cruisers, destroyers, tankers, tenders, barges, motor launches, and tugs everywhere, and all had guns that were soon trained on his men.

Above Henebry, Jerry brought the 9th Squadron into the battle. Just past North Daughter, he and his men spotted aircraft taking off from Lakunai aerodrome—survivors from the first wave bravely going forth to carry on the fight. Jerry and his flight, barely 3,000 feet over the bombers, went down after the planes taking off, hoping to knock them down before they could get their gear up and go after Henebry's boys.

Then everything went to pieces. The mission had been planned so that the 9th Squadron would be down low enough to cover the 3rd Attack as it pressed home its wavetop runs on the ships in Simpson Harbor. That gave the bombers a good chance to escape interception, but without any high cover force over the 9th, Jerry and his men were terribly exposed to attack from above, and that was exactly what happened. Just as the squadron passed through a group of small clouds, scattering the P-38s, somebody called out, "Zekes! Six O'Clock High!"

They came down with all the impetus of a freight train, a dozen cannon-armed Zeroes lashing out at the Lightnings with terrible precision, guns chattering, tracers streaming forth. The P-38s broke wildly into their attackers, heeling over in tight chandelles as they put their own guns in the enemy's face.

Carl Plank, now leading Green Flight, was the first to go down. He broke into the Zekes, picked out one of the oncoming fighters and set up a head-on attack. Bob Wood lost Plank in the clouds, but Blev Lewelling stayed right on his wing, covering his new leader as they roared towards the Zeroes. Blev watched as Plank opened fire at about the same time the Japanese pilot did. Both held steady, closing the range to practically nothing in just a few short seconds. Neither pilot scored, but then neither pilot refused to break away. They collided, head-on, going flat out at a closure rate of over 500 miles per hour. Blev blinked and Plank had disappeared—his P-38 was replaced by a terrible orange fireball that soon dissipated, leaving in its wake a cloud of debris waffling downwards.

Seconds later, Wood emerged from the cloud into a sky full of enemy fighters. Being alone in such a situation invited disaster, so as he dodged attacks, he scanned the area for another P-38. Luckily, Blev Lewelling popped up and Wood headed straight for him. Reunited now, they clung to each other as Zeroes and Lightnings swirled around them in a tapestry of gunfire, burning aircraft, and black puffs of anti-aircraft fire. Zeroes and Oscars came at them from every direction, forcing them to twist and turn so violently that at times it seemed like they were not flying at all, but skidding through the sky. From time to time, as they gyrated madly over Lakunai aerodrome, a Zero would wander in front of them, and both men would take quick snap shots at the unwary Japanese pilot. Blev nailed one that way in a head-on pass. As it dived under Wood, the pilot bailed out. Though they both got a small sense of satisfaction out of the kill, that Zero was but one of seemingly hundreds. Several made quick passes on Bob's Lightning, and as he juked and jinked to avoid their fire, he could feel the *whoomp, whoomp* of shells striking home. One string of bullets walked along his top wing and shot away his fuel tank's gas cap. Fighting on, Bob kept turning into his attackers, giving them the worst possible angles while trying to bring his own guns to bear. Then, he lost Blev again, and was alone amid a scene of unimaginable chaos.

Francis Love got it next. Zeroes singled him out and chopped his P-38 to ribbons. He went in without anyone seeing his final, mortal dive. That left nine ships out of the twelve that had left Dobo earlier that morning—and the fight had just begun.

As Blev Lewelling and Bob Wood fought for their lives amidst the puffy clouds, Jerry and Stanley Johnson were busy trying to keep the Zeroes from Lakunai off of the 3rd Attack Group. Jerry shot down two Zeroes, one with a 45-degree deflection shot. Then, with fighters zooming by everywhere, he and Stanley snapped out short bursts at anything that passed before their noses. The fight carried them inland, over the coconut plantations near Vunakanua aerodrome, where Stanley managed to flame an Oscar. The Japanese plane crashed into a grove of trees and exploded.

By this time, Jerry had only two guns firing. The rest had either jammed or run out of ammunition. He and Stanley were in no position to disengage, though. They had been fighting just off the treetops, and without any altitude they could not run away from the dozens of Japanese planes in the air around them. They would have to fight their way out. Jerry turned into another Zero as it made a pass at him, forcing a head-on approach that put the Japanese pilot at a distinct disadvantage, even though *Sooner* only had two .50s working. Jerry met every attack in that same manner, always turning into the Zeke, dishing it out as well as taking some lumps in the process. This happened five or six more times, until he spotted a lone P-38, smoke gushing out of one of its Allisons.

He closed on the crippled fighter, and saw that the damaged engine had been feathered. The Lightning had attracted the attention of a lone Zero, which intended to finish off the American. Jerry swept down on the Zero and chased it off with his remaining ammunition. Finally free from the Japanese interceptors, Jerry and Stanley turned for home.

Meanwhile, down on the water, John Henebry had set his sights on a freighter. His guns hosed down the vessel's decks, sweeping them clear of sailors, blowing holes in the bulkheads, and smashing gun positions. Just short of the target, John pickled off his first 1,000-pound bomb. It fell free from the open bomb bay doors and smacked into the water. Instead of sinking, though, it bounced, skipping like a stone off the wavetops until it slammed into the side of the freighter, burying itself deep in the ship's bowels before detonating.

A split second before the impact, John horsed the yoke back into his stomach, wrenching the Mitchell into a sudden climb that carried them right over the merchant ship, wings practically scraping the masts and rigging. John's tail gunner saw their first target explode in flames behind them as the bomb found its mark.

Ahead lay a huge merchant ship, a 10,000-tonner at least. Jock hosed it down with machine gun fire, keeping the sailors from throwing out accurate ack-ack. Again, he repeated his earlier performance, and released his other 1,000-pound bomb just before pulling up and thundering over the vessel at a perpendicular angle to it.

This time, he pulled up too hard, and before he could ease the nose down and onto the next target, the ship ahead cut loose on Henebry's B-25 with dozens of flak guns of every caliber. It was the heavy cruiser *Haguro*, swinging on its anchor chains like an ugly bulldog, ready to maul anything that came within its reach.

Shells slammed into the Mitchell, riddling the tail gunner's position and knocking out his guns. Miraculously, the gunner himself escaped untouched, but now Jock's stinger was gone. Worse, the same shells tore through the rudders. Instantly, the Mitchell began mushing around, forcing John and his copilot to give the aircraft right rudder to hold her steady.

The barrage continued, shells slamming into the Mitchell and churning up the water all around it as it sped towards the *Haguro,* nose high. This was the worst moment possible—down low with a gun-studded cruiser in the way to safety, and no way to strike back. So they took it, flying through the hailstorm of gunfire until the B-25 blazed right over the ship, so close that Jock and his crew could make out the binoculars around the captain's neck as he gazed up at them from the bridge.

Then they were over the ship, running for home with throttles wide and guns blazing. As they neared the south end of the harbor, John swung the nose slightly over to line up a small lugger chugging along nearby. He demolished it with his last bomb, a 500-pounder. That done, it was time to take the crippled Mitchell home.

All through the attack, Dick Ellis in *Seabiscuit* tried to stay close to Jock, though as they sped across the harbor Dick fell behind as his cursed engines could not keep up with the rest of the squadron. Though hit numerous times by ground fire, Ellis brought *Seabiscuit* out of the harbor in fairly decent shape. Even as Rabaul faded out of sight to the north, Lee Van Atta sat down in the navigator's compartment and began typing up his recollections of the attack. It would be published all over the world a short time later, becoming one of the war's best on-the-spot accounts of an air battle.

❧

Henebry made it out of the harbor area, limping along on a sick engine and a tattered rudder. Out of nowhere came a Zero, diving from above on his Mitchell. It made a single pass, but it was enough. The Zeke's cannon shells blasted the B-25's right engine into wreckage. Instinctively, John reached forward and hit the switch to feather the propeller. Nothing happened. The controls had been shot away, leaving them with a windmilling prop that added drag. Fortunately, the Japanese pilot decided not to stick around and finish off the cripple, turning instead for Rabaul and its relative safety.

Henebry flew that plane with every ounce of strength he possessed, standing on the right rudder along with his copilot, coaxing out every bit of power from the remaining engine while at the same time keeping an eye on the dead engine, making sure that it had not caught fire.

As they limped south for Kiriwina, the rest of Dick Ellis's squadron showed up. John ordered them on, as his B-25 could not even come close to matching their speed. Just to keep it airborne, John's crew had tossed everything they could overboard, but the B-25 still barely clung to the air. Chuck Howe, John's wingman, stayed with him doggedly, watching out for fighters and lending moral support to his group commander. The others, including Dick Ellis, headed for Dobo and home, wishing Jock luck as they passed his battered and scarred Mitchell over the Solomon Sea.

Notre Dame De Victoire brought Jock and his crew almost all the way home. As they closed on Kiriwina, the gunners continued to strip the fuselage of all nonessential gear. Everything went overboard—the remaining guns, ammo, and boxes—anything to lighten the load. They finally reached a sort of odd equilibrium. Now lightened, the B-25 stopped losing altitude, but its one remaining, overworked engine strained just to keep the bomber airborne, making it impossible to climb.

Practically scraping the whitecaps, Henebry dragged *Notre Dame De Victoire* to the Kiriwina shoreline. As he tried to make an approach on the runway, he found the bomber could not climb over the palm trees at the end of the strip. With no other recourse, he bellied the Mitchell into the surf right offshore. Though banged up in the crash, he and the rest of crew were picked up by a PT boat only a few minutes later.

⚓

Back over Rabaul, Bob Wood knew it was time to get home. Shot-up, low on fuel, and separated from the squadron, he fought his way south over the harbor, dodging and weaving as the Zeroes kept pressing home attacks on him. They were everywhere, attacking any plane in range with a white star on its wings. There simply was no way to avoid them. Carefully, though, he picked his way through the dogfight, breaking into every attack launched at him, picking up a few more holes as he went. Finally, he broke out the other side and ran for Kiriwina.

⚓

Kiriwina was a mess. Crippled planes were coming in one after another, landing practically on top of each other as the pilots tried to bring their wrecked ships down. The situation soon got out of hand as the air filled with desperate pilots, low on fuel, with wounded crewmen aboard. One P-38 ran out of gas on its final approach, and crashed in flames a bare hundred feet from the runway. Another exhausted Lightning pilot put his plane down on the runway and slammed into a Jeep parked along the flight line. Others tried to land at the same time from different directions. Amazingly, no collisions took place, but the near misses gave the ground controllers fits. By dusk, every square inch of the field was filled with wrecked or damaged airplanes. B-25s stood in revetments, their metal skins peppered with bullets, hydraulic fluid and oil dripping from them to form puddles in the dust.

All this for twelve minutes of combat over Simpson Harbor. Ever after, the Fifth called the raid "Bloody Tuesday."

❧

The next morning, Bob Wood awoke at Kiriwina to find his temporary tentmate, another P-38 pilot from a different group, was already stirring. He sat up on the edge of his cot, and as he threw his clothes on, he made small talk with the other pilot. Before bedding down the night before, the two had chatted and Bob had found him to be a likable, decent fellow.

Suddenly, the other pilot stopped talking, leaned back onto his cot and raised his arms slightly. Before Bob could reach over and help, the man fell right over onto the tent floor on the other side of the cot. Bob stood, going to his aid. The pilot lay on the wooden floor, convulsing wildly, his body shaking as his arms flailed around him. The sight terrified Bob, who had no idea what was going on. He fled the tent in search of help.

A few minutes later, he was back with several others. The pilot still lay on the floor, but his seizure had passed. When they tried talking with him, though, they discovered that the man remembered nothing—it was as if his entire memory had been wiped clean by the sudden attack. He had no idea who he was, where he was, or why he was there. The doctors examined him and concluded that he had suffered a complete nervous breakdown. The stress of that last Rabaul mission had pushed the poor man right over the edge. The pilot was gingerly carried from the tent.

Bob never saw him or heard about him again. He was probably returned to the States with the designation, LMF—Lack of Moral Fiber, the Army Air Force's way of classifying breakdowns.

"God," thought Bob as he watched the broken pilot being carried out of the tent, "Am I that close to the edge, too?"

Whatever the answer was, he was terrified to find out.

PART FIVE

Fighter Leader

FIFTEEN

Republic's Abortion

Dearest Mother and Dad,

You get the news there and know what our men are doing down here. Sometimes things are tough and they know they may not return to their homes, yet they do not flinch. We who fight believe in our liberty. We thank God that we can serve in the capacity for which we've been trained. I have told you before that I am happy here. My happiness is not based on the vision of the future when peace is here again, but on the faith I have in you, in Barbara, and the men in my squadron. I have no regrets or complaints in my heart, why should I? I have known the companionship of fellow men, the feel of a trout on a line and the warmth of a real and genuine love. On earth and in heaven, I shall be with men who have meant more to me than these pleasures of life. The things we believe in are greater than ourselves. We pray only for the courage, strength and a task to perform.

Your Loving Son,
Gerald

The Flying Knights continued to fight and die over Rabaul. Three days after Bloody Tuesday, Dick Bong led ten other patched together P-38s on a high-altitude escort mission to the Japanese base. On his wing that day was George Haniotis, the squadron's fitness freak, who could always be seen jogging around Dobo or lifting weights. George was a recent arrival to the squadron, but had proved to be a good pilot. He had shot an Oscar down over Wewak on October 16 while flying with Wally Jordan.

On this day, November 5, the Japanese hit the 9th Squadron with a formation of dirty green-brown Zekes. Dick flung his Lightning at the attackers and downed two of them in a confusing melee. Somehow during the fight, George got separated from Dick, and a Zero shot him up. Blev Lewelling saw him limping away from Rabaul with one engine feathered. After the squadron reformed out of the target area, George's voice came over the radio. He called out a Mayday and announced he had to bail out. George Haniotis splashed down into the Solomon Sea, somewhere east of Arawe. Climbing into his life raft, he settled down to wait for rescue. Without the fuel to search for him, the 9th headed for home, hoping that the air-sea rescue outfit at Kiriwina would fish him out.

Later that evening, word came through to Dobo that George had not been found. Over the next four days, the 9th flew daily search missions to find Haniotis. More than once, they located him adrift in his yellow life raft, frantically waving to his airborne buddies as they passed overhead. Each time, the squadron called in his location, but for some inexplicable reason, air-sea rescue never located him.

Finally, on November 9th, Jerry gathered the squadron to tell his men that they were going out to find him and make sure he got picked up. Eight P-38s fanned out over the Solomon Sea, flying in line abreast a few hundred feet above the whitecaps. Somewhere between New Guinea and New Britain, they caught sight of his bobbing little raft. Jerry got on the radio and called out the exact location to the air-sea guys at Kiriwina, then ordered his men to circle George until help arrived.

The men waited for a flying boat to show up, but one never did. Blev Lewelling, flying wing on Jerry that morning, later learned that all the seaplanes at Kiriwina were committed elsewhere. As time dragged by, the P-38s began running low on fuel. Jerry sent most of the squadron home, though he and Blev remained, hoping somebody would come and get their friend. Finally, a PT boat showed up. Jerry contacted it and talked them over to George's life raft. Somebody on the PT boat announced they had George's raft in sight. Convinced they had done all they could, Jerry and Blev turned for home, nursing their dwindling fuel supply.

After they left, the PT boat lost sight of George. Despite an exhaustive search, the crew never found him. Three weeks later, George's raft washed ashore near Cape Ward Hunt—his body was not in it.

The Flying Knights returned to Rabaul on November 7. This time, Captain Jump O'Neil led the squadron—or what was left of it. The outfit was down to eight flyable birds, and all were in bad shape. Among those flying with Jump that day were Dick Bong and Stanley Johnson. Stanley had become quite a close friend of Jerry's over the past few months, and Jerry usually selected him as his wingman. He "loaned" Stanley to Dick that morning and made the Wisconsin-born ace promise to take good care of him.

They ran into a small group of Zekes over Rabaul. Dick made several passes, but grew frustrated when he missed each time. Somewhere in the course of the fight, he caught sight of Del Moore's P-38 below. Del was being attacked by no fewer than nine Zeroes. Leading Stanley down after them, Dick managed to clear Del's tail and break up the Japanese attacks. Stanley Johnson went after a Zero and chased it inland. He was never seen again.

The loss of his third wingman in three months was too much for Dick to take. Stanley Johnson had been a close friend, and his loss prompted Dick to swear that he would never fly with a wingman again. Meanwhile, gossip in the squadron focused on Dick's ordeal, though nobody seemed to blame him. He was such a marvelous pilot that few others could hang with him in a fight. A few weeks later, after Dick had returned to the States, he felt compelled to visit Stanley's wife in Michigan. He sat with her for an afternoon, explaining as best he could what had happened to her husband. It had to have been one of the toughest things Dick had ever done.

❧

The Flying Knights were just about out of business. Assigned to another escort mission to Rabaul on November 11, the mechanics were able to get only six P-38s flyable. One or two more missions, and they would not have any planes left at all. Replacements were not available, as most of Lockheed's Lightning production was earmarked for the Eighth Air Force over in England. The Eighth's heavy bombers were getting mauled over Germany, and every available long-range fighter was needed to staunch the bloodletting.

Though hardly any P-38s were making it to the Southwest Pacific

Area, the Fifth Air Force had recently received a large batch of Republic P-47D Thunderbolts. There were enough "Jugs"—as the pilots called the P-47—on hand to re-equip several of the battered P-38 squadrons. As a result, in mid-November, Kenney ordered the 9th Fighter Squadron to turn over their last few P-38s and to accept delivery of twenty-five factory-fresh P-47s. When Jerry learned of the decision, he was livid. To him, the Jug was an oversized, bloated, and unresponsive monster that lacked climb rate and acceleration; it could not possibly compare with his beloved P-38. With several of his closest friends, he brooded over this development, though there was nothing they could do about it.

Kenney recognized that the switch might cause morale problems, so he sent Colonel Neel Kirby over to the 9th to give them a pep talk about the Thunderbolt's better qualities. Kirby's 348th Fighter Group had introduced the Jug to combat in the theater back in August 1943. Kirby proved to be a bad choice. Earlier that summer, Kirby had rubbed Jerry and some of the other pilots of the 49th Fighter Group the wrong way with his brash and arrogant manner. One 49th pilot recalled years later how the 348th showed up, fresh and fiery, full of braggadocio. That was knocked out of them in the first few weeks of operations, when they kept pranging their Jugs during landing and take-off accidents. Another 49th pilot recalls how their bragging diminished considerably one day, after the 9th Squadron returned from a hot mission to execute numerous victory rolls right over their stretch of the airfield.

Whether these things actually happened is not particularly relevant. What matters is this: the 9th did not like the P-47, and Neel Kirby was not the man to sell it to them. In fact, when Neel and Jerry began discussing the merits of the Thunderbolt over the Lightning, tempers flared almost immediately. As the heated exchange turned to a red-faced shouting match, they challenged each other to a duel—Jerry in his P-38, Kirby in his P-47. Though the proposed match never occurred, Dick Bong and Neel Kirby squared-off against each other over Port Moresby. Exactly when this took place is in doubt, but those who witnessed the fight, including Wally Jordan, recalled that it was an epic struggle. Kirby threw his P-47 all over the sky, doing things with it that nobody thought possible. Bong, on the other hand, was silk-smooth, precise, and aggressive in his P-38. By all accounts, they fought each other to a standstill.

Though no clear winner emerged, the Flying Knights who witnessed the scene gave the edge to Dick Bong, probably out of loyalty to their top ace.

After November 12 when the first batch of Jugs arrived, Jerry knew he had to stop complaining about the new aircraft, lest he damage morale even further. Walter Markey, who had been flying with the 9th since January, 1943, recalled that when the P-47s arrived, morale in the squadron plummeted. He remembered that Jerry decided to buck everyone up by showing them what the Thunderbolt could do. With many of his pilots watching, Jerry dashed over to a Jug and took it out onto the runway at Dobodura. Standing on the brakes, he opened the throttle and let the enormous Pratt & Whitney engine run up to full power. When the engine's roar reached its peak, he released the brakes and stormed down the runway. Halfway down, he sucked the stick right into his gut, and the Jug suddenly barreled upwards into a 45-degree climb. Markey gasped at such a reckless take-off, which nearly did Jerry in. Overestimating the power and acceleration of this new fighter, Jerry suddenly found himself on the verge of a stall. The nose wallowed, then dropped. The entire plane mushed downward until Jerry managed to recover—barely fifty feet off the ground.

Needless to say, the demonstration did little to cheer the men up. Most of the old-timers in the squadron remained committed P-38 pilots, though some of them grudgingly admitted later that they liked the Jug's firepower. Eight .50-caliber machine guns could turn any Japanese fighter into a greasy flaming smear with just the shortest of bursts.

Most, however, remained unreconstructed. When Ralph Wandrey received his P-47, he ordered his crew chief to name it *Republic's Abortion*. For his part, Jerry somehow managed to snare a wayward P-40N, and he used it on a several occasions as his personal hack, as well as for unofficial combat missions. Though exactly where this Tomahawk came from is uncertain; most evidence points to it having been a 7th Squadron aircraft.

Jerry also found time to get some experience in the right seat of a B-25, probably a 3rd Attack Group aircraft, and even took a flight in an A-20G Havoc at Dobodura. He later learned to fly A-20s, and accumulated several hours in them. Months later, at Biak, 8th Squadron pilot Oliver Atchison recalled seeing Jerry slow-roll an A-20 right down Mokmer aerodrome's main runway. Whatever plane he flew, Jerry always managed to wring every bit of performance out of it.

From November 12 until early December, the 9th generally remained out of combat as it re-equipped. During the change-over to Jugs, many of the squadron's old hands went home. Among them was Dick Bong, who returned to his native Wisconsin and a hero's welcome. While this transition period kept most everyone out of battle, Jerry got into all sorts of trouble.

Unable to stay out of combat, he began flying missions with other squadrons. Exactly how many is unclear, but he flew an escort mission to Hansa Bay on the morning of November 17, 1943 in a P-38. Later that same afternoon, he flew a patrol to Finschhafen, again in a Lightning. Both missions were probably with the 39th Fighter Squadron, which still had its twin-engined fighters. The second mission of November 17 has been shrouded in mystery and controversy ever since the war. Exactly what took place, if anything, on this afternoon mission may never be known for sure. The various versions of the story, however, are described below.

According to most secondary sources, this mission actually occurred on November 15, though Jerry's Form 5 has no entry for that day. During the flight up to Finschhafen, he spotted a single, radial-engined aircraft coming straight at him. He pulled the nose of his P-38 up and gave the onrushing aircraft a quick burst. The plane began smoking, then rolled slightly as it blew past him. To his horror, Jerry saw the plane's markings were not Japanese but Australian.

There are many different versions of what happened next. Most secondary sources state that the pilot bailed out or crash-landed his Wirraway at Lae. Pilot Officer R. M. Stewart survived the engagement, but Jerry was later forced to surrender a bottle of gin to make amends. Recent interviews with pilots from the 49th Fighter Group paint a slightly different picture. All of those who spoke directly with Jerry about the mission agree that the aircraft he downed was not a Wirraway at all, but instead a Commonwealth Boomerang. That would make sense, as the Wirraway was a two-seat aircraft and no mention has ever been made to a second crewman being involved in this unfortunate incident.

Ralph Wandrey, who spent considerable time with Jerry in November and December 1943, has the most different recollection of the event.

According to Ralph, Jerry was up at Gusap, flying a P-40 around the mountains north of the airfield, when he caught sight of a column of Japanese troops below. They were working their way along mountain path and were ripe for a good strafing. Jerry dived down in his P-40 and began working the column over with his six .50s. He stayed on his strafing run, then banked to follow the trail around a steep cliff. As he leveled out to begin a second strafing run, he caught sight of an onrushing radial-engined fighter. From head-on, it looked just like an Oscar or a Zero. He could see little twinkles of flame on the wings as the pilot fired his guns. Realizing it was a kill-or-be-killed scenario, Jerry pulled his nose up, got the plane in his sights and fired. He struck it in the engine, which began to smoke. As the aircraft rushed by him, he saw the Australian markings on it, and was horrified at what he'd just done. He later found out that the Aussie was strafing the same column from the opposite direction.

Intensely worried, Jerry pulled up and swung around to see what had happened to the Aussie. As he did so, he saw the pilot bail out and land in the scrub a short distance from Gusap's main runway. He rushed over to the area and called Gusap Control, telling them to send a patrol out to get the Aussie before the Japanese got him.

After he returned home, he took Wandrey aside and said, "Jesus, I just shot down an Aussie. I feel really bad. But, he bailed out—he flipped her around and I saw him bail out. I called it in and told them to send some help there. I sure hope the Japs don't get him."

A few weeks later, according to Ralph's recollections, he was sitting in his tent when the Aussie showed up. He said to Ralph, "I'm looking for the guy who shot down the Boomerang."

Ralph studied him for minute, then asked, "Oh? What's the deal?"

The Aussie gamely replied, "I was the pilot he shot down and I want to give him a piece of my mind."

Jerry was at the Officers' Club at the time, so Ralph went on up there with the Aussie in tow. Leaving the irritated pilot outside, Ralph went in to prepare Jerry for what was about to happen.

"Hey Johnny," he said to Jerry, "that guy you shot down is here looking for you." Startled, Jerry tried to make an escape. "I got to get out of here, stall him for me Ralph." he blurted out as he stood up to leave.

Too late. In walked the Aussie and Ralph pointed to Jerry and announced, "Here's the guy!"

What are friends for, after all?

Rather than an ugly scene, the two pilots soon settled down and became fast friends over a few drinks. To smooth things over, Jerry surrendered a bottle of liquor, but there were few hard feelings. Wally Jordan recalled the meeting as well, noting that the Aussie was not really all that upset as he got a leave back to Sydney out of the whole deal. In the process, he got to visit his wife. And, his minor leg injury was a small price to pay for a few days of peace away from the war.

Jerry's Form 5 lists him as flying a P-40 from Dobodura up to Gusap on December 5, 1943. He landed, refueled, and took off again and flew around Gusap for about ninety minutes before landing. If Jerry knocked the Aussie down at Gusap while flying a P-40, this was the day he did it.

However, yet another version exists. On November 24, Jerry flew up to Gusap. The 9th Squadron was supposed to move to this forward base in a few weeks, and Jerry wanted to get the lay of the land. Around noon, he wandered into the 8th Fighter Squadron's Operations shack and asked to see the roster of personnel. He studied the roster, looking for anyone he might have known in flight school, or from Oregon. As his finger ran down the list, he came across a pilot named William A. Runey. The address listed for him was on 13th Street in Eugene. Jerry couldn't believe it. A fellow pilot from his hometown. Eagerly, he left the shack and went off to search for Runey.

Later that day, he wrote to Barbara of this chance encounter with a fellow Oregonian so many miles from home:

> I visited another squadron in our group today, and met a young pilot named Rooney [*sic*]. He went to Roosevelt Jr. High and Uni Hi with you. For once I became quite a bit homesick and that is not usual with me.

William A. Runey—Bill—turned out to be a soft-spoken young man of twenty-two who had been with the 8th for only a few months. He and Jerry hit it off right away, and when Jerry learned of Bill's connection with Barbara, he was delighted. He and Bill spent the entire afternoon sitting under the wing of a P-40, chatting away about Eugene, Barbara, and flying. Bill recalled that Jerry became quite nostalgic, and he was surprised at how personal some of Jerry's revelations became. He spoke of his intense love for Barbara, and his plans to marry her when he returned home. Bill told Jerry about his admiration for her. He remembered she was an excellent public speaker. Bill had always been shy, so he looked up to her for that ability. Indeed, Barbara was one of the few girls Bill had ever been able to talk with without feeling awkward or out of place.

The two of them delighted in their shared memories of Barbara for quite a while, but then their conversation turned to flying and the killing all around them. As they began swapping stories about the missions each had flown, Jerry suddenly confessed to shooting down an Australian pilot. As Bill recalled years later, the incident had, in fact, taken place near Finschhafen. Jerry was flying along when he spotted a couple of Japanese soldiers ducking into some brush below him. He went down and strafed them, but as he did, he caught sight of an unidentified plane rushing straight at him. He gave it a quick shot, saw the Aussie markings as it went past him, then watched as the Aussie crash-landed his Boomerang fighter in the kuni grass below.

By Bill Runey's account, the mission must have been flown sometime before November 24. The only flight Jerry took up to Finschhafen that month was on the afternoon of the 17th. Bill's memory of that long, lazy afternoon with Jerry remains quite clear, as it was one of the only times the two men met while overseas.

Australian records contain an interesting case that potentially adds insight into what might have occurred. Though no Wirraways were lost in action during November or December 1943, Australian sources state that a Lockheed P-38 chased a Boomerang from Lae to Salamaua, forcing the pilot to make a crash landing. This took place sometime in November of 1943. Though it does not agree with the basic details of Jerry's mission, it is the closest thing to verification of the incident found in Australian records.

∾

In early December, Jerry and George Alber were scrambled from Gusap and vectored onto a single bogey in poor weather. When they ran down the aircraft, they discovered it was a B-25. Jerry spotted it below them, cruising along over the Markham Valley. Being young and irrepressible, he rolled his P-47 over and swooped down on the lone Mitchell, intending to give it a good buzzing. He pulled up level with it then drew up alongside. To his astonishment, the waist gunner opened fire on him— .50-caliber rounds stitched into his engine cowling, then walked back along the fuselage. The bullets missed the cockpit area, but cut into the rear part of the fuselage and tail. With two cylinders shot out of his Pratt & Whitney, and his hydraulic lines severed, Jerry had to pull off and make an emergency landing at Gusap. At the time, there were two strips. One was covered with PSP, the other was a smaller grass strip. Jerry belly-landed his crippled Jug on the grass strip, figuring there would be less chance of a fire that way. He walked away unharmed from the crash, though his P-47 was badly banged up.

Jerry's interesting luck with the P-47 continued. Back at Dobodura one day about this time, Jerry asked Wally Jordan to fly up to Gusap with him. The two pilots climbed into their Jugs and taxied out to the PSP-covered strip that intersected the dirt one they usually used. They tried taking off in formation, with Wally off to Jerry's left and slightly ahead. Just as Wally's tail came up, his right tire blew. The Jug slewed over to the right and almost collided with Jerry's plane. Wally fought with the controls and tried to hold the heavy fighter steady until Jerry could get off the ground. Jerry's Jug lifted off the ground just as Wally's plane swerved to the right again. A collision was inevitable at this point. Wally heard a terrible crunching sound and felt a tremendous thump as Jerry's propeller chopped out a V-shaped section of his horizontal stabilizer. Then they were clear of each other, Jerry getting just high enough to come around and land, while Wally cut his throttles and began touching the brakes.

With Jerry making a circuit around Dobodura, Wally's right gear collapsed. His Jug bounced and vibrated on the PSP as if he were sliding along a corrugated tin roof. Terrified of a fire—he was carrying a full load of fuel—Wally shut off all of the switches, then braced himself in the cockpit. The Jug careened down the runway for several hundred yards before finally coming to a stop. Mechanics later judged it to be a total wash out.

Meanwhile, Jerry swung into his final approach and landed his damaged Jug. When the two friends met there on the runway, Jerry burst into laughter. Wally, still shaken, smiled at first. They had both come close to buying the farm, but that did not phase Jerry, and soon, his infectious laughter had Wally in stitches as well. Years later, he would remember, "We laughed like hell over it."

On another flight back to Dobodura from Gusap, Jerry discovered his Jug's airspeed indicator had failed. Worried about this, he entered the landing pattern over Dobodura and inadvertently got too close to the guy in front of him. As he did, his hand jerked away from the landing gear level, releasing the little dog that kept the gear down. Without realizing it, his gear retracted—that caused him to accidentally belly-land a perfectly good P-47. Chagrined, he climbed out of the cockpit to face Wally Jordan's needling. Wally could not get away with too much harassment over this incident, however, as he himself had done the exact same thing just a few weeks before.

Aside from bent propeller blades, the Jug was hardly even damaged. At least he had made a soft landing! Jerry just shook it off with his good-natured humor and went back to the task of keeping his squadron running.

❧

A few days later, on December 10, 1943, Ralph Wandrey climbed onto his Jug's wing just as a jeep pulled up alongside with an anxious enlisted man behind the wheel. "Hey, lieutenant!" called out the enlisted man, "you better take Huckleberry along with you, 'cause he'll get killed here and somebody will eat him."

Ralph looked down at the man and saw he was holding the squadron's mascot, a white duck who had been with the Knights since their days at Darwin. Years later, recalling Huckleberry, Wandrey quipped, "He had more time in the outfit than I had!"

After considering the situation, Ralph decided that he could not take Huckleberry along without wrapping the duck in something. He popped open his Jug's tiny baggage compartment and began digging around. Jerry had told him the night before to pack all his belongings, as they were heading up to Gusap with Ray Swift and Walter Markey, and they would not be coming back. Ralph had crammed everything he owned into the tiny baggage space; now, as he poked around, he found one of his prized possessions—a white linen bed sheet. He only owned one set, and he was reluctant to use it on Huckleberry. There did not seem to be anything else he had that would work, however, and Jerry had just taxied by on his way to the runway. Ralph did not have any more time to waste, so, pulling the sheet out, he tossed it down to the enlisted man, who bundled Huckleberry up in it. After having the duck handed up to him, Ralph climbed into the cockpit and stuffed his companion down between his legs. Huckleberry, who had only his head poking out of the sheet, was not sure what to think about the whole scene. To calm him, Ralph stroked his head from time to time. A panicked duck was the last thing he needed in the cockpit with him.

A few minutes later, the four Flying Knights were airborne, winging their way north for Gusap. At first, the arrangement in Ralph's cockpit did not cause too much trouble. The Jug was a huge aircraft with a roomy interior, which allowed Ralph to stretch his legs out a little and give Huckleberry some breathing space. All the while, he kept rubbing the duck's head, making sure he would stay calm. As Ralph struggled to keep Huckleberry happy, Jerry took the flight up to 10,000 feet for the trip up to Gusap.

Four minutes from their destination, the trouble started. All four Flying Knights heard the ground controller at Gusap suddenly yell out over the radio, "All C-47s, clear the area, we're being attacked!"

Jerry keyed his throat mike and called out to the controller, "This is Captive Red, I have four Captives three minutes south of you. We'll come in and help. How many are there?"

As the four Flying Knights dropped their external tanks, the scared voice of the controller crackled in their ears again, "Captive Red, it looks like there are about sixty of 'em. And here come about twenty to strafe the field. I'm outta here!"

The radio went silent. All four pilots opened their throttles and spread out into their standard tactical formation. Minutes later, Jerry and Ralph spotted the airstrip. Japanese aircraft were swarming around, making strafing passes down the runway. Another cluster of planes, probably bombers, were high above.

Jerry saw the two groups and called out to Ralph, "Which ones should we take?" Wandrey, who was low on gas, figured it would take way too long and use too much gas to climb up to the bombers. He keyed his mike and replied, "Johnny, let's get the ones strafing the field."

"Roger, let's go."

About 5,000 feet below, eight Ki 61 Tonys were coming down the Ramu Valley. Jerry's flight was in a perfect position to drop down on these fighters and make a head-on pass. All four Knights pushed their sticks forward. Their Jugs fell out of the sky, gaining so much speed that none of the pilots had time to set up effective attacks. Jerry wrote later, "Our speed was so great on our initial attack that we only broke up their flight."

Ralph closed quickly on one of the Ki 61s. He had the range, and the deflection was low, making this a perfect killing position. He pulled his trigger, expecting to feel the comforting vibration of his eight guns doing their grisly work. Nothing. He tried again—the guns were dead. In fact, the gun switches had not even been installed. Furious, Wandrey decided that he would ram his target. He pointed his prop at the Tony's tail and tried to stay with the Japanese pilot. Years later, he recalled, "I thought I would just saw his tail off, and since this is the first time I'd ever got into a fight over our own airfield, I'd just roll this clunker over and bail out after I collided with him."

He missed by only a few feet as the Tony pilot saw the danger and broke hard to avoid Ralph's onrushing Jug. Seconds later, all four American planes had cleared the Japanese formation and were zooming back for altitude. That's when Ralph's voice came over the radio, "Hey Johnny, I don't have any guns!" he cried. Ray Swift, flying wing on Jerry that day, echoed the lament, "Neither do I!"

Even without his guns, Ralph stuck with Walter Markey as he swung around and made another head-on pass. Markey took a snap-shot on one of the Tonys from three-quarters head-on and watched in astonishment as his eight .50s buzz sawed into the fighter, instantly blowing it apart. He remembered later how much of an impression his Jug's firepower made on him during that fight. It was simply awe-inspiring.

Then they were through the Tony formation and racing for altitude so they could make another pass. The Japanese turned hard and tried to come around behind the four Americans, but they had zoomed out of range. Once clear, Jerry led the quartet back down in a swinging, slashing attack. Markey nailed a second Tony with a quick burst. This one blew up, throwing debris all over the sky. A few hundred yards away, Jerry lined up on one of the other Tonys and unleashed a fusillade of bullets on it. The rounds turned its engine into flaming wreckage. The Ki 61 rolled and began to go down. As Jerry passed it, he watched the pilot bail out.

Meanwhile, Ralph Wandrey was having a tough time staying with Walter Markey. Huckleberry was fussing around between his legs, making it very clear that ducks do not do well in high-G turns. Every few seconds, Ralph had to pull his hand of the throttle controls to stuff the fowl back down in the sheet. The terrified duck was squawking away, doing everything he could to escape from his predicament. Then a canny Japanese pilot took a high deflection shot at Ralph and scored. A tremendous thump shook his Jug. A cannon shell had skipped along the wing and exploded a few feet from the cockpit. It left a huge hole in his wing.

Wandrey broke into the attack, hoping the feint would force the Ki 61 to break off. No luck, the Japanese pilot grimly hung in there and shot up Ralph's P-47 even more. A split second later, the two fighters careened past each other. Ralph threw his Jug into a steep, diving turn that would bring him back over Gusap.

Meanwhile, Markey thought he had cleared the fight as he sought to extend out and make another pass. He began circling to the right, getting ready to re-engage. Suddenly, his Thunderbolt shook and he could hear the hail-on-a-tin-roof sound of bullets smacking into his fuselage. Desperately, he searched for his attacker. A Tony was behind him, right on his tail, guns flaming. Walter slammed the stick hard to the left. The Jug lurched over in a hard, breaking turn; then he dived for Gusap. The Tony could not stay with him and went off in search of other prey.

Markey came out of his dive and discovered that he was totally alone. He could not see another aircraft anywhere in the area. Enough was enough—it was time to get down. He swung into the pattern at Gusap and lowered his landing gear. As he did, the landing gear warning light came on, telling him that the gear had not fully extended. Gingerly, he set the fighter onto the runway. Fortunately, the Jug's main landing gear held as he rumbled along the strip. When Markey came to a stop, he jumped out to inspect the damage. The Tony had hit him in the rear fuselage, severing the hydraulic line to the tail wheel, which was why the warning light had come down. The tail wheel hadn't extended at all. Breathing a sigh of relief, Walter headed over to join Ralph Wandrey and wait for the other two pilots to come home.

Jerry and Ray Swift stayed in the fight until the Tonys broke for home. Though Swift's guns hadn't worked, he stayed on Jerry's wing through the entire engagement. The Oregon ace would never forget that devotion, and would later refer to Swift as "one of my best pilots."

Once the Tonys had cleared the scene, Jerry went off in search of the Japanese pilot he saw bail out. According to Ralph Wandrey, Jerry spotted the chute and called its location into Gusap. He was very excited about this rarest of opportunities—if they could interrogate the Japanese pilot, they might learn more about the Ki 61. Though the 9th had tangled with the plane on several occasions, its capabilities were still mainly a mystery to the Americans. Now this pilot's survival gave them a golden opportunity to learn more.

When Jerry heard that an Aussie infantry patrol would be combing the area for the pilot, he took Swift back to Gusap, where they both landed. The first thing Jerry noticed was how unhappy Ralph Wandrey was. Huckleberry had spent the whole dogfight frantically trying to get out of the sheet and to fly away from the terrible ruckus. Ralph almost had more trouble keeping the duck under control than he did with fighting the Japanese. Almost, but not quite. As the four pilots looked over Wandrey's Jug, they saw that the 20mm round that had exploded in the wing had actually skipped once before exploding. It had gouged a little furrow out of the wing a few feet from where it had detonated. The men followed the round's course and discovered that, had it been a fraction of an inch higher, it would have slammed into the side of the cockpit right above Ralph's thigh. Had that happened, both fowl and pilot would have been horribly maimed.

Huckleberry, in the meantime, was no wiser. All he knew was that the humans were very angry at him. He had fouled Ralph's sheet so thoroughly that the Arizonan had to throw it away. Nevertheless, Huckleberry earned the distinction of being perhaps the only duck in aviation history to participate in a dogfight. Based on that, Ralph and the others didn't have the heart to commit any acts of malice against him. He was given a place of honor at their new camp at Gusap, and he remained with the squadron for over a year. Then, sometime while the Knights were fighting in the Philippines, one of the squadron's dogs caught Huckleberry and ate him. It was his second, and unfortunately last, dogfight.

❦

Carl Estes knew he must be dreaming. Here they were, on their way to war, and the Aussies were busy milking cows out in the middle of nowhere. No sense of urgency, no sense of duty. Carl, a conscientious New Englander, was at a loss for words. They had been on this troop train for two days now, traveling from Sydney to Townsville, where they were supposed to catch a flight to New Guinea. At the rate they were going, it would take forever just to get to Townsville. Combat seemed more appealing than another minute on that train.

They had averaged ten miles an hour since leaving Sydney. At times, he and the other replacement pilots were so bored that they jumped out of the cars and ran alongside the train; it helped burn off energy and ease the monotony. At the small towns they passed through, some of the Aussie women would turn out along the tracks and try to sell the pilots cucumber sandwiches. *Cucumber sandwiches.*

Now, the locomotive's crew had stopped the train. At first, Carl thought something might have gone wrong. But when he peered out the window of his car, he saw the engineer squat down next to a grazing cow and began to milk her.

A few minutes later, the train's crew sat down and began brewing tea. As Carl gaped at them, the same thought kept running through his mind: *What a way to go to war.*

❦

Carl finally got to his war in early January 1944. He reached Gusap in a Gooney Bird that transported him and six other replacement pilots up from a transition center at Port Moresby. When he arrived, Wally Jordan greeted them in the O Club. Wally was the Operations Officer by then— Jerry's number two—and his informal style appealed to the new men. They were the squadron's first draft of P-47-qualified pilots, so Wally was glad to see them.

After their reception, Carl and the others were given tent assignments. He ended up in the worst tent in the squadron. This one belonged to Blev Lewelling and Charlie "Mac" McElroy. Apparently, neither had been a Boy Scout in their younger days, so the finer points of tent construction had been lost on them. Their abode sagged and drooped so badly it was almost impossible to stand up inside it. The pole was never straight, and the two pilots had all the housekeeping skills of a cyclone in a college dorm room.

Whatever their shortcomings at keeping house, Carl felt right at home with Blev and Mac. They were outlandish companions, always coming up with goofy ideas and plans. Blev had an especially good sense of humor, which eased the tension before missions. It did not take long for Carl to get into the air. On January 7, he flew his first combat patrol, as wingman to Ralph Wandrey. He flew again on the 10th, then came down with dengue fever. That January, the 9th Squadron was almost knocked out of action by this disease. Many of the pilots became infected and fell critically ill, and Carl was among the worst affected. He lay in his cot, day after day, sweat streaming off of his fever-wracked body. Whenever the doctor came to check on him, Carl would moan, "Just let me die. Go away!"

On the morning of January 15, at about 7:30, Carl lay in his bed in absolute agony. All of a sudden, several Japanese planes came tearing through the camp area, strafing the tents. Stumbling outside, Carl looked up just in time to see a Tony zoom by not fifty feet in front and above him. The Japanese pilot looked down at him and waved. It went on past his area and along with his comrades, shot up a 3rd Attack Group A-20 sitting in the dispersal area. Two 9th Squadron Jugs were also shot up, and Mac McElroy cracked a few ribs when he jumped into an already overcrowded slit trench after escaping from his swaybacked tent.

It took almost two weeks for Carl's fever to break finally. When it did, Carl went back on flight status almost immediately. He flew a mission on the 20th, then was assigned to a sweep against Wewak on the 24th. Carl heard a lot about Wewak from the other pilots, and this particular mission made him very nervous. When morning came, he dressed quickly, managed to get a bit of pancake and powdered eggs into his stomach, then headed down to the flight line. As he was sitting on a cot outside the Operations shack, Major Gerald Johnson came over to see him.

Carl had heard many stories about Jerry's antics with the squadron, but this was the first chance he had to really talk with him. Jerry had been bumped up to Group headquarters only a short time before, so he was not flying with the 9th as much now. This mission to Wewak, however, would be an important one, and Jerry had come to talk to the new guys in the outfit.

As Carl sat on his cot, Jerry knelt down in front of him and began chatting away. "Est, you want to know how to beat a Jap Zero?" he asked. Carl, who held Jerry in awe after all the stories he had heard, nodded his head eagerly. Jerry smiled, then launched into a discussion of tactics that had Carl's head spinning. Then, all of a sudden, he felt a searing pain in his foot. He jumped up from the cot to discover that Jerry had given him a hotfoot. Confused and a bit angry, Carl looked at the major, who looked him square in the eyes and said, "Est, none of that tactics stuff means a damn if you don't keep track of everything around you. If you keep your eyes open, your head on a swivel, and know what's going on at all times, no Jap will ever sneak up on you. Remember that."

Carl never forgot that lesson. He flew 116 combat missions and never suffered any combat damage.

❧

The week before he gave Carl a lesson in Situational Awareness, Jerry had flown up to Wewak with the entire group. The 49th had been assigned to escort the 22nd Bomb Group, which had recently traded their B-26s for B-24 Liberators. The 9th Squadron flew high cover that day, with the 7th and 8th Squadrons spread out below to give close escort to the heavies.

As the strike left the target area, a lone Ki 43 appeared above the 9th Squadron. Coming in from the north, it swung around George Alber's Green Flight, which was trailing the other three flights that the 9th had up that day. Alber watched it come right down behind his men and make a pass before breaking hard to the left and climbing away. Whoever was flying this Ki 43 had guts and brains. His nimble little fighter could outclimb the P-47 all day, and his quick grab for altitude made it impossible for Alber's men to follow.

When the Japanese came back down for another pass, however, Jerry broke into him and caught him in the dive. There was no way that an Oscar could escape from a Jug while diving. Jerry walked right up behind him and blew the Japanese plane to pieces with a concentrated torrent of .50-caliber fire. Several thousand feet below, with the 8th Squadron, Bill Runey looked up just in time to see Jerry flame the Oscar. He watched as the plane exploded, throwing a cascade of avgas across the sky that formed a rainbow. The image of the debris fluttering downward, bracketed by this odd, shimmering band of colors, stayed with Bill his entire life. When he found out later that his new friend Gerald Johnson got the kill, it became a treasured memory.

After that mission to Wewak, Jerry did not score again for the rest of this tour. His assignment with 49th Fighter Group headquarters kept him very busy, and as a result he did not get to fly nearly as many combat missions as he would have liked. Throughout the spring, though, he managed to pick up plenty of twin-engine time as he flew from base to base as part of his administrative duties. His exposure to A-20s and B-26s did not make him any less reckless. In fact, he began to develop quite a reputation in these twin-engined aircraft, as he would get quite a rush from slow-rolling them right on the deck. Other times, he would cut both engines and buzz a field—a feat that nearly got him killed a year later in the Philippines while flying a B-25.

His position at Group gave him one advantage that he surely enjoyed a great deal. Through the winter of 1944, the 9th Squadron remained chained to their P-47 Thunderbolts—a plane Jerry didn't particularly like. The 7th and 8th Squadrons, however, were equipped with P-40s. He flew frequent combat missions in a P-40N, usually with the 7th Squadron, throughout this period. Once, after going up to Mt. Hagen to buy fresh fruit from the locals, Jerry hit a tree with his P-40's wing on takeoff. Somehow, he managed to drag the crippled plane back to Gusap and put it down on the runway—minus three feet of the wing and part of the aileron!

By this time, the air war in New Guinea had been all but won by the Fifth Air Force. Most of the JAAF units around Wewak and Hollandia had been utterly smashed by Kenney's repeated hit-'em-low, hit-'em-high bombing tactics. The 68th Sentai, one of the 9th Squadron's most frequent enemies, would be officially disbanded a few months later during the summer of 1944. Few of its pilots or ground crew would survive the war, as they remained isolated in the jungle for almost a full year. Other units fared much the same, and as the Americans prepared to make the final series of landings needed to set the stage for the invasion of the

Philippines, the entire Japanese air defense system in the southwest Pacific collapsed under the constant torrent of bombs and bullets. By April of 1944, sighting a Japanese plane in the air over New Guinea became almost a novelty.

෴

On April 22, 1944, General Douglas MacArthur executed his most spectacular end-around of WWII. With the help of Nimitz's aircraft carriers, he swung an entire corps around the Japanese stronghold at Wewak and put it ashore at Hollandia. Some 84,000 GIs stormed the airfield complex there, which was defended by about 11,000 men under General Hatazo Adachi. The move caught the Japanese totally by surprise, and most of the area's defenders fled into the New Guinea interior, leaving behind equipment, supplies, and a few grisly surprises for the Americans.

As soon as the airfields were secured, the 49th Fighter Group moved up there to Hollandia. At the end of March, the Fifth Air Force finally had enough P-38s to re-equip the 9th Squadron, so the Knights came to Hollandia with a batch of brand-new P-38Js. The 7th and 8th Squadron continued to make do with P-40s. It would be several more months before they received P-38s.

Jerry settled the group down at Hollandia, in a stretch of battle-scarred terrain not far from the airstrip. The men slept in tents pitched amongst the wreckage of uncounted Japanese aircraft. A creek, half-filled with mangled wings and fuselages, lay a few yards from the camp. A dead Japanese soldier lay sprawled on the far bank, decomposing in the equatorial heat. The smell emanating from the corpse proved so disgusting that none of the ground-pounders would dispose of it. Jerry and his men suffered through several days of the nauseating stench before they finally waded through the metal-strewn creek and set fire to the body with gasoline.

The men could hardly have liked their new surroundings. Japanese snipers still dotted the area, and a couple of times GIs from the 41st Infantry Division swept their camp to clear the Japanese stragglers out. At night, the men slept with their side arms and tried to ignore the sounds of battle boiling from the jungle only a few miles away. One night, as Jerry lay asleep in his bunk, a gun shot rang out in the camp.

The pilots woke instantly, reaching for their .45s and hoping that they were not about to be overrun.

Jerry grabbed his Colt automatic, cocked it, and swung off his cot. Without hesitating, he charged out into the night, pistol at the ready. If he were going to die, it would not be in bed. He stumbled all over the camp looking for some Japanese to kill before discovering the source of the noise. One of the other pilots had been attacked by a snake, and he had used his pistol to kill it.

Though the incident turned out to be a false alarm, everyone was impressed with Jerry's quick reaction. He showed them he was as brave on the ground as he was in the air. Later, he would get another chance to prove it.

❧

Jerry knew many of the men in the 41st Infantry Division, since it had been the Oregon National Guard unit before the war. His days in ROTC at the University of Oregon had acquainted him with many of the officers and men in the combat regiments. With the 41st at Hollandia, it struck Jerry as a perfect time to see how the infantry lived. Several times, he left the airfield and drove out into the jungle to find his old friends. When he did, they took him on patrol with them. On one such occasion, Jerry's escorts ran into some opposition and a fierce firefight erupted. Rather than keeping his head down, Jerry joined in and killed a Japanese soldier.

Jerry was not alone in his desire to spend time with the infantry. Bill Runey's old National Guard company was at Hollandia, and all of his old friends from his year in the outfit were still alive and active. One day, he borrowed a jeep and drove off in search of them. When he came to the 41st's general area, he was stopped at a road block flanked by machine guns. He asked the GIs if they knew where M Company had set up shop. At first, nobody knew. Suddenly, there came a cry from across the road: "Runey, is that you?"

Bill turned and discovered that one of the sergeants he had served with was manning the other machine-gun emplacement. He could not believe that, after two years, the man had still recognized Bill's voice!

They had a quick reunion, then Bill got directions to M Company. He went out on several patrols with them, though they never saw any action.

Some of the other pilots from the 8th Squadron also went out with the infantry. One pilot Bill Runey knew ended up in a sharp engagement with a grizzled old sergeant and his squad. They had been moving along a jungle trail, when a burst of fire ahead of them caused everyone to dive for cover. The pilot hit the dirt right next to this veteran NCO, who lay on his back with a Tommy gun clutched against his chest. The sergeant, who used to spend much of his off-duty time with the 8th Squadron down at the flight line, looked quite casual as the bullets zinged and cracked overhead. Suddenly, he jumped to his feet and sprayed some bushes a few yards away. He half-turned and fired another quick burst. Just like that, he wiped out all of the opposition in front of them, hitting three Japanese soldiers.

The men crept over to one who had been badly wounded and was writhing in agony in the jungle muck. To their disappointment, the Japanese was clothed in rags and had almost nothing on him. The Americans were all searching for souvenirs, and he did not even have any shoes. The other two were in similar shape, though both were dead.

The sergeant pushed his way past his men and knelt down beside the wounded Japanese soldier. He patted the man's buttocks twice, then said to him in a conversational tone, "You're a good Jappy now, aren't you?" Horrified, the pilot returned to the airfield to share the experience with his fellow aviators.

Such outings against the Japanese infantry were bound to lead to some sort of calamity. According to some of the remaining 49th pilots, one recent replacement pilot went out one night on a patrol with some GIs and ended up on the receiving end of a banzai charge. The fighting became hand-to-hand in the darkness, and when the pilot returned the following morning, he had completely snapped. He stumbled around with a wide, hollow-eyed look, mumbling unintelligibly. He was evacuated later that day, and never returned to the group. Shortly after that, all pilots and ground crew were banned from joining in on infantry patrols.

Nevertheless, Jerry and his men continued to explore their surroundings. Not far from their camp area stood a small thatch-roofed shack built on stilts. A gruesome stench radiated from it, which kept the men from exploring it at first. Finally, however, curiosity overcame disgust and Jerry, Ralph Wandrey, and a couple of other pilots walked over and explored the inside. The shack had clearly been used as quarters for the "comfort women" the Japanese kept at the base. The Army had forced these women—mostly Chinese or Southeast Asian—into sexual slavery. They were frequently kidnapped and then taken to far-flung bases, where their sole function was to submit to the local garrison's sexual desires.

This squalid little shack gave Jerry and his comrades a window into the lives of these hapless women. The floor was scattered with broken and used condoms; the bedding was sullied and gray with filth. Wandrey later wrote that he saw "evidence of several miscarriages" inside the shack. Revolted, the men retreated and Jerry ordered the foul place burned to the ground and the order was quickly executed. The men were left wondering what had happened to these poor women. They were not left behind when the Japanese fled Hollandia—could they be out in the jungle?

About this time, Bill Runey was driving around in another borrowed jeep, looking for more friends from his days in the Oregon National Guard. He had served from September of 1940 through the fall of 1941 with two different companies, so he had a lot of friends in the infantry at Hollandia. As he was poking around, he ran into an ashen-faced lieutenant. Bill stopped the vehicle and asked him if he needed a lift.

The man stared at Bill with an odd, sort of off-kilter look. "You want to see something?" the lieutenant asked him. Bill shrugged and said, "Sure." The lieutenant led him beyond a copse of trees and out into a clearing. There, the Japanese had dug long trenches near a garbage dump. Inside the trenches were hundreds of corpses piled one on top of another. Flies swarmed over the bloated, decomposing bodies, and the stench was so powerful it nearly knocked Bill off his feet. Faces poking through the jumble of limbs and torsos were wracked in frozen anguish—they had not died quickly.

"They're Koreans," said the lieutenant, "From a labor battalion the Japs massacred when they bugged out of here."

The lieutenant led Bill to another clearing a few hundred yards from the hellish scene at the garbage dump. What lay in this little field was far worse. Here were the comfort women, butchered and laid out in odd patterns that appeared to Bill to have been meant as some sort of message to the GIs. The Japanese had arranged the murdered women in precise stacks all over the field. Each stack was layered with bodies facing different directions, so that legs jutted out every few levels, while heads hung grotesquely in between.

At that moment, Bill came the closest to feeling hate than at any other time in his life. How could humans do this? He fled the scene with the lieutenant, thinking "There was about as much humanity in a bunch of Japanese as there was in a swarm of fire ants."

SIXTEEN

Summer Homecoming

Barbara Darling,

I have seen and experienced many things in this fighting Darling—I will tell you a lot about it. If anything ever happened to me I'd want you to know how I think and feel and believe.

I have seen the might of our armies—waves of bombers dropping their death dealing and destructive load in the middle of enemy troops, ships and airfields. I have seen our fighters drive Nippon from the sky and have seen brave boys go down in flames while fighting to save their comrades.

I've seen men burn in crashed planes, gunners cut and bleeding from shrapnel wounds and soldiers shaking with uncontrollable nerves shattered by shock. I have fought side-by-side with the highest and the lowest—in battle, every man is equal. You command or obey according to your duty and responsibility and you are calm and deliberate.

You never worry about being killed or even wounded. You worry more about getting sick and being temporarily knocked out of commission.

Most of all though, we hold in our hearts one hope and one fear—will we get home? Will we get home even for a day or a week, just come home again to see in another's eyes the honest of deep and abiding faith and love.

All My Love,
Gerald

Jerry left the States in early 1943, still more a boy than a man. By the spring of 1944, he was more man than boy, a fact that his family back home would never fully understand. For three years, he wanted more than anything to marry Barbara Hall, but each time he tried, her mother Hazel had intervened. He had honored her insistent refusal to sanction the marriage, just as Jerry honored his own parents' wishes and orders. By the spring of 1944, though, he had been the one issuing commands and giving orders for over half a year. The challenge of being a squadron leader had matured him—no longer did he look upon his parents as his higher authority. In fact, by April 1944, Jerry had come to realize that he was his own higher authority when it came to the details of how he would run his life.

This sense of independence grew in the weeks before Jerry returned home in the late spring of 1944. General Kenney told him he would be going home on a sixty-day leave, in part to attend the Command and General Staff College at Fort Leavenworth, Kansas. When he would actually leave was not clear until May, but as Jerry began to think of home, he grew determined that he would marry Barbara, regardless of any obstacles either family threw in his way. He made his desire very clear in his letters home to Barbara.

His father's attempts to direct Jerry's life became an increasing nuisance. Here he was, helping to lead one of the most successful fighter outfits in the Pacific, and his father continued to treat him as if he were a child still living in the old house on Broadway. While H. V. fully supported Jerry's desire to marry Barbara, he sent letters to New Guinea that implied they would live at home when he returned from the war. To Jerry, the idea of living with his parents while married made no sense at all. In a blistering letter to Barbara, he made his feelings on that matter abundantly clear. They would be married, and they would have a place of their own, where they could be alone to choose their own course in life. Major Gerald Johnson would not be bullied or presided over by anyone, especially not his father.

His father never did come to accept this. Even a year later, he continued to send letters to Jerry, full of his plans for his son. It nettled Jerry and made him increasingly determined to be totally independent from his father, though fortunately the conflict never grew severe enough to damage their love for each other.

After a year of intensive combat in New Guinea, Jerry's respect for those who fought continued to grow, as did his derision for those who remained at home. He had seen so many friends die in action that his respect and love for those in the fight with him gradually became the pillars that defined his character. He was proud to be among the men who were giving everything they had to the war effort; he was even more proud to be their leader. To him, serving in combat was the highest form of duty, the pinnacle of devotion to one's country. It was the yardstick that he use to measure everyone else—and that caused problems.

Jerry respected those that measured up to his new yardstick; he held in contempt those that did not. By the spring of 1944, some of his closest friends back home had felt the sting of Jerry's derision. The letters he received from his friends who had yet to don a uniform aggravated him to no end. Here he was, out in the middle of nowhere, watching his men die in action, and he would get a letter from an old friend extolling his latest camping trip into the Cascades. Or, he would get another letter telling him how wonderful things were back home. Far from helping his morale, these notes made him bristle with contempt. If they were real Americans, he thought, like the ones he flew with every day, they would be out here fighting the Japanese, or over in Europe wiping out the Nazis.

❧

Jerry learned at the end of May 1944 that he would be going home for his sixty-day leave. Delighted, he sent a telegram to Barbara, announcing his imminent return and asking her to make wedding plans. The telegram threw the Hall household into a flurry of activity. Barbara's mother realized that, this time, there was no way she could delay or postpone the marriage. Jerry coming home as a war hero with thirteen planes to his credit and a promotion to lieutenant colonel on the horizon—he had finally proved himself worthy of Barbara in her mother's eyes. Rather than standing in the way again, she helped Barbara make the wedding arrangements.

Jerry arrived in Eugene on Memorial Day, 1944. A crowd of friends and family greeted him at the railroad station downtown. For the occasion, Jerry had worn his dress uniform. Two years ago, he'd left Eugene on the way to war in the Aleutians as a mere first lieutenant. Now he was a major, an ace with a distinguished record and lots of press clippings. Gene McNeese rushed forward to greet his old friend. He had always idolized Jerry, but now, seeing him in his splendid uniform, he blurted out, "Jeez, Jerry, you look like Napoleon with all those medals on your chest!" Jerry gave Gene a hearty handshake, then was soon swamped by other friends and family.

Later that day, Jerry gave a speech at the McDonald Theater in downtown Eugene, urging his fellow countrymen to keep up the hard work in support of the troops overseas. It was a subject about which he felt quite passionately, and his speech proved quite rousing. The next day, he visited his old high school and spoke to several of the classes. Ross Guiley Jr., a senior at Eugene High in 1944, was so inspired by Jerry's talk that he joined the Army Air Force upon graduation and became a B-17 pilot. Other students were similarly inspired and vowed to join in their country's defense.

Jerry spent his first nights home at his parents' house on Broadway. His folks hosted a barbecue his first night back. The whole neighborhood turned out, and the scene was festive and mellow. For Jerry, it must have been a little unsettling, going from the misery of jungle life to this civilian world again. In fact, during the course of the evening, he lost his temper with his old friend John Skillern. Skillern had been drafted a short time before and was home on leave. He had been teaching mountaineering skills to the troops of the 10th Mountain Division. Though he had several years of college, John enlisted as a buck private and had deliberately avoided responsibility and promotion. In fact, in Jerry's eyes, John was trying to skate through the war with a minimum of effort or personal risk.

As they talked that evening, Jerry became quite angry with John. He rode him hard for not trying to become an officer and better his position in the Army. John, who now saw his old friend as arrogant and overbearing, ignored Jerry's derisive remarks, as he had no interest in doing anything more than what he had been doing. Jerry's feelings towards those he considered slackers back home had probably caused him to attack John in this manner. Whatever the reason, it virtually ruined their friendship. In John's defense, he and the rest of his division were sent to Italy later in 1944, where he saw intensive combat in the infantry. When Jerry heard the news of his departure, he wrote Barbara and told her how glad he was to hear John was finally doing his part for the war effort. Though John had redeemed himself in Jerry's eyes, the two never got a chance to patch things up.

There were other friends Jerry would never see again. Tom Taylor, a fellow high school and college classmate, had been killed in a B-26 over France the previous year. Aaron Cuddeback, the kid who couldn't look cross-eyed and was thus disqualified from the AAF at first, also became a casualty of the European air war. He was forced to ditch his battle-damaged B-17 in the North Sea, and he was lost at sea with the rest of his crew.

The cost of the war had become intensely personal to Jerry. As he heard these bits of bad news, he grew even more resolved to get back into the fighting, and stay there until final victory. He would have liked nothing more than to settled down with Barbara and live a normal life, but his inner compass would have never allowed that. As long as men he knew and respected were fighting, dying, and sacrificing in squalid hellholes the world over, he felt compelled to be there with them, giving everything he had to see this terrible ordeal through.

On June 1, 1944, Jerry and Barbara finally got married. Barbara had selected the First Congregational Church for the ceremony. It was a small church a few blocks from the University of Oregon campus that neither of them had attended, but it had been available on short notice. Gene McNeese sang for them, and Howard stood up for Jerry as his best man.

There would be no time for a honeymoon. Jerry had orders to attend the Command and General Staff College, and he and Barbara had to leave Eugene and head east for this new assignment soon after the wedding. They drove Jerry's 1937 Plymouth, spending the long journey getting reacquainted. When they reached Fort Leavenworth, they moved into a quaint little red brick house a few blocks from the post.

For the next two months, Jerry and Barbara spent every free moment together. They were utterly content, totally fulfilled, and hopelessly in love with each other. The moments they shared that summer became some of the best memories either would ever have. After all of the long months of separation, after all of the sad farewells, neither Jerry nor Barbara ever got used to the sheer joy of waking up next to the other in the morning during that long, hot summer. They had waited so long for that wonderful aspect of marriage that it just seemed like all their dreams had finally been realized.

It was one of those rare moments in life when everything good comes together at once. Barbara and Jerry had loved each other for so long that they already had a solid foundation upon which to build their marriage. Yet, the excitement of living together, of taking their love to another level as they grew to know each other in ways nobody else ever would, gave their relationship a sense of breathlessness, a sense that no matter how long they would wake up beside each other in the morning, they would always learn something new from one another.

Sometime that summer, Jerry flew up to North Dakota for a few days to visit Harold. Harold had been serving as a gunnery instructor since graduating from flight school, and had yet to see action overseas. In 1942, he married a woman he had met in Florida while in training. He and his young wife Betty Jo had been stationed in North Dakota for over a year. Jerry was eager to see his brother again, though he was disappointed that Harold had not done everything possible to secure a combat slot. Nevertheless, the two had a happy reunion and regaled Betty Jo with stories of their youth. Betty Jo, who had not met any of the Johnson family so far, tried her best to play hostess, without showing any of the nervousness she felt. Jerry picked up on her discomfort and decided to try and set her at ease. When she excused herself to go into the kitchen and check on dinner, Jerry swapped shirts with Harold. Wearing Harold's shirt, Jerry walked into the kitchen and put his arm around Betty Jo. Chatting to her as if he were Harold, Jerry hugged Betty Jo to him. She confided in him that she was terribly nervous and deathly afraid Jerry would not like her. "Relax," Jerry said to her, "Gerald likes you just fine." At that point, Harold walked into the kitchen with a huge grin on his face. Jerry began laughing hysterically, and pretty soon Betty Jo joined in. After that ice-breaker, the three had a great weekend together.

Jerry completed his tour at Leavenworth at the end of August. They drove back to Oregon, where they honeymooned in the Steens Mountains. A friend of the Halls had a cabin in the woods there, and they borrowed it for a week as Jerry waited for orders. Without running water, electricity, or anything more modern than an outhouse, the cabin was perfect for their getaway from the real world. For a week, they explored the mountains, fished, filmed each other with Jerry's home-movie camera, and just enjoyed each other's company for one last time before he had to return to the Pacific.

A few days after they returned to Eugene after their honeymoon, Barbara and Jerry were strolling through downtown, arms locked, when they ran into Bill Runey. Bill was delighted to see his two friends, and they stood together on the sidewalk for several minutes catching up. Bill mentioned that the 49th Fighter Group's commanding officer had been shot down and killed just a few days before he had returned home in June. Colonel Campbell had gone down on a mission to Babo, leaving Colonel George Walker in command of the group. That would probably change, Bill thought, when Jerry returned to the group. He was a natural for the job, and told Jerry as much. The chatted for a few more minutes before Bill had to meet a friend at the YMCA bowling alley across the street. Then, they said their good-byes and went on their way. It would be the last time Bill would see Barbara for almost thirty years.

All too soon, this wonderful little interlude from the war came to an end. Jerry received orders sending him to San Francisco, where he would await final orders sending him overseas. With Barbara, Jerry caught a train down to San Francisco and took up residence in the Saint Francis Hotel. They spent the nights on the town, going to different clubs to dance and dine. They met many of Jerry's service buddies there, and frequently their twosome grew into a crowd of six or eight. They had a roaring good time every night, though their imminent parting always lay in the background, like storm clouds on the horizon.

One morning, Barbara got out of bed and felt absolutely awful. Dizzy and disoriented, she stumbled into the bathroom. She had not been drinking the night before, and whatever this was, it did not feel like food poisoning. She called for help, which sent Jerry flying out of bed to her side. It was none too soon, either, as she fainted. Jerry lowered her into bed, then called for the hotel doctor. When he arrived, he gave Barbara a thorough examination.

"My dear," he said after finishing up, "you are going to have a baby."

The words hit Jerry and Barbara like a thunderclap. They could not have possibly hoped for better news. Jerry was beside himself with happiness—becoming a father had always been one of his most treasured goals. Now he would be returning to combat knowing that a little one would soon be depending on him. He loved that, and he could not have been happier. Barbara too was overjoyed. She and Jerry had discussed having children for almost six years. Now that their long cherished dream was at last coming true, Jerry's return to combat seemed somehow easier to take. He would have a family waiting for him, and she would have a part of him with her while he was gone.

It did not take long for Jerry to begin to dote on her. He hustled her here and there, taking care of everything for her so that she almost felt like royalty. As the day of his departure grew nearer, however, he became convinced that she could be cared for better up in Eugene. To Jerry, living in a hotel far from home while pregnant just did not seem like the right thing for Barbara to do, so he insisted that she go back home to live with her folks. Reluctantly, she agreed, and in early September 1944, Jerry helped Barbara pack her things, then they caught a cab to the train station in Oakland. Once again, they said good-bye to each other on a railway platform. Jerry waved from the platform while Barbara smiled and blew kisses from her Pullman car until they lost sight of one another. It was the exact same scene they had played out together in 1941—only this time the roles had been reversed.

Jerry shipped out a few days later.

PART SIX

Puck in a P-38

SEVENTEEN

Knights Over Balikpapan

October 19, 1944

Dearest Mother and Dad,

I haven't been too busy but lack of activity often precludes [sic]
a storm.

*The war has improved considerably since I first came over
here and everything is done on a pretty grand scale. We are more
amused than ever at the reports of Radio Tokyo. We wonder
what effect will have on the little yellow people when they realize
how their war lords have misrepresented every phase of the war
to them.*

*Our teamwork and cooperation continues to improve and we
can strike the enemy with devastating force. He is yet undefeated,
however, for his soldiers and airmen fight with all their cunning
and strength.*

*I would not be satisfied to remain at home while this war is
in its most interesting course. I believe in the men here and I
take considerable pride in being a soldier among them.*

Your Loving Son,
Gerald

When Jerry returned to New Guinea in late September 1944, he found the Fifth Air Force in rough shape. Morale in most squadrons had dropped since the spring, as the men were being forced to fly far more missions than the crews in any other theater. General Kenney had wanted to send pilots and crews home after about 300 combat hours, as he had found the men's abilities started to decline at that point. The low replacement rate from the States, however, had prevented this for quite some time, and now some of the men were not even going home after 500 combat hours. The results were clear: Kenney's men were tired. Replacement pilots and crews trickled into New Guinea in fits and starts, which, combined with the overall fatigue of his aircrews, caused an overall decline in effectiveness.

The famed 345th Bomb Group, for example, had to ground almost half of its crews due to combat fatigue during the late summer of 1944. Other units were in similar straits, and the problem was exacerbated by the sporadic arrival of new aircraft. Weary pilots, flying weary aircraft, did not add up to peak combat efficiency.

The arrival of the Thirteenth Air Force in New Guinea had helped to ease the situation, as there were more units to execute the required missions. However, the Thirteenth's replacement rate remained equal to the Fifth's—their pilots and crews were being used up just as fast as those in the Fifth Air Force.

Jerry could see this in the 49th when he returned in September. There were many old hands still around who had yet to rotate home. Bill Williams and Bob Wood were two of the oldest hands left in the squadron, as was Ray Swift, Jerry's old wingman. Wally Jordan still commanded the 9th Squadron, though he would move up to Group soon and leave the outfit in the hands of Bill Williams. Carl Estes, Blev Lewelling, and 7th Squadron ace Bob DeHaven were also still with the group. All of these men, Estes excepted, had been out in New Guinea for well over a year and had tallied at least ninety missions.

Jerry caught up with the 49th at Momker aerodrome, a crushed-coral strip on Biak Island. His old friends in the 41st Infantry Division had gone ashore at Biak on May 27 and found that the Japanese had dug in among the honeycomb of volcanic caves in the hills overlooking the aerodrome. It took weeks of vicious fighting to clear the Japanese off of the island, and cost the 41st over a thousand casualties. More men from the Pacific Northwest died securing Biak than died during the Normandy invasion ten days later.

At Mokmer, the 49th's camp had been situated right along the beach. Jerry bunked down with the group commander, Colonel George Walker. Somehow, Jerry's old bed and mattress that he had used back at Gusap and Hollandia had made the trip to Biak, and he was able to reclaim both of them; not having to sleep on an army cot made life a little more tolerable. His hut even had a small refrigerator, which the pilots used to store beer and other essentials.

Jerry was made the deputy group commander. He worked very closely with Colonel Walker as a result, and while he found Walker to be an excellent administrator, he did not think much of his fighting skills. Walker's health had been all but ruined by his tour in the tropics, and he would eventually have to relinquish command of the 49th because of it. He was frequently too sick to fly, so Jerry became accustomed to leading the group into battle as a matter of course.

To get reacquainted with combat, on October 8 Jerry borrowed a P-38 and flew a combat patrol over Owi Island with his old friend Dick Bong. Bong was now attached to 5th Fighter Command HQ and could join in on whatever missions he wanted. This mission became one of the first "Fat Cat" flights, though that term came along later.

Throughout the fall, several of the Fifth Air Force's top aces would occasionally band together to fly sweeps. Somebody dubbed these missions "Fat Cat" flights and the name stuck. Jerry flew many missions that fall with Dick Bong, Tommy McGuire, and Bob DeHaven, always with the idea of getting into a good scrap so they could all run up their scores.

Jerry had rejoined the 49th just in time to take part in one of General Kenney's most important air operations of the war. For some time, Kenney had wanted to go after the oil refineries and storage facilities around Balikpapan, Borneo. Using B-24s, Kenney went after Balikpapan with daylight raids early that fall. Unescorted, the Liberator crews flew right into a maelstrom of flak and fighters. While damage was done to the oil facilities, the bomber groups took heavy losses.

Kenney believed if he could destroy Balikpapan's oil targets, he could shorten the war. Borneo's production sites provided the vast majority of Japan's oil supplies, so if they could be destroyed, the Emperor's military machine might just grind to a halt for want of fuel.

Kenney had originally wanted to go after Balikpapan with B-29 Super-fortresses based at Darwin, but Arnold refused to release any of these giant bombers to his command. That forced Kenney to use his B-24 groups in ultra-long range flights from western New Guinea and Darwin. The missions required flights of over 2,000 miles, and took a heavy toll on his already exhausted crews. When they actually reached the target area, they were set upon by swarms of Zeroes and Ki 44 Tojo interceptors. One outfit, the 307th Bomb Group, lost nine of its planes in two missions at the end of September and early October. Other units suffered similar beatings at the hands of these experienced Japanese pilots. On October 6, 1944, Kenney flew down to Noemfoor to check up on the Thirteenth Air Force's Liberator crews. Their heavy losses were of great concern to him, and as he chatted with his "kids" he could see that they were close to the breaking point. He cheered them up by promising to sending some fighter escort with them the next time they went to Balikpapan.

Fighter escort was clearly needed. The problem was how to get the P-38s over Balikpapan. The nearest American base to Borneo was the island of Morotai, some 850 miles away. That meant the fighter crews would have to fly at least 1700 miles round-trip, while spending time over the target engaging the Japanese. Up to that time, the longest fighter mission flown in the Theater had been a 1,650 mile flight from Sansapor to Davao and back to Biak earlier that summer. And even that was possible only after Charles Lindbergh visited the Fifth and Thirteenth Air Force fighter units and showed them how to lean their fuel mixtures in order to stretch their range.

Brigadier General Paul B. Wurtsmith approached Kenney with the first proposed solution. He wanted to get fifty volunteers from the fighter outfits to escort the bombers from Sansapor to Balikpapan. They would fly as far back toward home as possible, then they would all parachute out together. PBY Catalina rescue planes would then pick up the pilots. Kenney was incredulous: could fifty pilots even be found to try such a suicidal mission? Wurtsmith just responded that if he authorized the mission, he would have 200 pilots wanting to go inside of a half hour. Kenney considered the scheme, then vetoed it. Planes and pilots were both too precious to throw away in this manner, especially with the replacement situation being the way it was. Some other solution needed to be found.

Wurtsmith did some research and returned with another idea. If P-38s and P-47s could operate out of the freshly-captured field at Morotai, and if they could carry 300-gallon drop tanks instead of the usual 165-gallon tanks, they could just make it to Balikpapan and back. There was a catch, though: the field at Morotai was too short to handle the P-47s if they had the 300-gallon tanks under their wings.

Kenney immediately ordered the engineers at Morotai to get to work and lengthen the runway 500 feet by October 9. Meanwhile, a batch of 300-gallon ferry tanks were sent up to the fighter units slated for the escort missions. On October 10, 1944, the Liberators were dispatched to Balikpapan again. This time, they were escorted by the P-38s of the 49th Fighter Group, which could operate at Morotai without the lengthened strip. Over the target, 160 Liberators were hit by almost a hundred Japanese interceptors. The thirty-six Lightnings waded into the fray, heavily outnumbered, but managed to shoot down six Japanese fighters without loss. Four B-24s were lost, but heavy damage was done to the Pandasari oil refinery.

To Jerry's immense frustration, he missed the fight on October 10. Just after his "Fat Cat" patrol with Dick Bong, his teeth began bothering him. He had experienced various problems with his teeth on and off throughout his tour in the Southwest Pacific. This time, when he went to see the base dentist at Mokmer, and had several teeth pulled. He spent the 10th recovering from the oral surgery and could not have been more upset when he learned from his returning pilots that the skies over Balikpapan were studded with Japanese fighters. He resolved that one way or another—bad teeth or not—he would get in on the next Balikpapan raid.

He got his chance on October 14, 1944. On the afternoon of the 13th, the pilots from the 49th and 475th Fighter Groups climbed into their P-38s and flew up to Morotai, where the engineers had finished lengthening the runway on the 11th. As a result, the 35th Fighter Group's Thunderbolts flew up and joined the two P-38 groups. This time, the B-24s were going to be covered by almost sixty "Little Friends."

The night before the mission, Jerry visited the 475th and got to talking with Tommy McGuire. The two old friends had not seen much of each other since Jerry's return to the theater, but on this night they decided to bend the rules a little and fly together with the rest of the 49th Fighter Group. Early on the morning of the 14th, the pilots of the 49th Fighter Group settled into their cockpits and waited for word to taxi out to the runway. Each man was lost in his own thoughts. This would be the longest mission most of the men would ever fly, and over a hundred Japanese fighters were waiting for them at Balikpapan—more if Intelligence was right. According to John Spence, the Group's erudite intel officer, the Japanese had recently moved several crack naval fighter groups from Singapore to Balikpapan. They would be facing fresh opponents, who were among the best that the Japanese could still deploy in battle.

Colonel George Walker would be at the head of the 49th that day, while Major Wally Jordan would serve as the mission leader. With them would be some of his best veteran pilots: Bill Williams, Ed Cooper, Blev Lewelling, and Leslie Nelson. Jerry and Tommy McGuire had attached themselves to the 9th as part of White Flight. Looking around the airfield that day, Jerry must have realized that he would be flying with some of the best fighter pilots in the entire theater. If he didn't know it then, he sure knew it by the end of the day, some seven hours and forty-five minutes later.

After take off, the 49th formed up and headed out to rendezvous with the bombers. They were the lead on the day's escort mission, and would cover the Fifth Air Force's B-24 groups as they made their run over the target area. Behind them, the Thirteenth Air Force's Liberators would make the follow-up strike, escorted by the 475th and 35th groups. With the 9th Squadron's sixteen P-38s stacked from 11,000 feet up to 19,000 feet around the bomber boxes, the 49th approached Balikpapan from the west. Twenty miles out, around 10:30 A.M., the sky suddenly erupted with Japanese fighters. Oscars, Tojos, and Zeroes—some fifty in all—waded into the Americans from above and below. Jerry and Tommy were sitting above all the other 49'ers at 19,000 feet when the Japanese attacked. Overhead, they both could see a number of Ki 44s and Ki 43s getting ready to plunge down on the American formations. Reacting quickly, Jerry brought his Lightning around in a steep climbing turn, with McGuire tacked on his wing.

This could not have been a worse position to be in. The Japanese had the altitude advantage, were more maneuverable, and could engage or disengage at will at this point. Jerry knew that if they did not go after them, the P-38s already engaged below them would be ripe targets. Worse, these Japanese could get down on the bombers, trading altitude for energy and speed and blow past the fighters altogether.

Jerry's climbing left turn brought White Flight right into a flight of Oscars. McGuire went after one, snapping out a couple of short bursts until it broke hard and evaded his attack. Frustrated, he swung around, looking for Jerry and more trouble. The formation Jerry and Tommy had attacked had scattered by this point. A few of the Oscars had begun to dive down on the B-24s arrayed in tight formations below, taking advantage of the general confusion of the fight. Jerry spotted one of these Ki 43s arrowing down toward the Liberators and tore after it, with McGuire following in his wake.

The Oscar pilot saw the two P-38s on his tail, but held his course and made a run at the bombers anyway. Jerry ran him down and chased him right through a bomber box as hundreds of tracers from the bombers' guns streaked through the sky around them. Seconds after they passed through the formation, Jerry nailed the Oscar with a well-placed burst. The Japanese fighter slewed, then slowed, causing Jerry to overshoot it. McGuire saw his chance and pounced on the stricken Japanese—a long burst, and the Oscar was sent plummeting in flames.

Just then, another Oscar finished a diving pass on the bombers and zoomed past Jerry's P-38. Jerry banked hard, horsing his Lightning around in a tight turn that brought him right onto this second Oscar's tail. A quick burst, and the P-38's guns did their deadly work. Jerry saw hits on the plane's fuselage and wings, and cannon shells struck the Oscar's engine, prompting an oily tail of smoke to trail back from it. Jerry snapped out another short fusillade of fire, and the Oscar exploded.

McGuire caught up to Jerry just as the debris from this second plane began to rain down towards the water below. They turned back towards the bombers, looking for more trouble. They didn't take long to find it. A few hundred feet below, a Ki 44 zipped underneath their P-38s, going flat out on a perpendicular course. Jerry spotted the swift silvery fighter and rolled down on it after a sharp, diving right turn. From dead astern, he sprayed the Tojo with cannon and machine-gun fire, tearing pieces off of the hapless plane. He closed quickly with it, and saw that he was in danger of overshooting again. He held the trigger down and battered the Ki 44 until it suddenly exploded. Jerry flew right through the fireball and could hear and feel pieces of debris ricocheting off of his P-38's wings. When he emerged from the inferno, his Lightning was scorched, but otherwise intact.

It was a good thing, too, as more Tojos were on the way. McGuire went after one that had been skittering along below them. Jerry swung behind Tommy to cover his tail. It didn't take long for Tommy to drop this Ki 44, but then two more bounced them from above and behind. Jerry saw one Tojo latch onto his own tail—he was cold meat if he did not do something fast. Once again, his quick reactions saved his life. Instinctively, he shoved the stick forward and slammed the throttles to the stop. The Lightning fell out of the sky like an anvil, and while the Tojo tried to give chase, it was soon left far behind.

Alone now, Jerry eased out of his dive and ducked into a cloud northeast of Balikpapan. He checked his fuel gauge, decided that he had enough gas to get back into the fight, then plunged back into the stark blue sky in search of more prey. All around him, a sprawling fight played out. Japanese fighters swarmed and flitted around the bombers, while Thunderbolts and Lightnings ranged back and forth along the Liberator formations, driving the attackers away. Here and there, a sudden explosion would flare, and for an instant an incandescent orange glow would be cast across the morning sky. Smoke plumes left ugly smears behind the fight, marking the path of battle.

Jerry pulled his nose up and climbed back into the fray. In seconds, he was engaged again as Tojos and Oscars zipped back and forth all around him. The fight was so wild that he could not get a decent shot at anybody. Instead, he snapped out short, high-deflection bursts as targets presented themselves. At one point, three Oscars jumped him from behind and bored in after him. Jerry firewalled his throttles again and extended away in a shallow dive to the east. Eventually, the Oscars gave up the chase and turned around to get back into the main fight. When they did so, Jerry swung around and charged after them.

With his lone Lightning streaking after them, the Oscars all broke hard and came around in a head-on pass. Jerry concentrated on the lead Ki 43 and peppered it with .50-caliber fire. The Oscar began to smoke, but ducked into a nearby cloud and disappeared before he could finish it off. The other two beat a hasty retreat, and Jerry decided that he did not have the fuel to give further chase. He turned back eastwards and disengaged from what had to have been the wildest fight he had ever experienced.

On the way home, he spotted a crippled P-47 pilot ditch in the shallow water right off the western end of Celebes. The Thunderbolt pilot climbed out of the cockpit and inflated his rubber raft as Jerry circled protectively overhead. He remained over the downed aviator until a PBY came along and picked him up. With the pilot safe, Jerry dove down and fired his remaining ammunition into the half-sunk P-47, destroying it so that the Japanese could not recover it.

Seven hours and forty-five minutes after take-off, Jerry returned to Morotai and put his faithful Lightning down on the crushed-coral runway. As he taxied to the dispersal area, he could see that other pilots from the 49th had already returned. Climbing down out of his P-38, he linked up with McGuire and the other 49th pilots and began to compare notes. It soon became evident that they had wrought havoc on the Japanese units they had faced. Jerry had bagged two, and McGuire had nailed two as well. Ed Cooper got a Tojo, while Leslie Nelson flamed three and Oglesby got two more. Bill Williams picked off one, while Wally Jordan knocked down three and a probable between this mission and the one on the 10th.

And what of Balikpapan? Kenney's repeated raids had been costly, but the oil refineries had been savaged—at least in Kenney's mind. Postwar research showed that the refineries had suffered much less damage than Kenney described in his own book. Historian Thomas Griffith pointed out that, even had the refineries been destroyed, their loss to Japan's war machine would not have been significant, at least in the short term. The reason was this: the Japanese had more refined fuels sitting in storage sites throughout the Dutch East Indies than they had tankers to move them to needed places in the Empire. The fuel was available, but the transport system was not, thanks mainly to the American submarine campaign.

The Balikpapan raids turned out to be strategically insignificant. Kenney's knock-out blow did not work, and while it gave his fighter pilots valuable experience in ultra-long range missions, the losses frankly did not justify the results obtained. And after the 14th, Kenney could not concentrate on Balikpapan anymore, as another, much more important target lay just over the horizon: Leyte. For Jerry and the other 49th pilots, Leyte would soon make Rabaul look like a walk in the park.

EIGHTEEN

Storm Over Leyte

Dearest Mother and Father,

We have shot down over a hundred planes since our arrival. I hope that the people at home realize that Germany and Japan are not push-overs, that the cost of victory must be paid in pain, and fear, and sacrifice.

We are working harder than we ever have before. Men here who work from dawn to after dark then drag their exhausted bodies to an army cot put the CIO & AFL complainers to shame. I have never seen such an example of men lifting themselves up by their bootstraps.

Before dawn 'til after dusk, rain, mud, dust, flies, mosquitoes—we continue to work. Our morale is just as high as ever and everyone keeps pretty happy.

The boys are shooting them down every day and I guess people in the USA think these islands will be a push over. Well, we'll push the enemy over well enough—we have the men and the guts and the spirit to do so. I wish a few of the "when the war will end . . ." speculators would be here with me for a day and realize that several thousand men aren't as worried about when it will end as much as who will get home.

Your Loving Son,
Gerald

Just before the Leyte invasion Bill Williams, the 9th Squadron ops officer, approached Carl Estes and asked him to fly back to Nadzab with three other men from the squadron to pick up some brand new P-38s. Everyone knew that the 9th would soon be heavily engaged in the Philippines, and Kenney had wrangled new Lightnings out of Washington for his best fighter group. For the men of the 49th, this was a clear indication that, when the curtain went up in the Philippines, they would surely form the spear point of the aerial effort.

Estes, Fred Helterline, Jimmy Poston, and Don Fisher arrived at Nadzab and worked their way through a maze of red tape before a quartet of factory-fresh P-38L Lightnings were turned over to them. None of the four pilots knew anything about the "L" model, assuming that it was similar to the "J-15s" they had been flying. They soon got a rude shock.

Estes sat on the runway and watched as Jimmy Poston took off first. As soon as he was airborne, Poston's P-38 began wallowing and rolling all over the sky. Estes went next, and as his wheels left the ground, his Lightning seemed almost uncontrollable. As they all climbed to their cruising altitude, none of the pilots could hold their planes steady. Estes fought the yoke, wondering what could possibly be wrong with all their planes. He began to suspect that they had been rigged wrong. Finally, as they approached Hollandia, Don Fisher announced over the radio, "Well, there's no way I can land this son of a bitch. There's no way to control it. I'm going over the lake and bail out. Air-Sea Rescue can come and pick me up."

They flew on a little further, each pilot lost in thought, trying to figure a way out of their collective dilemma. Then somebody came over the radio and said, "Hey, there's a valve down here on the right hand side of the seat, way down almost on the floor. It says 'Hydraulic Boost' on it." Estes leaned over and looked around for the valve. When he found it, he saw that it was resting in the on position. He flipped the valve closed. Almost instantly, the P-38's controls became more solid and felt right to Estes. He called this out and the other pilots followed suit. That solved everyone's problems, and the four pilots were able to get to Mokmer aerodrome without further incident.

Back on the ground, they went to Frank Bertelli, Lockheed's tech rep in the area, and asked him what the hydraulic boost was all about. Frank had no idea, but he promised to look right into it. He came back to Estes and the others a few days later with a wealth of data, and after reading through it, the pilots became quite excited. The L model, as it turned out, was no average P-38.

First off, the tech specs stressed that under no circumstances should the hydraulic boost be used on takeoff or landing. If one aileron's hydraulics failed, the Lightning would slow roll right into the ground. Well, that was one lesson learned. All four of the pilots left the runway with the boost on when they took off at Nadzab.

What the hydraulic boost gave the Lightning was maneuverability. The controls were much lighter and took less effort to manipulate than earlier P-38s, and the pilots were soon able to execute radical maneuvers that would have been utterly impossible in every other variant. Carl Estes described the hydraulic boost as the difference between manual steering and power steering in an automobile. Light on the yoke, responsive as a thoroughbred, capable of a top speed of almost 420 mph, the P-38L was the ultimate Lightning. And it arrived just in time, for where the 49th was headed, they would need all of the help they could get.

⁓

General Douglas MacArthur, come hell or high water, was going back to the Philippines. His whole campaign in the southwest Pacific had been predicated on that goal. Every move he made since leaving Corregidor in March 1942 had been calculated to get him that much closer to avenging his defeat on Luzon. When the Navy tried to convince Roosevelt to bypass the Philippines and invade Formosa instead, MacArthur's powerful presence and rhetorical abilities convinced FDR to side with him. He would return to the Philippines.

MacArthur had originally planned to assault Mindanao as his initial step back into the islands, because it was in range of the Fifth Air Force's aircraft in western New Guinea and Morotai. Kenney's old command could cover the landing forces from afar, then move into freshly-prepared or captured strips on the island to project their power further north in the Philippines. After the experience with the Hollandia operation, however, MacArthur's staff reevaluated the situation. Rather than tackling Mindanao, the decision was made to land first in the central Philippines. MacArthur liked the idea, as it sped up the timetable to get troops on Luzon and recapture Manila. Leyte was selected as the first invasion site.

Leyte presented several problems for Kenney. First, his aircraft at Biak, Sansapor, and Morotai would be too far away to cover the landings and provide close support for the beachhead. Second, there were only a few good sites for airfields on Leyte. When the Fifth Air Force did move up to the island, the fighter and bomber groups would be crammed into three or four fields, at most. Meanwhile, they would be surrounded by Japanese-held islands that were dotted with almost 200 airfields.

The only way to pull off this giant leap to Leyte was to use the Navy's Third Fleet, the fast carriers under Admiral Bill Halsey, to provide air cover during the early phases of the invasion. Vice Admiral Thomas C. Kinkaid's Seventh Fleet and its escort carriers would also be needed to give the beachhead close support. Using the Navy in this manner grated against Kenney, as he absolutely detested Kinkaid and did not have much use for Admiral Halsey either. The Leyte operation would strain the relationships between these three men to the breaking point, with Kenney going so far as to threaten to bring Kinkaid up on formal charges.

Personality differences aside, the plan that the three air leaders formulated proved to be unsound from the outset. The carriers would strike the Japanese airfields with repeated attacks to suppress any aerial and naval opposition against the beachhead. However, Halsey's pilots and aircrew had been flying nonstop throughout the fall and were exhausted. Also, the carriers could stay on station for only about five days, then they would need to return to Ulithi to replenish fuel and ammunition stocks while giving the aircrews a desperately-needed rest. Kinkaid's escort carriers would also need a break about then as well.

Thus, the timetable was set for Kenney. He had to have fighter groups on Leyte by October 25—no later. The first airfield, the Japanese strip at Tacloban, had to be ready five days after the landing. If not, the GIs and the invasion force would be exposed to merciless air attack. With 200 airfields to operate from, the Japanese were in a position to shift their units around to avoid destruction on the ground. There was no way that the fast carriers or Kenney's Fifth and Thirteenth Air Forces could suppress every landing strip in the Philippines. That in itself would pose an insurmountable problem at the beginning of the campaign— one that was only solved when the Japanese eventually pulled their remaining units out of the islands in January 1945.

A few days after the Balikpapan raids ended, Colonel Walker sat down with Jerry and briefed him on the upcoming Leyte invasion. The 49th Fighter Group would pave the way into the Philippines. Kenney wanted his best men covering MacArthur's GIs as soon as possible. Thirty brand-new P-38L's would fly up to Tacloban as soon as the strip was ready for them, and Walker wanted the best pilots from the group in their cockpits.

Jerry put a list together of the men he wanted with him, for he knew this would be the toughest assignment the group had ever faced.

They would be thirty pilots against an unimaginable horde of Japanese aircraft. Intelligence estimated varied, but there were at least 1,500 Japanese Army and Navy aircraft based in the Philippines. Reinforcements could be rapidly deployed to the Philippines from Formosa, and even Japan itself, as soon as the invasion began. They could be facing over 2,000 planes! Granted, the Navy and its carriers would whittle these numbers down in the days before the first GIs splashed ashore on Leyte's beaches. Nevertheless, as the plan dictated, the Navy would be gone by the time the 49th moved up to Tacloban. Other units would follow, but the 49th would have to hold the line until they arrived.

Jerry and Colonel Walker deliberated for several hours before completing their list of thirty men. Most of the men would come from the 9th, an obvious bias of Jerry's. Wally Jordan, Bill Williams, Bob Wood, Blev Lewelling, Leslie Nelson, and Carl Estes were among the Flying Knights selected for this assignment. From the 7th Squadron came Bob DeHaven. Willy Drier, a close friend of Bill Runey's from the 8th Squadron, joined the mission, as did his buddy George Smerchek. From the group's headquarters, Jerry and George Walker both planned to make the flight. From 5th Fighter Command came Bob Morrissey and Dick Bong. Bending the rules again, Tommy McGuire from the 475th would be brought along as well.

The GIs stormed the beaches on October 20 and immediately ran into trouble. On one of the assigned beaches, a sandbar prevented the amphibious fleet's LSTs from unloading. This was noticed in the pre-invasion survey of the beach, but nothing was done about it. As it turned out, the only way to unload the LSTs was to push them right up to the small peninsula where Tacloban's airstrip had been constructed by the Japanese. The bluejackets beginning emptying the LSTs and soon the airstrip was cluttered with hundreds of tons of supplies. The engineers who came ashore that day found it impossible to work on the airfield—there was just too much stuff lying around. Worse, the PSP they planned to use on the airfield had not arrived, nor had the crushed coral that was needed on the runway.

While this mess developed, the Japanese struck with full fury. For the first time in the war, the Japanese Navy and Army air groups launched concentrated kamikaze attacks on the invasion fleet and Halsey's carriers. These terrifying attacks proved stunningly effective—throughout the Leyte campaign one in every three kamikazes hit an Allied ship. The Navy's fighter pilots were overwhelmed and overworked. Scores of Japanese planes were going down on every mission, but they still kept coming. Tacloban was bombed and strafed, and the invasion fleet suffered many bomb and kamikaze hits. Things were becoming increasingly desperate, and the strip at Tacloban was nowhere near ready for the 49th.

Then the Japanese fleet sortied. For two days, the two navies slugged it out from Surigao Strait to Cape Engano in what became the largest sea battle in history. When it was over at dusk on October 26, the Japanese Navy ceased to exist as a cohesive fighting force. Lost were its last four operational aircraft carriers and three battleships, as well as numerous cruisers and destroyers. It was a catastrophic defeat for the Japanese, but it did not stop their air effort against the Leyte beachhead. In fact, the attacks would soon intensify.

On October 25, while Halsey and Kinkaid were fighting the Battle of Leyte Gulf, General George Kenney was ready to pull his hair out. The strip at Tacloban was not only not ready, but work to finish it was being totally disrupted by a number of factors. First, almost seventy Navy planes crash-landed on the field throughout the 25th—refugees from Kinkaid's escort carriers that had been attacked by a Japanese surface force that included the battleship *Yamato*. Next, the LSTs were still dumping supplies on the runway, and the stacks of material kept getting in the way of the engineers. Kenney was so furious at this development that he threatened to bulldoze all of the stuff right into the bay if it was not removed immediately.

By the end of the 25th, Kenney realized there was no way he could take over from the Navy and assume responsibility for the beachhead's air operations. Halsey and Kinkaid, despite all their airmen had been through over the last week, would have to stay on station. Five days after the landing, the hand-picked pilots of the 49th Fighter Group fretted away the hours, waiting for the word to move forward. They were alone now, as the rest of the group had long since embarked on LSTs to make the journey to Leyte by sea. In fact, the 49th's ground crews were already up at Tacloban, helping the engineers get the field ready. For the pilots, time dragged by slowly, and the bored tension the wait created was only broken by the occasional bit of news dribbling out of the beachhead. The Navy had scored some tremendous victories, but the Japanese were really putting up a fight in the air—targets would definitely not be scarce.

On October 26, the 49th left Biak and flew up to Morotai in final preparation for the move to Leyte. At 9:00 A.M. on October 27, Walker received word from Leyte that the strip was operational. Within minutes, Jerry and the rest of the pilots left Morotai and headed into the maw of the raging battle. En route, Tommy McGuire suffered engine trouble and returned to Morotai, leaving twenty-nine P-38s. The 49th reached Tacloban around noon, in a driving rainstorm. Since there was no air cover over the airfield, the group would be terribly vulnerable as it landed and refueled. The decision was made to keep eight P-38s overhead while the rest of the outfit landed and refueled. Once they were ready to go, they would be launched again and the eight providing air cover would land.

Coming in from the north, the first P-38 touched down—and promptly skidded off the runway. To call Tacloban operational at this point turned out to be a stretch. Only 2,000 feet had been covered with PSP and crushed coral, while the rest of the strip was awash in a sea of gooey mud. The second P-38 came down and went right off the end of the runway as well, and two succeeding planes soon ended up in the mud as well. Fortunately, none of the planes were seriously damaged, but as Carl Estes and the others watched the near-disaster unfold from their perch in the landing pattern, it did not look like there was any safe way to get down on the strip. The remaining P-38s swung around and chose to land from south to north. That way, they splashed down in the mud first, then rolled up onto the PSP. Although two more P-38s slid off either side of the runway, the rest of the group got down without any major damage. When Estes climbed out of his Lightning, he was incredulous. "I'd never seen so much mud on an aircraft before in my life," he recalled years later.

Nearby, at MacArthur's headquarters at the Price House, Kenney and his commander were in the middle of lunch when they heard the roar of engines overhead. "Hello, what's that?" asked MacArthur. Kenney replied, "That's my P-38s from the 49th Fighter Group." MacArthur was on his feet at once, calling for his jeep. Together, he and Kenney drove out to the airstrip where they found the pilots milling around their

P-38s. They were surrounded by crowds of GIs, their own ground crews, and some local Filipinos. Their arrival had been like a shot of adrenaline to the beleaguered men in the beachhead, and now they were cheering the Army pilots.

Kenney walked over to the pilots and introduced them to General MacArthur. Everyone was suitably awed by the legendary man. Jerry later wrote home about the incident and described MacArthur as a great leader. When Kenney spotted Dick Bong in the group, he asked him who had given him permission to come up to Leyte. Bong told him that Generals Wurtsmith and Whitehead both had approved.

"Did they tell you that you could fly combat after you got up here?" asked Kenney lightly.

"No," Bong said, pausing for a moment before asking, "Can I?" Everybody, including MacArthur had a good laugh over that.

The meeting soon broke up as the planes had to be refueled and the pilots briefed on the local situation. By 4:00 P.M., the aircraft were fueled and ready to go. Jerry, Dick Bong, Bob Wood, and Bob Morrissey were among the first eleven pilots to fly the first combat patrol from Tacloban. The P-38s left the strip and sped south to Dulag village, where they bombed and strafed some Japanese fortifications. After the strafing runs, Bob Wood's P-38 began to run rough, so he turned over his flight to Bernie Krankowitz and returned to Tacloban. Krankowitz took the rest of Yellow Flight on a patrol around and over Tacloban.

Meanwhile, Jerry, Bong, and Morrissey were flying together as Captive Green Flight, off to the northwest of the rest of the squadron. Around 5:20, Tacloban's ground controller called and told them that there were enemy aircraft over the airfield. From 14,000 feet, the three pilots dived towards the strip, fighting to see the sky around them through the pouring rain. About twenty miles from the field, Morrissey spotted four Ki 43 Oscars heading towards them. Jerry, as the number three man in the flight, saw only two at first.

Using their speed and new maneuverability, Bong led Green Flight down and around behind the Oscars. He made the first pass from dead astern, but overshot his target. Jerry pounced on it and flayed it mercilessly with all five guns from point-blank range. The Oscar burst into flames, rolled over, and plunged into the water north of Tacloban. While Bong and Jerry teamed up on the lead Oscar, Morrissey went after another Ki 43. From ten degrees off to the left, he let loose with a fusillade of fire that ripped into the Oscar's engine and fuselage. The Japanese pilot dropped away, his plane smoking. Morrissey gave chase, but as he closed with it, the Oscar disappeared into a cloud at 1,500 feet. Nearby, Jerry had just finished off his own Oscar when he saw Morrissey's victim plunge out the bottom of the cloud. Suddenly, the engine exploded in flames and the plane went straight into the water.

Two down. Now it was Bong's turn. Just off to his left he spotted an Oscar and gave chase. Jerry slid behind him and covered his tail while he concentrated on his target. He nailed it cold with a well-aimed burst that scored hits all over the Ki 43's wings and fuselage. The Japanese fighter fell off on its right wing and crashed into the sea. Bong then spotted the fourth Oscar trying to get away. He dashed after it, determined to make a clean sweep of their formation. At about the same time, Jerry discovered a Val hugging the wavetops several thousand feet below him. The plane had obviously just come from the Tacloban area and was now trying to make its escape. He rolled down on it and closed quickly.

All three pilots were now scattered. Morrissey was poking around the cloud he'd lost his first target in some minutes before, while Bong was still chasing the last Oscar. Jerry had his own target and was about to unload on it. Morrissey had just climbed back up to 8,000 feet above his cloud when he caught sight of Jerry's Val. He thrust the yoke forward and barreled down on it from dead astern. As he dived, he saw Jerry ahead of him, coming down on the Aichi's beam as he prepared to make a run at it.

Jerry pressed his attack. Rolling his wings, he swung in behind the Val and from close behind cut loose with his guns. The barrage ripped pieces from the fragile dive bomber. It staggered, then headed for the sea in a shallow descent. Morrissey was on it in a flash. He noticed the tail gunner was still firing away, so he set his gunsight right on the man and pulled the trigger. The gunner died instantly, just seconds before the Val hit the water. The Japanese pilot managed to execute a reasonably good water landing despite the damage Jerry's bullets had wrought on his Val. Jerry and Morrissey both had pulled up to come around for another pass when they saw the Val splash into the northeast end of

Carigara Bay. Jerry swept down on it and made a single strafing pass to complete the kill. After all he had seen in New Guinea, there would be no mercy for his foe.

Without any more targets to knock down, Jerry and Morrissey linked up and returned to Tacloban. Bong found them on the way home, after having damaged the fourth Oscar. The Japanese pilot somehow managed to avoid destruction and got away in the clouds over Biliran Island.

Once back on the ground at Tacloban, Jerry learned that the rest of the squadron had also run into quite a scrap. Bernie Krankowitz knocked down a Val and damaged another, while Art Hufford zapped another Aichi. Altogether, the 49th downed six Japanese planes without loss. Not bad for the first day on the job.

After the day's activities, the pilots were understandably exhausted. With the rain still coming down around their ears, they retreated from the flight line to the Operations tent, located right alongside the runway, for a quick debriefing. They were wet, dirty, and ready for a warm blanket and a bit of shut-eye. Spence hurried them through their statements, then released them.

Together, the pilots piled into several jeeps that took them the four miles to their camp. The road between their new home and the airstrip was awash in mud, which made for slow going. Rumor had it that there were still snipers in the area, and some of the pilots later remembered getting shot at as they drove down the road. The camp proved to be no better. Everything was covered with mud, and the men were to be billeted in tents again. Unfortunately, the tents had not been set up, so the pilots ended their first afternoon on Leyte building their own quarters, working in ankle-deep mud. It would be another week or so before they could get some Filipinos to come in and build wooden floors in their tents, so for the time being, the men sloshed around in the muck even inside their own quarters.

Exhausted and dispirited, the men slogged to dinner and back, shucked off their boots and lay back within their mosquito netting, hoping that sleep would soon come. That night, as darkness enfolded the camp, the Japanese came. Single raiders, long ago dubbed "Washing Machine Charlies" by the veterans of Guadalcanal, crept over Tacloban. All night long, they buzzed around the strip and occasionally dropped a bomb or two. By morning, the pilots were filthy, having spent the night diving in and out of foxholes.

It was a depressing glimpse of what life would be like for the coming weeks. Mud, fatigue, mosquitoes, and more Japanese than even Dick Bong wanted to handle.

❧

Jerry flew two missions the next day. That morning, the rain poured down on Tacloban with an intensity that made storms in New Guinea look tame in comparison. Kenney fussed all morning, cursing the weather. Over in Ormoc Bay, on the other side of Leyte, the Japanese had brought in a reinforcement convoy, and he wanted to send the 49th after it, but the rain was so bad he could not ask his boys to go aloft. Grinding his teeth, he asked the Navy for help. They sent in a small strike that hit the docks, but more aircraft were needed over Ormoc to do any real damage.

The rain finally let up shortly after lunch. The pilots had been sitting around in the Ops tent, waiting for word to get going. When it came, they grabbed their gear and headed to their mud-encrusted Lightnings. Flying through heavy clouds, twelve pilots from the group dive-bombed the small town of Ormoc, hoping to destroy some of the supplies that had recently been landed. On the way home, Ray "Swifty" Swift, Jerry's faithful wingman from the old days over Rabaul and the Markham Valley, spotted an Oscar and shot it down. Swift was still flying, despite fracturing his skull in an accident some months before. His injury would not be properly diagnosed until his return to the States in the spring of 1945. When it was, it would force him from the service on disability.

Meanwhile, back at Tacloban, Bong, Morrissey, Walker, and Jerry remained behind as the Alert flight. At 4:00, they got word to scramble— Japanese aircraft were inbound. Jerry ran to his P-38, number #83, where Jack Hedgepeth, his crew chief, helped strap him in before he taxied out onto the strip and gunned the throttle. Bong and Morrissey had already left, so Jerry had to hustle to catch up to them.

With Bong leading, ground control vectored them right into an incoming Ki 43. Bong attacked it with a fury, but the canny Japanese pilot evaded him, turned west, and tried to escape. All four pilots gave chase,

Bong still in the lead. Somehow, that Oscar dragged the Americans all the way to the west side of Leyte. Inevitably, however, the Lightnings ran their quarry down, and Bong hit him from dead astern. The Oscar began to dive, but Bong stayed with him and kept firing until the Japanese fighter caught fire. Satisfied, Bong pulled off target and turned north. Just as he did, he caught sight of Jerry diving down after the stricken Oscar. Jerry followed it all the way down and watched it crash. As he did, though, the rest of the flight sped northward to a rally point known as "Point L," waiting for Jerry to join up with them.

He did not join them; exactly where Jerry went on this mission is unclear. What is clear is that he missed a large brawl when his flight mates continued north and began patrolling along Masbate Island's south coast. Bong encountered another Oscar and gave chase. As it tried to dive away, the Japanese pilot jettisoned his bomb. The bomb tumbled back under the Oscar's fuselage and slammed into the tail. Amazed, Bong watched as the entire fuselage broke off just aft of the cockpit. The dismembered Oscar tumbled wildly into the water, some 11,000 feet below.

Moments later, the three Americans ran into a swarm of seventeen Oscars. Morrissey turned for home, hoping to call up more Lightnings, while Walker and Bong waded into the Japanese. In the wild fight that followed, Bong damaged two more Oscars, but was then forced to dive out of the fight. His left radiator took a hit during the escape, which forced him to feather the engine. He limped home on one engine, with Walker providing escort. At one point, another Oscar showed up and tacked onto Walker's tail, but for some reason, the Japanese pilot didn't fire. He stayed behind Walker for several tense minutes, then zoomed up into the clouds and disappeared. Upon returning to Tacloban, Jerry was sorely disappointed to learn that he missed the later fight. He flew a second patrol, hoping to catch some of his own, but failed to spot any Japanese planes.

In two days, the 49th had destroyed ten Japanese planes without loss. The one-sided contest could not last; in fact, it lasted less than 24 hours.

❧

Staff Sergeant Jack Hedgepeth sat in the cockpit of Jerry's P-38, cleaning the windscreen and trying to get the grime out of the plane's interior.

STORM OVER LEYTE 199

He had been in the theater for over two years, and had been Jerry's crew since he had returned from the States. Jerry had long since learned to trust him implicitly. The ace was always amazed at the care and dedication his crew chief showed—how he babied #83 to keep it in top shape, even if he had to work through the night to get it ready for Jerry's next mission. October 29, 1944 was no different. Jack had made it down to the flight line before dawn to warm up the engines and put the final touches on the aircraft so that Jerry would find everything in order.

As Hedgepeth sat in the cockpit, the air raid siren burst to life. He paused in his cleaning, and looked up, scanning for the incoming raiders. He saw an empty sky dotted with clusters of clouds, but no aircraft. He waited a few minutes, then returned to his cleaning. Over the last week, there had been as many false alarms as there had been actual strikes, and Jack just assumed this was one of the former.

A single Oscar roared in from the bay, so low that his prop was practically scraping Tacloban's pierced steel planking. Its twin 12.7mm machine guns barked out a steady stream of tracers, which tore into the 49th's ready fighters. The Japanese pilot stitched his way down the runway, releasing a couple of light bombs as he went. As soon as he appeared, he was gone, speeding away in a climbing turn. In his wake, he left three destroyed P-38s, and four more badly damaged. Seven out of twelve Lightnings sitting along the runway had been knocked out by a single Oscar making one low-level pass.

When the ground crews rushed to the stricken aircraft, they found Jack Hedgepeth in Jerry's cockpit, bleeding profusely. They gently eased him out of the damaged P-38 and rushed him to the nearest aid station, where he died later that day. Jerry was devastated by Jack's loss. Heartbroken, he wrote a long letter home to his father that barely concealed his mourning.

Our men are fighting the most difficult battles of the war and we are flying against a force that has numbers, skill and dogged determination. Men are wounded or killed. Husbands, fathers, brothers and sons are giving their last full measure, Dad. There are no braver, more courageous men anywhere than these thousands of unsung heroes who are defeating the Japs. A few of us get the medals and become "heroes" yet we live well, and have a fighting occupation that suits our stomachs.

Every time I start to complain, I think how selfish, how little I am. Those men lie awake in a stinking water-filled foxhole, waiting for the rustle of a Jap crawling on his belly. Those men who crawl out of the mud in the midst of a lead-filled morning to find their buddy next to them is dead, his throat slit because he was too sleepy and exhausted to maintain constant vigilance. They are the real heroes, Dad.

Perhaps I told you of my crew chief who had been overseas for two and a half years. One early morning he was in my ship's cockpit cleaning it up, preparing it for my flight. An air raid alarm sounded, but he saw no airplanes so he continued with his duty/well, that's another story, but he was one of the bravest men I ever knew.

The day after Hedgepeth died, George Kenney and Pappy Gunn were walking along the runway at Tacloban when another Oscar skimmed the wavetops and came down the peninsula, all guns blazing. A fragmentation bomb exploded right by Kenney and Gunn. Pappy, one of the Fifth Air Force's greatest legends and the man who virtually invented the B-25 gunship, fell, gravely wounded with shrapnel wounds in his arm. The wound knocked him out of the war, and caused him intense pain for the rest of his life.

Later that day, the first of the season's monsoons struck Leyte. With gales approaching 50 mph, tents were blown over, shacks were flattened, and aircraft were destroyed or damaged. Waves four feet high swept over the peninsula and swamped the runway. The road between the airstrip and the 49th's camp was turned into a quagmire so severe that no vehicle could negotiate it. The pilots were only able to get to the runway in the following weeks by using a "duck" (an amphibious truck, or DUKW) to get across the bay. They were frequently strafed on their way to work each morning as they chugged through the water.

If storms were not enough, the Japanese certainly were. On the 31st, a day in which Jerry flew two more combat missions, the 9th Squadron's new commanding officer, Major Bob McComsey, died in a dive-bombing attack that struck Tacloban at dusk; he had been at Leyte for only three days. Jerry and Colonel Walker gave Wally Jordan the 9th Squadron again, and he commanded it until Bill Williams took over a few weeks later.

McComsey was the second 49th pilot killed on the 31st. Earlier in the day, American anti-aircraft gunners guarding Tacloban accidentally shot down Bob Searight, a pilot from the 7th, as he came back after a dawn patrol over Leyte. He had been trying to land in the middle of an air raid, but that did not ease the knot in everyone's stomach over the incident. Most of the pilots flying from Leyte in those early days of the invasion remember constantly getting shot at by American anti-aircraft gunners. Usually, the Navy's ships in San Pedro Bay were the culprits, but sometimes the field's own guns opened up on them. The infuriated pilots could not believe it—as if hundreds of Japanese planes in the area was not enough, their own gunners appeared incapable of identifying a P-38, the most recognizable aircraft of the Second World War.

The losses continued to mount. On November 2, Leslie Nelson was sitting in his P-38 at the end of Tacloban's wet runway, waiting for the signal to takeoff for a dusk patrol around San Pedro Bay. Three other P-38s were with him, and the flight was led by a non-49th Fighter Group ace.

As they sat waiting for the green light to start their takeoff rolls, another patrol came in to land. Bill Huisman's P-38 swung round on final approach with its gear and flaps down, when another Lightning dropped down on top of him from behind. Evidently, the second pilot did not even see Huisman as he came down towards the strip. The collision chopped Huisman's P-38 in half, sending the pieces careening down the runway spewing flaming avgas along the way. The other P-38 staggered off on one wing, barely missing the Ops tent where Jerry and the rest of the 49th watch the horrifying accident unfold. Everyone dived for cover as the second P-38 passed overhead, then exploded alongside the runway a short distance from the Operations tent. The explosion engulfed the area in flames, wounding several men. The pilot of the second P-38 died instantly, while an enlisted man who had been caught in the explosion and knocked unconscious suffered serious burns. Several other men from the 9th pulled this man to safety; they received the Soldier's Medal for their heroism.

Huisman's cockpit and the forward part of his Lightning, now totally bathed in flames, skidded to a halt alongside the runway. Huisman, who was best known for being a workout and body building fanatic much like George Haniotis, frantically tried to open the canopy and get out away from the fiery wreck. Sheer brute force popped the canopy free, and Huisman flung himself out of the cockpit—right into the middle of the burning wreckage.

At the end of the runway, Leslie Nelson watched in horror as his friend burst into a human torch. The crash had probably destroyed the fuel tank right behind the cockpit, which meant that in all likelihood Huisman had been covered with gasoline while still in the cockpit. Now, he staggered around, sheathed in flames. Leslie was grateful the noise of his engines masked his friend's anguished screams.

From the Operations tent, two 9th Squadron enlisted pilots charged across the runway and threw themselves into Huisman's burning plane. They grabbed Huisman and dragged him free of the P-38. They got him on the ground and began beating the flames off him as he roiled around in abject agony. As they did, the flight leader at the end of the runway suddenly opened his throttles and began thundering toward them. As he passed Huisman and the two scorched enlisted men, his P-38's prop wash pelted the three injured men with rocks, debris, and dust, contributing to their misery. The Lightning continued on, got airborne and then circled the strip to wait for the rest of his flight.

Leslie Nelson felt sick. The sight of what his flight leader had done would never leave him, and it permanently affected his opinion of the man. Despite the fact that he was overhead, waiting for Nelson to get off the ground and join up, Leslie remained at the end of the runway, refusing to move until medics had reached Huisman and the two enlisted men. When they had been picked up, Nelson let up on the brakes and headed off to join up with his flight leader.

Huisman died of his burns a few days later while aboard a hospital ship. The ship's crew buried him at sea with full honors. His death would haunt Leslie Nelson for the rest of his life.

❧

By November 10, 1944, the 49th Fighter Group had suffered seven dead and at least two missing during the two weeks they had been on Leyte. Bob Hamburger was the latest pilot to be lost. He had been strafing a truck convoy on Highway 2 along with the rest of the 9th Squadron on November 3 when his P-38 caught fire. When last seen, he'd hit the silk and landed in a rice paddy, not far from his burning Lightning. On that same mission, Dick Bates was shot down and killed. It was small consolation to the group when an army liaison officer showed up at the Ops tent to tell the pilots that they had destroyed at least twenty-five trucks and killed at least 2,400 Japanese troops.

Jerry and George Walker took each loss hard, but neither had much time to grieve. As the group's executive officer, Jerry spent much of his time dealing with all sorts of problems that arose as a result of their move to Leyte. Worst among the issues was the fact that several LSTs failed to show up at the beachhead. One of those LSTs had been carrying some critical parts for the 49th. For example, none of the group's oxygen adapters had arrived, which forced the some of the pilots to fly without oxygen. Carl Estes flew three missions without oxygen before replacements part finally arrived. As a result, most of the early missions the group flew from Tacloban occurred below 12,000 feet. The group's personal belongings had also failed to show up; that included Jerry's mattress and his refrigerator, two luxuries he had had on Biak.

During the days, Jerry worked hard with Colonel Walker to keep the group running, while still flying every mission he could manage. Nighttime brought no respite—he labored long into each night, sorting through paperwork, requisition forms, and red tape in an effort to get replacement parts, pilots, and planes. It was an overwhelming, never-ending struggle to keep the group running, and it began to take its toll on him.

Jerry lost weight, and his already skinny frame grew gaunt and haggard. In a letter home to Barbara in early November, he commented that he could not seem to stay clean. No wonder, there was no escape from the mud, and by the end of their first week at Tacloban, everyone in the group was filthy. Uniforms grew ragged and stained, and even the employment of local Filipinos as laundry help failed to keep them clean for long.

With this exhausting regimen, Jerry was rarely seen by the majority of the group. He spent most of his time with Walker and his tent mate, Doc Bas, the group's flight surgeon. Even Wally Jordan did not see much of Jerry, as both men were so busy trying to hold their respective commands together through the struggle they had found themselves in.

Jerry turned out for mail call one morning, and found a small package waiting for him. He held the small box, delighted to see that it was from Barbara. For a moment, he was lost in thought, his mind back in Eugene with his family and his pregnant young wife, far from the mud, the misery, and the exhaustion of Leyte. He returned to his tent alone to open his package.

Barbara could not have timed this one any better. Inside, Jerry not only found a letter, but Barbara had sent along a half-dozen photographs of herself in various seductive poses, covered only by a towel or skimpy bathing suit. Jerry's eyes nearly bulged out of their sockets as he studied the images. As he did, these slender threads that tied him to Barbara and his distant home made him both lonely and joyful at the same time. He read and reread the accompanying letter, as pangs of homesickness hit him for the first time in years. He had grown accustomed to separation from home and hearth long before while living in the New Guinea jungles, but for this one moment, he indulged himself in memory and nostalgia. He would have given anything to see Barbara, to hold her close and run his hands along her stomach as they quibbled over names for the baby.

The reality of his situation returned. As a leader of men, Jerry could not indulge himself in this sort of emotional outburst much anymore, so he gathered himself together. The photographs were pure gold, and he spent many more minutes staring at them before deciding he had to share them with some of his close friends. Off he went in search of Bong, Walker, and Doc Bas, all of whom were treated to stories of Barbara and news of the baby. By the time he climbed into his P-38 for an afternoon patrol, Jerry was feeling pretty darned good.

On this day, November 11, Jerry and Dick Bong had attached themselves to the 7th Fighter Squadron for an escort mission to Homohon Island, about fifty miles east of Tacloban. A group of C-47s were going to drop supplies to Allied troops on the island, and given the fact that Japanese aircraft were frequently in the area, the 7th was assigned to cover their run in and back with five P-38s.

The first part of the mission proved uneventful. The C-47s made their air drops without any trouble, and no Japanese aircraft showed up. After escorting the transports home, Jerry brought the flight around to the west and headed for Ormoc. A short time earlier, a Navy carrier strike had hit one of the frequent Japanese reinforcement convoys sent down from Manila, so when Jerry's flight arrived, they could see smoke billowing up from wrecked ships in the bay.

As it turned out, they arrived just in time. One of the ground controllers called out bogeys running along the southern part of Ormoc Bay. Jerry turned the flight to the right and climbed up to 13,000 feet, hoping that the controller would vector them in on the enemy planes. Along the way, they spotted a few Navy planes leaving the area following their strikes.

A few minutes later, they sighted six Grumman TBM Avengers—torpedo planes from one of the nearby carriers. Without any fighter escort, these planes had historically been slaughtered if intercepted by Japanese Zeroes. Sure enough, trailing behind them was a flight of seven Zeroes, getting ready to dive down and chew them up. Jerry immediately nosed down and charged after the lead Zero. A quick pull of the trigger, and the Japanese plane exploded. Behind him, Bong waded into the fray and nailed two Zeroes. Both dropped out of the fight with their engines smoking. Jerry, while swinging around to go after another target, saw both of Bong's victims hit the water.

Jerry lined up on another Zeke and cut loose with all his guns. He barreled towards the fighter, snapping out expert bursts until the Mitsubishi was so close it filled his windscreen. Suddenly, it exploded. Jerry had no way of evading the tremendous fireball in front of him, so for the second time in a month, he flew right through the flaming, smoky mess. Shaken, but unhurt, he stormed out the other side and waded back into the scrap.

No Zeroes were even able to make a run on the vulnerable Grumman torpedo planes. Bong and Jerry made quick work of the seven Zekes, shooting down four of them. Bob Morrissey hit another Zero, but it was able to get away. A half hour later, all five pilots were back in the Ops tent along side the runway at Tacloban, comparing notes with Spence. Later, the Navy tracked down Dick and Jerry and invited them aboard a destroyer in San Pedro Bay, where the two pilots were able to get their first decent meal in over two months. Jerry really appreciated eating off of china plates with real silverware—he had not done that since coming back to the theater in September.

November 11th had been an eventful day, and as the afternoon wound down, Jerry retreated to his tent to scribble a letter to Barbara. In part, it read:

Hello You Beautiful Body,

The boys have loosened the straight jacket enough for me to have a free arm for writing this letter. The pictures arrived today and I am completely unnerved.

I have the best damned wife in the world, Darling, and the most beautiful. Let me repeat that your pictures are even beyond my imagination and remind me of the luxury of your loveliness.

Well, I have 19 now. Seems they just get in front of me. One I shot down blew up before me and I flew through the flame. Haven't yet (ever) picked up any bullet holes. Bong and I have been knocking them down together. Hope those people back there don't think that I have become a "Fat Cat." I have every reason in the world to carry on with my work. One of these days, Colonel Johnson will tell you all about it.

I'm glad—as a matter of fact I'm tickled to death to hear Johnny is fine. It will be a thrilling experience for me to meet the two of you when I return. I love you, repeat, I love you Darling and to say I miss you terribly much doesn't even intimate how much that is.

Every memory I have of you is alive with warmth and happiness. Your faith, your purity, are to be found anywhere in this world. Barbara, I am the most fortunate husband in existence. Your letters are priceless, and your spirit and humor give me new energy and stronger faith. I belong only to you alone Darling, beyond all eternity—and you know how long that is.

> *Whatever I am I Belong to You*
> *Just a Fighter Pilot in Love,*
> *Gerald*

❧

And so it went at Leyte, day after day. The pilots flew to the brink of exhaustion, then beyond. Every night they collapsed in their cots to grab what sleep they could. Air attacks came with depressing regularity, forcing the men out of bed and into nearby muddy slit trenches. In the morning, the cycle would repeat itself once again. All the while, the losses piled up as the days blurred into a sort of surreal nightmare existence. Friends came and went, killed in flaming wrecks or attacking Japanese convoys. Others—a few—simply collapsed and couldn't go on. The 8th Squadron lost half its pilots through November, and the group as a whole wrote off sixty planes in the first forty-five days at Leyte—200 percent of its original strength on October 27th. Replacement pilots came in, but they frequently lasted only a mission or two. Nelson Flack, one of the 8th Squadron's old hands, recalled assigning a brand-new replacement pilot to a mission on November 18. Flack gave him the assignment that morning—his first with the squadron—and he was dead before nightfall. Most of the 8th had never even had a chance to meet him.

At one point, according to Flack, combat had whittled the 49th down to twenty able-bodied pilots and just nine P-38s. In fact, the group lost so many Lightnings that Hap Arnold jumped all over Kenney, telling him that he was losing too many airplanes and warning him he would not be getting the kind of replacements he would need if the wastage continued. That was an easy thing to tell Kenney from Washington, but the reality of Leyte was very similar to the early days of Guadalcanal. In this instance, however, the Japanese had bases all around Tacloban, and hundreds of aircraft to throw at the beachhead.

The strip at Tacloban remained about the only USAAF sanctuary in the Philippines. Kenney's engineers had tried to build several more strips, but the sites chosen proved unsuitable and the monsoon soon flooded them out. Only a short strip at Dulag helped alleviate the congestion at Tacloban as other units began moving up. Unfortunately, neither the Dulag nor Tacloban could handle bombers, so Kenney's fighter groups were forced into double-duty. The constant grind wore everybody out, to the point that even the fiercest Tigers at Tacloban—Bong, McGuire, and Jerry among them—were losing their eagerness for combat.

At the end of November, Jerry was so exhausted that George Walker ordered him back to New Guinea on leave. He flew back to Nadzab and stayed a few days with Jock Henebry, his old friend from his Dobodura days. Jock was running an in-theater training command now, taking fresh crews from the States and giving them tactical combat experience by sending them after bypassed Japanese garrisons. It gave the crews a chance to get their feet wet, and Jock devoted most of his time to imparting his own vast knowledge to his young students. This was Jerry's first trip back to Nadzab, but he would visit Jock periodically throughout the rest of the war when he needed to get away from the killing for awhile.

❦

By December 7, 1944, Jerry was back at the killing game. Flying with Bob Morrissey, George Walker, and Harry Harris, the Oregon ace headed over Ormoc Bay for one more fight. This time, they were supposed to provide air cover for the American landing force in Ormoc Bay. For an hour that morning, they circled over the destroyers and transports below without seeing anything. Jerry was flying in the number four slot that day on George Walker's wing. Morrissey, who was leading the flight that day, and Harry Harris made up the other element.

Five minutes before 10:00, Harry Harris called in a formation of nine twin-engine aircraft off the flight's left side. These were Nakajima Ki 49 Helen bombers. Bob Morrissey saw them as well, and he broke left to lead the flight into them. As they closed on the Japanese, however, the four Americans spotted a trio of Oscars heading away from them. The Helen formation could wait. With throttles to the stops, the Lightnings charged the Oscars. Morrissey bored in first, but the three Japanese saw him coming and made simultaneous hard right turns, just like a school of scared fish. Morrissey overshot just as Harry Harris and George Walker came in next. The Oscars' right break put them in a perfect position for a head-on pass, but just as Harris and Walker got into firing range, they flitted up and to the left in a steep chandelle.

Sitting slightly above the fight, Jerry was a little surprised that all three P-38s had missed. "Watch this!" he called out on the radio, then began a run of his own. Down he came after the trailing Oscar, which had just blown most of its energy in the steep chandelle. Jerry ducked under it, then pulled up sharply. The Oscar filled his sight—sitting at the top of a half-loop, the Ki 43 had nowhere to go and no power or speed to even maneuver. Jerry had him dead to rights. A quick burst and the Oscar erupted in flames.

Jerry zoomed above the other two Oscars, then came back down like a runaway train. The two Japanese pilots tried to get away by chandelling to the right. Jerry had the energy to follow, and he bolted up after them, coming into range quickly. The Oscars broke hard right presenting a difficult high deflection shot, but Jerry was right on them. He zapped the first one, tapped his rudder and touched the trigger just as his sight crossed in front of the second. Both Oscars splashed into Ormoc Bay within a few hundred feet of each other. Jerry had knocked down all three enemy fighters in just forty-five seconds. Exultant, he cried out on the radio, "Count 'em! One, two, three!" Walker and Morrissey later said that Jerry's two passes were the best displays of aerial gunner they had ever seen. After the war, Kenney recalled that Jerry's gun camera footage from that mission was still being used in gunnery training schools.

But the mission was not over. The Oscars had been trying to escort a force of Ki 49 Helen twin-engined bombers. In two side by side Vees, the bombers headed towards the invasion force off Ormoc, diving for the deck as they went in hopes of evading the P-38s overhead. Morrissey waited for Jerry to join up, then the flight lit into the Helens in a furious effort to break up their attack.

Jerry went after the left Vee on his first pass, targeting the far left Ki 49 in the formation. He got good strikes with his first pass, then pulled up and sped ahead of the bombers. He extended away, then swung back down and made a front quarter pass on the Helen he had already hit. The bomber, engines smoking, was straggling along behind the rest of the formation and did not stand a chance. Jerry hit him again, then watched as the Ki 49 dug a crater just off the beach near Talingon.

The American fighters slaughtered the bomber formation. After Jerry's went down, three of the Helens tried to crash-dive a nearby destroyer. Walker went after one of those, and from dead astern poured fire into its apparently empty tail turret. The rounds tore through the fuselage, probably killing the pilots. It overshot the destroyer and plunged into the water a few hundred yards from its intended target. Morrissey picked off another one, wrecking its right engine with concentrated machine gun and cannon fire. That Helen rolled over and crashed. Harry Harris nailed that Ki 49's wingman, knocking pieces off it and causing its right engine to smoke. The Ki 49 tried to reach the destroyer, but smacked into the waves just in front of the ship.

In a furious fight that lasted only a few minutes, the American quartet had picked off four bombers and three fighters, effectively ruining a suicide attack on the American task force. Jerry nailed four of the seven planes, which gave him an official total of twenty-three air-to-air kills. In three months of combat, he'd knocked down ten planes.

In the minds of many 49th members, Jerry's December 7th mission proved he was one of the best pilots in the Far East Air Force. Most felt he was Bong's equal in the air, while on the ground his leadership skills and his ability to inspire his fellow pilots were unsurpassed. Recalling Jerry years later, Leslie Nelson remarked that he had the ability to elevate everyone around him, making them believe they were probably better than they were. He instilled confidence into every mission, into every person in the group, with his mere presence. To some in the group, their respect for Jerry bordered on awe. He was a hero amongst them, but he was never arrogant and never let his own ambition affect his combat flying. And, they never forgot that in all of his fights against the Japanese, he'd always brought his wingmen home. To Fifth Air Force commander Gen. Enis Whitehead, there could be no finer tribute to this young Oregonian.

A year after joining the squadron, Leslie Nelson knew he'd had it. Back in New Guinea, he tipped the scales at 185 pounds, but since the summer, he had been steadily losing weight. By December of 1944, he was a walking stick, barely 115 pounds. Weak and easily exhausted, he found the rigors of manhandling a P-38 around the sky increasingly daunting. Finally, it all came to a head one day.

Nelson had left Tacloban on a local patrol when one of his engines exploded. Pieces of the fan went flying in all directions, and a chunk of the engine smashed through the canopy where it gouged Leslie's head. Leslie could barely keep the crippled Lightning aloft, but he somehow managed to limp back to Tacloban and get it down on the runway. When he shut down his remaining engine, he was so exhausted by the ordeal he could hardly get out of the cockpit. When ground crews helped him off the wing, they saw that his flight suit was soaked with sweat.

That did it—he went off to see Doc Bas and told him that he had no energy and no strength left. Sooner or later, he would kill himself in the air, or get somebody else killed. Doc Bas examined him and could not believe how much weight Nelson had lost. He grounded him at once, diagnosing Leslie with combat fatigue, and got him orders to return home. Actually, Leslie had contracted amoebic dysentery in New Guinea, but that fact would slip by numerous doctors in the ensuing weeks.

Leslie went by Group headquarters after he packed his gear. He said goodbye to Jerry, perhaps recalling that, how a year earlier, Jerry had welcomed him to the 9th Squadron. Here he was fresh from the States, standing before ace and legend Jerry Johnson at Gusap, not sure what to expect. Jerry shook his hand, then sternly barked, "We don't need pilots here, we need planes. So when you fly, remember that. Bring your plane back or I'll kill you myself." Leslie didn't know what to think of this welcome, until he saw a slight, mischievous grin lace across Jerry's face. After that first meeting, Jerry was all right as far as Leslie was concerned. Now they said their good-byes on Leyte, Jerry wishing his fellow 49'er luck back home. A short time later, Leslie boarded an LST thinking that his combat days were over. He could not have been more wrong.

❦

One afternoon, as some of the 49th's off-duty pilots lounged around the camp area, Bob Hamburger miraculously showed up after being posted missing for several weeks. Exactly what happened has become a part of 49th Fighter Group lore, and how much truth there is to the story is debatable. However, Hamburger reached Tacloban with the aid of local Filipino guerrillas, who spirited him away from the Japanese near Highway 2 on the day he was shot down. During an epic trek across Leyte, dodging enemy patrols with the guerrillas, Hamburger ended up married to a Filipino girl. When he entered camp, eyewitnesses claim he was being carried by natives on a throne-litter, with his wife beside him and a monkey on his shoulder. He looked positively piratical—something right out of a Gilbert and Sullivan musical.

The monkey became the stuff of legends as well. Shortly after he returned to the squadron, the monkey ripped open an entire months worth of cigarette rations stored in Hamburger's tent. When he came back after a mission and found the monkey ripping apart his smokes, he exploded. Drawing his Colt automatic, he blasted away at the monkey, who skittered around inside the tent, then scampered up the center pole. Hamburger emptied his clip at the beast, but somehow managed to miss every time. That night, when it rained, water poured into tent from the numerous bullet holes in the canvas. Wet and smokeless, Hamburger swore that he would never own another monkey again.

When Jerry returned to the group in early December, major changes were afoot, as many of the old-timers were about to be sent home. Among them were Carl Estes, Leslie Nelson, and Dick Bong. For quite some time, Kenney had been telling Bong he'd be sent home after he got forty kills; by the first week of December, he had scored thirty-eight. About that time, Carl Estes learned he would be sent to Australia sometime before Christmas, then after New Year's, he would be put on a ship for home. He had been out for almost a year and had flown more missions than most of the other pilots in the squadron. The news delighted him, and he relayed it to Dick Bong.

Estes and his tentmates had set up their quarters next to Bong's tent. The two tents were then connected by lifting the flaps on either side and creating a tunnel. He, Charlie McElroy, and Leslie Nelson had all joined the squadron about the same time and had roomed together throughout much of their tour. Across the tunnel, Bong and McGuire were bunking together, a kind of an odd mix in that McGuire was all nervous energy and Dick was the essence of cool and sedate. On top of that, McGuire's burning desire to catch Dick's score fostered some smoldering resentment toward the top ace.

Estes ducked his head and passed through the tent tunnel to tell Bong that he'd be going home, but he would first get a chance to spend Christmas and New Year's in Sydney. He found the top ace lying in his cot, staring at the ceiling. He congratulated Carl, then mumbled, "I think I'll go home, too."

On December 12, Carl and Dick were lounging in their tent in the late afternoon when somebody came by and said that General MacArthur was down at the airstrip and wanted to see Bong. Dick looked at the guy and just said, "Yeah, sure he is." The man left, and Dick did not seem inclined to move. Ten minutes later, the phone in their tent rang. Estes answered it and heard a voice on the other end say, "The General has to leave in a little while, is Bong on his way down?" Carl just answered, "No, he's still here." Both pilots thought a joke was being played on them, but when Carl turned the phone over to Bong, he saw right away that he had been mistaken. Bong repeatedly snapped "Yes sir! Right away, sir!" into the phone, before hanging it up and heading out for the strip. It was a terrible, rainy day, and as usual, the trip to the runway was an adventure in itself.

When Bong finally arrived, MacArthur personally awarded him the Congressional Medal of Honor in an impromptu ceremony. The enlisted men and pilots who were at the airfield gathered around to watch the moment, which reporters captured on film. Fifteen minutes after he received his award, Bong retreated to the Headquarters shack off the airstrip, where he found Colonel Walker and a reporter, who later documented the conversation that followed.

"Congratulations," said Walker.

Nonchalantly, Bong answered, "Thanks."

The two pilots got to talking, and Walker served him some tuna fish that his wife had sent along in a care package. While wolfing down tuna fish sandwiches, Jerry walked in. "Congratulations, Bing," he said, but Bong only nodded as his mouth was full of tuna.

The conversation soon turned to home, and Bong told Jerry he wanted to get back by January 15 so he could see his fiancée, Marge, graduate from college. They'd get married right after that. "I can see what's going to happen. Pretty soon they'll be married and then pretty soon we'll get a letter that Bing Bong is going to be a papa," Jerry replied.

Walker joined in, "Bong is going to put out!"

"He's got to prove himself first," added Jerry.

Bong ignored them both, and began making another sandwich. "My mom puts onions in this."

The banter continued for some time, with Jerry kidding Bong about a postwar visit to his family's farm. Jerry expected full service, including feasts for breakfast and a warm, cozy room for he and Barbara. For his part, Bong was looking forward to a trip out to Oregon to go fishing with Jerry up in the Cascades.

Jerry joked that someday he'd meet Marge, slap her on the back and ask her, "What in the hell did you every marry that guy for?"

Walker continued the ribbing, "She'll answer 'I don't know. I love him I guess.'"

Bong changed the subject and asked Jerry if he'd been to Washington yet. When the Oregonian said no, Bong opined, "When you get back, you'll be called to Washington." Turning to Walker, he added, "I've been telling him how they're going to make a fuss over him."

Jerry answered, "January 15th . . . Say, when you get home, tell them we're doing a job here. Mention Okie and Nelson and Brisbane. And you might say a word about Johnson. Nobody knows me there."

The conversation continued, wandering along as the three close friends puttered around inside the Headquarters shack. Sitting nearby was a writer named Don Hough. He later included most of the conversation in his book, *Big Distance*, amazed that only fifteen minutes earlier, Bong had received the Medal of Honor. Even that award had not changed him; he was still the old farm boy from Wisconsin.

Don Hough missed the other significance of the conversation. A little over a week later, Kenney sent Bong back to the States. This chat was one of the last Bong and Jerry would have, as the two old friends would never see each other again.

◈

With the ground campaign on Leyte coming to a successful conclusion, MacArthur looked to make another leap up toward Luzon by taking Mindoro Island. At first, his timetable for the invasion was so aggressive that all of the major commanders, including Kenney and Halsey, asked him to delay the operation. The fleet carriers had been on station virtually without rest for almost ninety days. Far from being able to turn over air responsibility in the Philippines to Kenney's Far East Air Force, Halsey's flat-tops were forced to stick around, striking targets all over Luzon to help suppress the Japanese air effort over Leyte. Numerous carriers and other ships were hit by kamikazes as a result. Relations between Kenney and the Navy took a hit every time a kamikaze struck one of the fleet carriers, and accusations flew back and forth between the two services over who was to blame for the mess.

The reality was this: Kenney simply did not have the airfield capacity on Leyte to deploy the majority of his command into the Philippines. As a result, the 49th and the other fighter units on Tacloban and Dulag were the only forces he had to face in what had to have been the largest concentration of Japanese air power to this point in the war. Not surprisingly, for the first month of the Leyte operation, the Japanese held air superiority, though they paid for it dearly in planes and pilots. It was an odd situation, here in late 1944, to have an American operation lack total command of the air. In fact, it was the last time in history that this happened.

With a shortage of fighter and bomber groups, Kenney could not possibly protect the Mindoro invasion fleet from what was surely to be a fierce Japanese aerial counterattack. Once again, he had to call on Kinkaid's jeep carriers and Halsey's Third Fleet to help cover the operation. On December 13, 1944, as the invasion force worked its way through the Sulu Sea, the sky came alive with diving, screeching kamikazes. Several ships were hit and seriously damaged, including the light cruiser *Nashville*, which had been MacArthur's flagship for the Leyte invasion.

The 49th pilots provided cover as best they could. Little did they know that somewhere in that mass of ships spread out on the azure sea below, one of their own was fighting for his life.

❧

"Going home, my ass," thought Leslie Nelson as he stood on the deck of his LST in the middle of kamikaze raid. Expecting a slow trip to Pearl, Leslie got a shrapnel-studded voyage to Mindoro on this particular LST. The ship had already suffered many losses among its crew during the Leyte operation, and it was short of officers. The skipper enlisted both Leslie and another pilot to direct the 20mm anti-aircraft guns that lined the sides of the ship. On this day in mid-December, Leslie found himself with a pitching deck under his feet, a microphone in his hand, and a helmet on his head, yelling to the gunners to increase their lead on their targets. Kamikazes were falling out of the sky like flaming autumn leaves. All around them, ships were being hit despite the thousands of ugly black anti-aircraft smudges that studded the air over the task force. It seemed

inevitable that Leslie's own LST would be hit, with so much carnage being inflicted around them.

A single-engined kamikaze zoomed by on the port side, attracting the attention of Leslie's gunners. They pounded it with 20mm hits, and though it staggered, it stayed aloft. Time slowed for Leslie until it seemed the seconds were just crawling along like ants in a hurricane. Slowly, ever so slowly, that Japanese fighter banked and came around in front of the LST. The nose dropped until Leslie was sure the Japanese pilot had targeted him personally. Coming right down the length of the ship, Leslie knew the kamikaze could not miss. He turned and began aft, but had only taken a few steps when the plane struck the LST's bridge, only a few feet from where he was. A tremendous explosion rocked the ship as flames and debris blew outwards, scything down everyone nearby.

Somebody was looking out for Leslie this day. Part of the kamikaze's propeller hub, with a stub of the crankshaft still attached, skidded along the deck and bounced right between Leslie's legs without touching him. Shrapnel shredded his pants and his arm. He collapsed on the deck, bleeding from numerous wounds.

One of the ship's medics saved his life that December day. The corpsman stopped the bleeding and cleaned up Leslie's shattered arm. Had it not been for the corpsman's quick actions, Leslie would have surely had to have his arm amputated. Even so, he almost lost it later.

The LST survived the kamikaze attack and off-loaded Leslie and the other wounded at San José, Mindoro. There, in the middle of the perimeter, he was dumped at an overworked aid station, where the medics were so overwhelmed they were triaging the new arrivals. Leslie languished there for several days until his arm grew gangrenous as he drifted in and out of delirium brought on by a raging fever. The medics soon decided that he was not going to make it—they even said so in front of him. One day, they wrapped him up in a sheet, then tossed him on a stretcher as he kept shouting, "I'm not through yet you bastards!" Ignoring his curses, they took him to the death tent where all of the hopeless cases were gathered. He would be given antibiotics, but no other medical attention. "If you're still alive in a few days, we'll see what we can do with you," one of the medics told him.

For the next several days, Leslie fought to live while men all around him died gruesome, painful deaths. Each morning and night, an orderly would come in with a blunt 20-gauge needle and shoot him full of penicillin. The six-inch needles were being reused as medical supplies were so short, so each stab in his rear brought about incredible pain—the needles were that dull. Through the entire ordeal, he simply refused to die. Finally, the medics took notice. "I'll be damned, you're still alive?" one of them marveled. The massive doses of penicillin he received had worked. They pulled him out of the death tent and put him back in one of the main wards, where he slowly began to recover. He was eventually evacuated from Mindoro and sent home, where doctors at a Stateside naval hospital diagnosed and cured his amoebic dysentery with a highly toxic, but effective, experimental drug.

Both Dick Bong and Carl Estes flew their last combat missions of World War II on December 17, 1944. Dick downed his fortieth kill that day over Mindoro, and as Kenney had promised, that figure got him sent Stateside. Jerry, McGuire, and many of the old-timers from the 49th saw Bong off. Bong went home to marry his fiancée Marge, then become a test pilot on the new Lockheed P-80 Shooting Star jet fighter program.

Estes, Ed Cooper, Fred Helterline, and Peg Ellis were all sent to Sydney on leave just before Christmas. Before they left, Jerry gave Carl rent money for the Buckingham. The squadron had been using it for almost three years, and it became a treasured sanctuary for its pilots from the stress of combat flying. Estes and the others spent part of their leave in an apartment on the beach, while the rest of the time they set up shop at the Buckingham's seven-bedroom flat, thoroughly enjoying the hospitality the Australians always showed them. And the women . . . well, the women of Sydney were some of the finest in the world as far as the 49th fliers were concerned.

The pilots returned to the group after the New Year, to discover that their outfit had been moved up to Mindoro. When they caught up to the 9th Squadron, the four old hands were given the option of sticking around and flying seventeen more missions, which would earn them all promotions to captain, or they could go home immediately as first lieutenants. All four had had enough. They went home via Biak a few days later.

When they left, Jerry realized how much the Philippine campaign was changing his beloved 49th Fighter Group. As more and more of the old-timers went home or were killed, they were replaced by young pilots fresh from Stateside training schools. As the group changed, so did Jerry—he grew into himself a little bit and did not really get close with any of the new pilots, regardless of their rank. Instead, he withdrew into the ever-diminishing circle of fellow old hands, growing closer to them than ever before. He and McGuire became especially close during those final weeks of 1944.

McGuire visited Jerry's tent the night of Bong's final combat mission, and the two old friends stayed up until the early morning hours, reminiscing about times past. They laughed over the guys they had known in the old 54th, talked about their days in Alaska and their time together en route to New Guinea. Jerry was as smooth and controlled as McGuire was emotional and erratic, so they made kind of an odd pair. They chatted through the night, McGuire chain-smoking as always, until talk turned to Dick Bong. Both men liked Bong a lot, but they were a little surprised by all of the attention that he received at the hands of a group of fawning reporters. They had been following Dick around ever since he had been awarded the Medal of Honor the week before, and the stuff they were printing was beginning to wear thin on both pilots.

This was especially true of McGuire, who was more determined than ever to break Bong's score—something Kenney did not want him to do. Tommy knew that he would only have a few more chances to get in fights, so he was bound and determined to knock down every Japanese plane that crossed his path.

Jerry wrote a letter to Barbara the next day and mentioned some of the grousing they had done. In it, he lightheartedly described the evening before:

> *I'm getting tired of everyone telling me what a superman Bong is. He is a very fine fellow, but the publicity boys are making it appear to the gullible public that such things ain't done by normal hoomans. McGuire (score 31) and I had a big blow-off last night and decided that he (McGuire) and I were still the hottest pilots of hot pilots, as hot pilots go. At any rate, I am your own little hot pilot even if I am still only 3rd man on the totem pole.*

You know I am kidding Barbie, you and several other things,
all of them are more important to me than pushing a throttle.
I just want to be the head of the house and the hero of my children.
How could I be happier and not be so lonely?

Always, Darling, Your First Husband,
Gerald

On January 7, 1945, McGuire died fighting a single Oscar. He refused to jettison his drop tanks, hoping to finish off this one Ki 43 off and continue on patrol. Instead, the Oscar turned the tables and got behind one of McGuire's flightmates. McGuire and another pilot rushed to save their comrade, but ended up in a turning dogfight with the Oscar. With nearly full drop tanks, there was no way their P-38s were going to cut inside the nimble Ki 43, but McGuire threw caution to the winds and pulled back even harder on the stick. At 1,500 feet, his P-38 entered a high-speed stall. He flipped over and went straight in, exploding on impact at Negros Island. As the remaining members of the flight chased the Ki 43, piloted by 54th Sentai veteran Warrant Officer Akira Sugimoto, a Ki 84 Frank from the 71st Sentai showed up and shot down Major Jack Rittmayer, one of McGuire's most experienced pilots.

The 475th never really recovered from the two blows. McGuire's death, especially, affected morale for the rest of the war. For Jerry, the loss of one of his last remaining close friends proved a bitter thing to take. At the same time, it shook him up enough to realize that there were more important things than the "ace race." He was going to be a father soon, which he realized was far more important than his final kill tally. He resolved to be more careful in the future, for now he had two people counting on his return home.

The day after McGuire's death, Jerry sat down at a makeshift table he had built in his new quarters at Mindoro and penned a letter to Barbara.

I have really slowed down in the flying game, Darling—I intend
to be the father of several children and am satisfied with my
present score.

McGuire got his 40th and thereby caught Bong. Of course,
Bong got his in a more leisurely fashion. McGuire was out the
other day and made a fatal mistake, so now he is gone.

I've lost many of my closest friends. They were some of the best pilots I've known, yet each one became too eager to do the fighting and consequently stuck their necks out too far. Be assured, Barbara, I intend to die from chronic old age with great grandchildren well through the tooth-cutting stage.

Your Faithful Husband,
Gerald

NINETEEN

Wingtip to Wingtip, Wave after Wave

January 1, 1945

Dearest Mother and Dad,

Here it is the beginning of another year. I hope and pray that the people back home are determined to work harder this year in order to give us the supplies and equipment needed to defeat the Nip.

I have seen more fighting and greater displays of courage in the last two months than all my years overseas. These men are fighting a determined and fanatical enemy, yet they do not hesitate. Some day, Dad, I can tell you stories of courage and heroism that will thrill your very soul.

We know too well the tremendous task before us for we are here where every day, every night, our lives are a series of vivid experiences.

Take care of my brown-eyed sweetheart, for her well-being is vital to my existence.

Your misbehaved Son,
Gerald

The January landings at Lingayen Gulf, Luzon, broke the back of Japan's airpower in the Philippines. Scores of kamikazes attacked the American fleet as it operated in support of the invasion, hitting numerous carriers and battleships. In the process, though, American fighter pilots devastated entire formations of Japanese planes. By mid-January, the decimated units were finally withdrawn from the Philippines and sent north to Japan itself, where they would soon be expended in suicide and suicidal attacks against the Allied navies during the spring and summer of 1945.

With no more Japanese planes in the area, the 49th settled in at a new strip built along the beach at Lingayen Gulf. Jerry moved into a small hut with one of the most spectacular ocean views anyone could every want. The men flew ground attack missions on a daily basis, something that Jerry absolutely detested. The missions were long, dreary affairs, and afterward Jerry usually had a hard time sitting down due to "pilot's ass." The pilots usually flew missions while sitting on their inflatable rafts and parachutes, and no matter how much the pilots fidgeted, the raft's valve stem always seemed to poke them in the most sensitive places. The lumpy cushion of the two survival devices grew hard as concrete after five or more hours aloft. As a result, Jerry would sometimes come home and hardly be able to sit down for the rest of the day after these missions.

Even so, life at Lingayen was considerably more tolerable than anything they had endured since the group first moved to New Guinea from Darwin back in 1942. The weather was terrific, warm and lush. The swimming was great, the quarters much more livable than the mud-spattered tents of Leyte, and the local Filipinos were delighted to have them in the area.

The pilots took to singing again, usually down at the beach at night as bottles were passed around. Many new songs were composed to mark some of the memorable incidents in group history. Wally Jordan, who was Jerry's last close friend in the group by this point, was lampooned for his belly landing back in the days when the 9th Squadron had P-47s. The verse went:

> *Just ask Captain Jordan, our second in command*
> *How to pull up the wheels and come in to land!*
> *Oh my! I'm too young to die!*
> *I just wanna go home.*

One night, as the gang was getting a little too rowdy out there on the beach, Jerry came out of his hut and gently scolded the men, telling them to keep it down. Indignant that their deputy group commander could ask such a thing of them, a bunch of the pilots charged Jerry and picked him up. As he struggled to get away, they carried him into the Gulf and tossed him into the surf. Soaking wet, he plodded ashore, feigning outrage. He ended up joining the boys and having a rousing time with them. Clearly, even to the new men of the 49th, he was much beloved.

Even to the unofficial members of the 49th, he was admired. While on Leyte, Jerry had hired a local kid named Carl Martinez to be his houseboy. Jerry paid him to keep his quarters clean and to do his laundry, as well as other odd jobs around the camp. Carl idolized his boss, and Jerry became very fond of the boy in return. As they grew to know each other, their relationship became one of mutual friendship. After the war, Carl wrote about working for Jerry, saying that the Oregon ace treated him like one of his buddies, and never as a servant. As a result, Carl followed the group to Mindoro, then on to Luzon, remaining with the outfit for almost a year.

At some point, Jerry asked Carl what he wanted to do with his life once the war was over. Carl thought about that for a moment, then said that he had always dreamed of going to the United States. He wanted to study at an American university, earn a college degree, and then return home to help improve his poverty-ridden country. Jerry was surprised at Carl's dream, but as he thought about it, he decided he would help him out. One day, he asked Carl if he would like to come live with him in Eugene, where he could go to school at the University of Oregon. Carl was stunned by the offer, and was nearly overwhelmed with emotion. Gratefully, he accepted Jerry's offer, and the two made plans for a postwar reunion in Eugene.

In the meantime, there was still a war to be won. While Jerry spent more and more time on the ground through the early part of 1945, he did find time to fly the occasional combat mission. Regular dive-bombing missions bored him to tears, so he took to lone-wolf night intruder missions. He would go hunting for nocturnal truck and tank convoys by moonlight, a difficult and hazardous task. He once caught a pair of Japanese trucks plodding along a back country road somewhere on Luzon. He made a pass that hit both trucks and sent soldiers flying in all directions. He went down the road back and forth, strafing them mercilessly until all were dead. While it was not air combat, such missions helped him feel like he was still contributing to final victory.

Jerry went back down on leave to Nadzab in February, and stayed with his old buddy, Jock Henebry. By this point in the war, Nadzab had started to acquire all the trappings of home. Jerry stayed in a real house that had running water—the first time he had had such luxurious accommodations since coming back for his third combat tour. For the first few days of his stay, songwriter Irving Berlin stayed with him in the little house. The two men became quick friends, and along with Jock Henebry did a great deal of exploring around the countryside. Before Berlin left, he and Jerry had made plans to meet in Oregon after the war to do a little fishing. The friendship even extended to Barbara, to whom Berlin wrote several times after he got back to the United States.

That March, George Walker was promoted out of the group and joined the 308th Bomb Wing's headquarters staff. Jerry took over the group and was promoted to full colonel. He was only twenty-four years old!

The group lost its remaining nucleus of old hands about this time. Bill Williams, Bob Wood, and Ray Swift all went home. Of the New Guinea bunch, only Jerry and Bob DeHaven were left. Things were getting very lonely for Jerry, as even Wally Jordan, who had left in January for Command and General Staff College, was now gone until May. Fortunately, just as all the old hands were leaving, Jim Watkins showed back up and rejoined the 49th, eager to fly another combat tour after his Stateside assignment. Delighted to have his old friend and flight commander back, he and Jerry began flying together again. Jerry wrote home to Barbara and described Duckbutt Watkins as "a capable officer in addition to being a top notch fighter pilot. Now at last I have somebody to fly with again." Watkins became Jerry's deputy group commander, and it did not take them long to run into trouble together.

On April 1, 1945, Jerry and Watkins attached themselves to the 9th Squadron for an escort mission to Hong Kong. It was just like old times, though this time Jerry led the mission, with Watkins on his wing. Along with fourteen other fighters, they covered a formation of Liberators assigned to bomb the docks and airfields around the former British crown colony.

The bombers reached their targets and scored many good hits on both the docks and the nearby airstrip. No interceptors rose to challenge the raiders, so after the B-24s headed for home, Jerry stayed over Hong

Kong and circled for forty-five minutes, hoping to find something to attack. Finally, a pair of Ki 44 Tojos showed up, unaware of the American P-38s in the area. Jerry and Jim pounced on them and shot them both down almost simultaneously. By the time the rest of the squadron joined them, the Tojos were but burning wrecks on the ground below.

Minutes later, several Oscars showed up and a young second lieutenant, Walt Koby, shot one of them down for what became the squadron's 254th and final kill. Jerry confirmed it for Koby, as he saw it burning on a hillside after it crashed. The Flying Knights would finish the war as the highest-scoring squadron of the Pacific War.

❧

On the morning of May 17, 1945, Jerry jumped on the wing of his P-38, pumped his fists in the air and shouted out, "Men, today we're going in wave after wave, wingtip to wingtip! Let's go get 'em!" Brimming with enthusiasm, Jerry bounded into his Lightning's cockpit and began getting it ready for take off. All around him, the rest of the 49th followed suit.

Jerry had assembled all the group's flight leaders the night before, and gave them a detailed briefing for this special mission. Following the capture of Manila, General Walter Krueger's Sixth Army had been pushing into the heart of Luzon, intent on wresting the Ipo Dam from the Japanese. As long as the enemy held the dam, Manila's water supply was threatened. As Krueger's GI's worked their way towards their target, they ran into ferocious opposition; the Japanese had studded the Ipo Dam area with concentrated networks of bunkers, pillboxes, and other fortifications. Taking the dam was sure to be a bloody, costly affair.

Following several 5th Fighter Command attacks on the Ipo Dam area through early May, somebody came up with the idea to saturate the Japanese defenses with napalm. If enough napalm could be dropped in the target area at one time, even the Japanese hunkered down deep inside their pillboxes might be killed by suffocation. But how to create such a mini-firestorm? Fifth Air Force headquarters settled on a massive strike with all five of its fighter groups—some 208 P-38s, P-51s, and P-47s.

Jerry explained to the pilots how the mission was to be executed. Each group would go in with its squadrons in line-abreast formation, one squadron behind the next. At the target area, each squadron would release its napalm tanks simultaneously, then clear the area as the next squadron followed suit. The 49th would go in, sixteen planes abreast with wingtips nearly touching. Jerry would lead the strike.

The strike turned the Ipo Dam area into a furnace of hell. Succeeding waves of fighter-bombers flew right into the conflagration to add their deadly cargo to the inferno. Smoke and fire swirled around them as they reached their release points, and the thermals created by the raging firestorm below buffeted their P-38s and tossed them all over the sky. Somehow, all of the pilots made it through the eerie, surreal scene unscathed, though the stench of the slaughter rose even to their cockpits, and none would ever forget its nauseating effects. When they landed, Jerry was ecstatic, for they had executed the mission perfectly and inflicted tremendous damage to the Japanese. They later found out that Krueger's men had found over 2,000 charred corpses in the killing zone, along with tons of equipment and supplies. The Ipo Dam was taken with minimal casualties.

As much as the group loved their commander, Jerry's rousing speech from atop his P-38 before the Ipo Dam strike had struck some as a bit overenthusiastic. Others picked up on the "wave after wave, wingtip to wingtip" line and began using it in all sorts of ways. It became a part of the group's lexicon, a sort of running joke that all would laugh at, including Jerry. For weeks after the mission, the pilots would ask him, "Are we going in wingtip to wingtip today colonel?" Jerry would just smile and quip, "Wave after wave!" The men loved him that much more when they found that Jerry could laugh at himself along with everyone else. To find that attribute in a twenty-four-year-old Colonel was an amazing thing.

≈

Lt. Ehrman Giustina could hardly stay awake at the controls of his Lockheed PV-2 Harpoon. The former member of the University of Oregon's Sigma Chi fraternity struggled to fend off sleep by willing his eyes to remain open. His eyelids felt as if lead weights were attached to them, so most of his energy was concentrated in fighting to stay awake.

Giustina had been in the air for hours, and his plane was still at least a couple of hours away from its base on Luzon. He shook his head, recalling that his family would be devastated if they lost another beloved son to the air war. Tom Taylor, the friend of Jerry's who had joined the Air Corps just before he had, was Erhman's brother-in-law. Two years before, Tom had been killed over France when a 20mm cannon shell hit him in the chest. Somehow, the copilot brought their B-26 Marauder back home, saving the rest of the crew; Tom, however, died instantly from his wound. Aaron Cuddeback, another friend of the Giustina family, had died after he ditched his damaged B-17 after a raid over Hamm, Germany, a short time before Tom's death. Jim Bennett, a high school classmate and neighbor of the Johnson family, had recently been killed aboard a PT boat during the invasion of Iwo Jima. A fraternity brother, Ralph Lafferty, was laying in a hospital somewhere in Europe, fighting to survive shrapnel wounds he received while fighting beside John Skillern in the 10th Mountain Division. So Erhman knew he had to keep himself awake, to be alert, to protect himself and his crew.

The heat in the cockpit was nothing short of stifling. It made him drowsy, even as the sweat dripped from his forehead. He looked over at his copilot. He was in the same state, looking nearly catatonic. These patrol missions could be so dreary. Nothing ever happened. Then something did. A shadow flashed over the canopy. Suddenly every nerve, every sense in Erhman's body went rigid and alert. He sat up, clutched the controls with both hands, then jammed down on the rudder pedals. That shadow could only have been a fighter. Obviously, his two gunners were asleep, or otherwise they would have called it in.

The PV-2 sloughed wildly, skidding left, then right as Erhman tried to throw off the enemy pilot's aim while waking up his gunners at the same time. Everyone inside the bomber was thrown about, which totally disoriented them.

Erhman looked out over his left wing, peering around for the Japanese plane. What he saw shocked him even more. Not three feet off his left wingtip sat a beautiful natural metal P-38 Lightning. And tucked right there in the Lightning's cockpit was none other than Gerald R. Johnson, fellow classmate and long-time friend. Jerry, of course, had no way of knowing that Erhman was piloting the PV-2; it was just dumb luck that he had stumbled across them out here over the South China Sea.

Jerry made a gun with his finger, pointed it at Erhman and mouthed the words "Bang bang, you're dead." Then in a flash, he rolled the P-38 into a steep chandelle and climbed away.

Lesson learned. Erhman stayed particularly attentive for the rest of the mission—as did the rest of his crew. Every flight after that, he made sure nobody fell asleep at their positions. Erhman would make it through the war and would later become one of the wealthiest men in the Pacific Northwest, building a timber empire that has few peers.

❦

While the final stages of Barbara's pregnancy unfolded in the States, Harold V. Johnson arrived in the theater at the end of May. Jerry nearly exploded with happiness at his arrival. The two brothers spent four short days together before Harold was assigned to the 348th Fighter Group and had to leave. Harold brought fresh news from home; he had visited Eugene on his way to his embarkation point at San Francisco at the beginning of May. He related to Jerry all of the latest events he had seen. He mentioned how big Barbara's tummy had become, and how well she was doing. Their younger brother Art was spending considerable time with Barbara, tending to whatever she needed, and Jerry was extremely grateful. The twins talked long into the night of the first day Harold arrived, catching up on all the news. Then, all too soon, Harold left to begin his combat career flying with Neel Kearby's old outfit.

Jerry wrote to Barbara:

> Harold is having a big time. Course he is as different from me as day and night. We have certain mannerisms and ways of speaking which are similar, but our emotions, ideas and thoughts are not alike.

Their wartime experiences had heightened some of their older differences. Jerry noticed how much more independent he was than Harold, and how Harold still lived under the influence of their father. Jerry could not conceive of running his family that way, and remarked so to Barbara a few days later. A little of the brotherly rivalry they had had as children also came out once Harold arrived in the Philippines. Jerry was now the well-blooded combat veteran, a fighter pilot with an international reputation. His brother was just entering the fight, and as Harold went through all the emotions and stages that Jerry had experienced back in the Aleutians, Jerry could not help but feel a little amused. Harold was eager to begin flying combat, to shoot down his first Japanese plane. "Harold is fine and just as eager as I used to be. I'm getting so that I spend most of my time looking forward to seeing you . . ." Jerry wrote to Barbara in late June.

Later, when the war ended in August, Jerry noted that his twin wanted to get home right away. He noted wryly, "Already Harold talks about going home. Naturally he doesn't expect to for quite a few months, but I am amused when I think of his 4 months (overseas) and my <u>29</u>." Still, though Jerry had changed, and Harold had as well, the two brothers remained very close and saw each other at least twice a week throughout the summer of 1945. The twins had quite a bit of fun together, and often staged mock dogfights with one another over their respective airfields. Jerry gained a healthy respect for Harold's potential combat abilities, and especially for his flying. In August, Jerry wrote to Barbara about Harold's combat talents:

> Harold is getting along extra well. He is a superior pilot and has a keen sense of observation. He knows a great deal already about the enemy's tactics, his capabilities, how to fight successfully against them.

Jerry and Harold did spend many good days together on Luzon. One of the most memorable was Harold's very first visit to Clark Field at the end of May. Jerry had been entertaining the comedian and film star Joey Brown, and the three men had a hilarious time together. Before Brown left, Jerry actually took him on a dive-bombing mission. The short, wiry actor was stuffed in behind Jerry's seat where the radios were normally placed. The ground crew had removed them so there was just enough space for Joey to wedge himself in and see what combat flying was really like. Of course, if General Kenney had caught them, both would have been in deep trouble, but, as Jerry knew, what the old man did not know would not hurt him.

Meanwhile, back in Oregon, Barbara went into labor on June 1, 1945—her one-year wedding anniversary. Several hours later, she gave birth to a healthy baby boy, whom she named Jerry. Following the delivery, she fell asleep in her hospital room, exhausted but totally content.

When she awoke some time later, she found herself surrounded by a hundred long-stemmed red roses. She later discovered that Jerry had called the local florist, Chase Gardens, just before he left for New Guinea in September the previous year. He had ordered the roses delivered for Barbara's one-year wedding anniversary present. The timing proved excellent, and when the folks at Chase Gardens learned of where Barbara was on June 1, they took the roses to her hospital room and had a terrific time decorating it as she slept.

Meanwhile, throughout June, Jerry sweated through each day, waiting for news from home. The 49th had recently moved to Clark Field, which put Jerry closer to Manila—or what was left of that war-torn city. Jerry started to make frequent trips to the capital to try and get some news through unofficial sources. He had befriended most of the war correspondents staying in Manila, and he had asked them to try and find out if Barbara had given birth yet.

Each day was agony for Jerry. Was his wife okay? Was the baby healthy? Boy or girl? Had it even happened yet? He finally gave up trying to get any work down at Group headquarters. He drove back into Manila and spent several nights sleeping on the floor of a bomb-damaged hotel, just so he could be closer to his reporter buddies in case they learned anything. He had amassed over $1,000, both through his pay and through many late-night poker games, which he had carefully tucked away in his pants pocket so he could send a money order to Barbara the moment he heard any news. It would be the best gift he could possibly send to her.

While he slept on that cold hotel floor, a very accomplished thief robbed him one night and made off with over $750.00. Jerry was livid and totally upset with himself. That, combined with the dreadful wait made him just about insufferable. He eventually gave up and returned to Clark Field, where he could at least grit-out the wait among his friends and comrades.

Finally, a week after Jerry's birth, Lee Van Atta called him from Manila with great news. Lee had been in New Guinea since 1943, reporting on Kenney's pilots and earning their respect by flying combat missions to Rabaul with them. During the November 2, 1943 raid on Simpson Harbor, Lee had witnessed the entire battle from the cockpit of Dick Ellis's legendary B-25, *Seabiscuit*. After the war, Lee would go on to conduct a live radio broadcast from a ship during the Bikini atomic bomb tests.

That evening, Lee told Jerry that Barbara had given birth to a baby boy. Jerry was beside himself with joy when he learned that she had named him Jerry. That night, he scribbled out a hasty letter to Barbara and his son,

My Darling Barbara and Jerry,

I have begun a new life tonight. I cannot yet realize that this wonderful thing has happened to me. Lee Van Atta phoned this eve and said that Gerald R. Johnson, 7½ lbs has been born June 1ˢᵗ. I won't hardly be able to believe it until I see your letter. I am wearing a wider smile than I've had for three weeks, Barbie. To even think that this marvelous thing has happened to us after these years of hoping and planning . . .

I intend to be careful, Barbara. I'm going to teach our son to be the best pilot ever. All these tales you hear about my flying are over-exaggerated. I have never done any tricks in an airplane that I didn't know how to do beforehand and had done safely. I want to return to you in one piece and I want to live with you beyond the space of time.

Well sweetheart, all the cigars have been consumed. I burned two of them and my head is swimming!

Barbara, I can in no way tell you how exuberant I am—I can only look at our star and watch the merry twinkle as it says, "You need never worry, Gerald, I am taking good care of Barbara." Yes Darling, as I go to sleep tonight, I wear a smile on my lips.

Jerry's Daddy,
Gerald

Later, in honor of the event, he asked his ground crew to change the name of his personal P-38. Carefully, they took off the red letters that spelled "Barbara" on the Lightning's nose and replaced them with a round baby picture with "Jerry" printed above it. Jerry was delighted and wasted no time in taking photos to send home to his family. In return, he barraged Barbara with demands for photographs of mother and son. When a few snapshots began trickling in to his mail slot at Clark Field, he wasted no time putting them into a scrapbook made from an administrative binder. His son became his greatest pride, and he shared his joy with everyone around him. Being a father made him happier than anything else ever had—or ever would.

TWENTY

Last Leave, Last Look

Somewhere in New Guinea

My Darling Barbara and Jerry,

Through all my experiences and memories there has been a warmth of love and true faith that have kept me going through it all. Yes, my beloved Barbara, you have actually made all the living worth while. Kiss Jerry for me tonight, I'll scribble another note soon.

Yours alone,
Gerald

In the middle of July, Jerry took his last seven-day leave to New Guinea. He returned to Nadzab and once again stayed with Jock Henebry. The changes at Nadzab shocked him. The airfield had originally been a single dusty strip hacked out of the jungle by the Japanese. When the Allies had captured it back in 1943, the combat engineers had expanded the runway, added several others, and turned it into a major base. Miles of taxiways, dispersal areas and revetments stretched across the floor of Markham Valley, and every square foot of the base was taken up with B-25s, P-40s, C-47s, Thunderbolts, Marauders, Liberators, Flying Fortresses, Lightnings, and countless other types of aircraft. Now, with the war thousands of miles away, the field had fallen into disuse and was slowly withering away. Only a few C-47s sat on the deserted runways. Few personnel remained; most everyone had moved up to Okinawa or Luzon. The roads that had been cut out of the thick scrub lay unused, and the jungle was gradually reclaiming them. Weeds poked through the pierced steel planking on the runways, and some of the old living areas had become almost overgrown with bushes and scrub. The scene depressed Jerry. He had fought hard for this place in 1943, and to see it wasting away after all of the death and killing made all of his effort seem senseless.

One afternoon, Jerry tramped down one of the old lanes, picked his way around shrubs that had sprouted in the roadway, and headed for a nearby hill. He hiked up the slopes and sat on the top of the butte, remembering all the things that had occurred two years before. He recalled the fight he had in July 1943, when he shot down his first two planes in New Guinea. "One of them nearly cut my tail off," he thought.

The field was silent that day—a far cry from the old days when the thunderous roar of hundreds of engines echoed through the valley. Now, every few hours, a plane would drop in, and its lonely engine would only accentuate the changes. The camp areas seemed almost haunted. Vines and grass covered what was left of the huts and shacks that had once housed thousands of sweating, exhausted men. The roads and taxiways were equally deserted. Jerry remembered the days when the trails had been clogged with trucks, troops, and even Japanese. Now, only the rare and forlorn jeep traveled the narrow pathways through the jungle. The days when Jerry could walk down the flight line, passing friends old and new, were long gone. Only Jock Henebry and a few others had stayed on to keep the field open.

Jerry remembered how he used to buzz the field in his P-40 in late 1943. He would zoom over Jock's place, and waggle his wings to signal his old friend to come down and meet him at the dispersal area. Then, he would swing into the pattern and bounce his P-40 down the runway. Often, in that P-40, or in his faithful old P-38, #83, he would protect Jock and Don "Buck" Good as they strafed and bombed a Japanese strip just up the valley. That enemy field was nothing but vines and kuni grass now. Only a few rusting, weed-filled aircraft hulks to mark the scene of many battles.

Then, there were the dead. It seemed impossible to him that so many of his friends from those days were gone. McGuire was dead, killed by his own recklessness. Jerry's old wingman, Stanley Johnson, had been killed long ago on a mission with Dick Bong. Price had died over Rabaul. Fanning had been killed as well. Morrissey had been terribly wounded, along with Leslie Nelson, in the kamikaze attack on that LST. Morrissey was still at Fort Vancouver's base hospital. Harry Lidstrom was long gone, killed in that terrible storm not far from Nadzab during that bloody fall of 1943. There were so many others, and thinking about them caused a wave of grief to sweep over Jerry. He later wrote to Barbara:

> Many of the brave, fine men I knew here are gone, never to fly as earthlings again. Yet the memory of their comradeship is as alive as though they were here by me now.

Of his inner circle of friends, only Wally Jordan, Jim Watkins, and Dick Bong were left. Everyone else was dead or horribly wounded. And death would strike one more time.

A few weeks after he returned from his last trip to Nadzab, Jerry learned that Dick Bong had been killed test-flying a P-80 in California. Jerry and the rest of the Fifth Air Force was stunned and shaken by the news. Jerry was practically alone now, and even as the clock was ticking down the final days of the war, he must have wondered which of the remaining three men in his group would be the next to die.

It had been a long, long war.

❧

As the war wound down and finally came to an end in August, Jerry grew increasingly eager to return home to his family. General Kenney, who respected Jerry so much, made arrangements for him to be sent back to the States to undergo further staff training. In the meantime, Jerry spent most of August and September flying all over Japan in order to locate Allied prisoners of war. The work proved very gratifying, as the men he found were in very bad shape. They had been through a terrible ordeal, and Jerry felt a compelling sense of duty to remain with them to ensure that they would get quick transport home.

All the while, however, he himself longed to return to Eugene and hold his son for the first time, to see Barbara once again and to wake up beside her each day. Duty overruled his own desires, however, and he brushed aside more than one chance to go home. Finally, at the end of September, Kenney's arrangements with USAAF Headquarters in Washington were finalized, and Jerry was informed that orders sending him home would be coming through within a few weeks. Whether he wanted to or not, Kenney was going to send Jerry home. He had done more than his share, as proven by his 262 combat missions, five Distinguished Flying Crosses, eleven Air Medals, the Legion of Merit, two Distinguished Service Crosses, the Silver Star, and the Soldier's Medal, which he received for saving a drowning GI at Lingayen Gulf one afternoon in the spring of 1945.

Jerry finally agreed to go home, and though he still felt torn by his sense of duty, there would be other days, with many more challenges ahead. The biggest one on the horizon was undoubtedly the confrontation he was sure to have with his father when he got home. H. V. had been bugging Jerry all spring about his plans for the future. He assumed Jerry would leave the service, finish his undergraduate degree, and go on to law school. Jerry did not want to have any of that. He had a great career in the Army Air Force; in fact, at age twenty-four, he was one of the youngest full colonels in the Pacific. In Kenney, he had a very powerful mentor, who seemed intent on steering Jerry to a general's star someday soon.

Law school would never be an option. Flying was Jerry's life now, and the Army Air Force would be his career. Five years after sitting on that front stoop and reading his rejection letter from Oregon Health Sciences University, Jerry had finally decided what he wanted to do with his life.

PART SEVEN

Point of Departure,

Point of Despair

Goodnight, Sweetheart

Hello You Two Civilians,

October 7, 1945

I guess you and Jerry are really having some times by now. He is 4 months & 1 week old and still I can't realize that he is our son. Well Darling, right now I am flying 10,000 feet high over the mountains east of Manila. I flew from Atsugi down to Tacloban, Leyte, to take some material to General Wirtsmith [sic]. En route somewhere, we blew the exhaust stack off my B-25 and so we were hung up at Leyte for 2 days putting in a new cylinder. The second evening there, I borrowed a B-25 from the General and flew up to Manila and back after dark to pick up a new cylinder. During the afternoon I had been having a tooth filled and as I crossed the hospital area someone called "Well, Jerry!" There was Bob Gregary, my young cousin. He has been transferred from the infantry to the medical corps. He is a member of the general hospital military band. I took him with me on the night flight to Manila and he really got a kick out of it!

Right now I'm on my way back to Japan via Laoag (Northern Luzon), Okinawa, and may stop over at Kanoya on Kyushu to see Harold. I imagine this darn pen will bleed ink when we begin to descend.

I have a 2nd Lt. copilot, a sergeant radio operator, a corporal who is a crew chief on board. Also, Lt. Col. Underwood, whom I met last spring. He is going up to Japan with me to at least see the place. After being overseas for about three years, he doesn't want to go home without seeing the conquered land.

Yup, Barbie, you and Jerry are cause enough for all my

happiness for a lifetime. I love you both with all my heart. The greatest experience of my life will be my return to you.

I am in high hopes of having quite a stack of mail awaiting me when I get back to Japan. We are over the mountains now & Laoag is in sight. Guess I better take over and get this baby on the ground. It is 8:00 AM and I'm hungry!

Your Lovingest Husband, Always
Gerald

Jerry landed the B-25 at Laoag, where he mailed his letter to Barbara as the plane was refueled for the long trip to Okinawa. By early afternoon, Jerry's B-25 had made it Ie Shima, a small island off the coast of Okinawa that had been turned into a giant American airfield complex. They refueled there and ate lunch. Jerry discussed the next leg of their journey with the other passengers and crew of the B-25. He wanted to fly over to Kanoya to see his twin brother Harold. Nobody seemed to mind, so Jerry decided to go ahead and do it. He was not sure if Harold's unit, the 348th Fighter Group, was still at that base, but he thought he would at least give it a shot.

The six men piled back aboard the B-25—the four-man crew (including Jerry) and two passengers they had picked up in the Philippines. Jerry flew on up to Kyushu, reaching Kanoya by late afternoon. In the gathering dusk, he circled the airfield and called down to the tower, asking the controller if the 348th was still stationed there. The controller, who had only recently arrived at the base, told him the 348th had rotated home. That was not true—Harold and the rest of the group were still at Kanoya.

Disappointed, Jerry turned the B-25 for Honshu. As they continued northward, the weather deteriorated. Jerry pushed on, thinking that they had just hit a local squall. In reality, they were flying right into the middle of an unreported typhoon. Without any warning from the ground controllers, Jerry and his copilot, Lt. Jim Nolan, had no idea what they were flying into. By now, darkness had fallen, and they were getting low on fuel.

As the typhoon seethed around them, the B-25 rocked and shuddered as fierce winds and driving rain struck the big bomber. Jerry and Jim

Nolan had to use every ounce of strength they possessed to keep the B-25 flying level. Then the gyrocompass failed—without it, there was no way they would find their way to Atsugi, at night in a typhoon, unless they could be vectored in by a radar controller. Jerry got on the radio and tried to reach Atsugi—no luck. He and the crew kept trying, and they finally gained contact with a C-46 Commando that was approaching Atsugi from another direction. The C-46 began relying communications between the radar operator in Atsugi's tower to Jerry's B-25.

In the meantime, visibility dropped to a few hundred feet. Messages between the C-46 and Jerry's B-25 were garbled and unclear. The tenuous link with the ground was soon severed when the Commando had to land, as it was out of fuel. Alone now, with no contact with the ground, Jerry continued to send radio messages in the hope that somebody would pick them up. In fact, the tower at Atsugi could hear him, but their transmissions were not getting through to the B-25.

For three hours, Jerry and Jim wandered through the rain-lashed skies over Suruga Bay in hope of finding some familiar landmark. They dropped down on the deck, searching for lights or any signs of civilization. Visibility remained so bad, though, that they brushed a mountain top with one wing. With the plane now damaged, it became even tougher to keep it in the air. All the while, the storm ranged around them.

With twenty minutes of fuel left, Jerry ordered everyone in the plane to put their parachutes on. His three crew members promptly did as they were told. His two passengers, however, had not brought any along. A quick search of the B-25 revealed that they had only four chutes for six men.

Jerry didn't hesitate. He unstrapped himself from his chute and handed it over to Lieutenant Colonel Robert Underwood. Nolan unbuckled his and gave it to First Lieutenant Herbert A. Schaeffler. At first, the two passengers protested and suggested everyone draw straws to see who would get the chutes. Jerry refused to consider it. "I'm in charge of this ship," he shouted over the roar of the engine and the tat-tat-tat of hail against the aluminum fuselage.

Silently, Underwood and Schaeffler put the chutes on and crawled towards the bomb bay. Jerry and Nolan swung the B-25 around so they could make a run over an open stretch of beach they had just spotted.

Jerry ordered the four men in the back of the plane to bail out over the sandy spit of land. One by one, each bailed out, though the typhoon scattered them along the coast for several miles.

Schaeffler was the last man to jump out. He tumbled down into the inky night, popped his chute open, and watched as the storm quickly swallowed up the B-25. When he hit the ground, he couldn't even hear the B-25's engine over the shriek of the typhoon.

Jerry and Jim had told everyone that they would make one pass over the beach so they could get out, then they were going to come back around and belly-land the B-25 right on the sand. After Schaeffler hit the ground, he kept waiting for the aircraft to come back into view, to swing around and mush onto the beach nearby. When it did not appear, he gathered his chute and headed inland.

Jerry and Jim Nolan were never seen again.

EPILOGUE

December 16, 1945

Dear Barbara,

I suppose Harold has returned by now and given you all the information about Jerry, so I shan't go into that except to say that we've found nothing more.

One thing of which I want you to be sure of is that no effort was spared in the search for him. Nothing could have been closer to the hearts of the boys in the 49th than locating Johnny's airplane. He was not only one of the most respected men in the theater, but also one of the most well-liked commanders. Rather impulsive at times, perhaps, but that very quality was an integral part his fighter pilot ability that made it possible for him to do far more than his share over here.

The incident hit me harder than most because I had flown and lived with Johnny for nearly four years—I sort of tagged along behind him in a way, getting my promotions a month or two later than he did, took over his squadron when he stepped up a little higher—things like that. We all become a little callous in this business, labeling fatal crashes as the "Luck of the game" and so forth, but when Harold came in up here, so much like Johnny, I found that the shell tends to crack at times.

At Lingayen one time, I heard him say that a boy who had gone in an airplane must have been happy to check out that way, if he had to go, and I'm absolutely sure that Johnny felt that way.

Although we've never met, I hope we shall some time. I have a picture of you and the baby and of course have been the recipient of many verbal descriptions.

Please give my love to Harold and the rest of the family, and reserve a generous share for yourself. I shall certainly drop by your place whenever I return.

Wally Jordan

Dear Barbara,

Harold is probably home by now, and has told you all that happened to Johnnie. In this letter I've no intention of extending unwanted sympathy, nor of making a lament. Merely let me state that your husband was one of the best-loved and bravest men that I or any man had the honor to know.

I want first of all, to assure you that Johnnie's friends and his old outfit, the 49th, did everything they could to try and locate him. Needless to say, no man in this theater was surprised when they heard that Johnnie Johnson rode his ship down when there were only enough chutes for the passengers.

The two of us had formed a team that was unbeatable, and everywhere I've gone since then people have asked me to send you their regards and regrets and asked numerous questions to which there will never be an answer. Mere men cannot begin to understand what happened that night. The only thing we can comprehend is that "No greater love hath any man than to lay down his life for a friend."

It is with tears in my eyes, and an unmovable lump in my throat that I thank God for the privilege of knowing Johnnie Johnson, a man's man.

Someday I'm coming back to the States, after I've kinda gotten used to not having Johnnie around. When I do, I'd consider it an honor if I may call in person and have a short chat with you and Jerry Jr. I have waited this long to write because of many reasons and at present none of them make sense. So, I'll sign off with no apology.

Always Your Friend,
Jimmie Watkins

Despite an exhaustive search by Japanese authorities and the Fifth Air Force, no trace of the B-25 was ever found. When Harold learned that Jerry's plane had gone down, he took off in a Piper L-4 Grasshopper and went searching for him by himself in the middle of the typhoon. After he landed, General Kenney grounded him. He didn't want the Johnson family to lose two of its sons. Harold was sent home almost immediately afterwards.

Barbara received the dreadful telegram a few days later. The message only listed him as missing, however, so she held out hope. For several weeks, she clung to the hope that he might still be found, indomitable as ever. His letters continued to arrive, the ones that he had sent before the crash, and each one gave her hope that he might still be alive, that this letter might be the one telling her all was well.

That letter never came. Gerald Johnson would never see his son or feel the joy of cradling his little boy against his chest.

❧

The years went by, but the pain never left. Barbara eventually married one of Jerry's high school friends, David Curtis. Dave had been out in the Pacific as a night fighter pilot, and he had actually encountered Jerry a few times out there. Barbara and Dave had four kids together, but Jerry's death cast a fifty-year shadow across both their lives. Barbara remained lost without the only man she ever really loved. They divorced in the mid-1980s, and Dave died of a heart attack less than six months later while swimming in a local public pool.

Harold never forgave himself for Jerry's loss. If only the controller at Kanoya had known the 348th was still there, Jerry never would have flown into the typhoon. Though Harold lived the life of a pillar in his community, working with disadvantaged kids through his church and serving as the Civil Defense Coordinator for Eugene, he too could never escape from the pain of Jerry's death. One day in 1975, he killed himself in his family's garage. Two weeks later, H. V. died of a heart attack while fishing on the McKenzie River, his soul broken by the loss of his second son, who had followed him into the legal profession as he had always hoped Jerry would have.

Barbara retreated into herself as each terrible incident unfolded. Her thoughts remained with Jerry through it all. He had been her rock, she had been his inspiration. As the decades passed, the pain of his loss remained the most terrible of all, and never seemed to fade. That short, wonderful summer of 1944 remained the best time in her life, and the years of happiness that fate had denied her was perhaps the most difficult thing of all to understand.

As the years passed, time claimed many of the things around town that reminded Barbara of Jerry's love. His old neighborhood, once very gentrified, grew seedy and crime-ridden. The church where they were married is now a run-down movie theater that shows art films for the local college crowd. Chase Gardens went out of business in the early 1990s, and their rose-growing greenhouses have been replaced by apartment complexes.

After the war, Jerry's many medals were placed on display at the local YMCA. General Kenney came to town and delivered a speech in Jerry's honor after Jene McNeese established a YMCA scholarship in his friend's name. But not long after, thieves broke into the display cabinet and stole all his decorations as well a bronze bust of Jerry. Aside from a plaque at the chapel named in his honor, Gerald Johnson's hometown has forgotten all about him.

The rest of the country has not forgotten. Over the years, many books have mentioned the exploits of Gerald R. Johnson, and articles in magazines have sought to capture Johnson's mystique. Men from the squadron who have written their memoirs generally speak lovingly of their former commanding officer. Profiles of his aircraft have been painted, as have scenes from his career. One recent painting has Jerry fleeing Rabaul on the deck after that memorable November 2, 1943 raid. If Eugene has forgotten him, the nation he defended certainly has not; if anything, he is more famous now than he was during the war.

None of that would have mattered to Jerry if he had survived the war. Unlike some other aces, such as his friend Tommy McGuire, he did not seek the limelight, and felt uncomfortable in it. Friendship, loyalty, and devotion were what mattered to Gerald Richard Johnson. Five decades later, the loyalty and devotion his friends showed him during the war has yet to wane. All remember him with fondness, respect bordering on hero worship, and with a sense of grief over his loss that they have never quite shaken.

Carl Martinez owed so much to Jerry and his family that he held them in the highest esteem until his death in 1997. After the war, H. V. honored Jerry's promise to help get Carl to the United States. He came and studied at the University of Oregon and lived with the Johnsons' in their house on Broadway for four years. Upon graduating, he returned home and ran a sugar mill until his death in 1997. From time to time, he would visit Eugene, where he was welcomed back with open arms. He had long since become a member of the Johnson family.

Wally Jordan, perhaps Jerry's closest friend through his service days, stayed in the Air Force after the war and retired as a full colonel. Gruff, irascible, and full of beans, Wally Jordan never had anything but kind words when talking about Jerry. To him, he was the best of the best, a reflection of youthful vigor that he could always look back on an laugh. They had some wild times together, and they were some of the best he had ever known. Wally died in the fall of 1999.

Jim Watkins stayed in the Air Force as well. He and his wife, Charlcie Jean, became friends with Barbara after the war, and would occasionally bump into her and Dave Curtis as their Air Force careers took them here and there. Jim's regard and love for his old comrade never diminished, though he grew distant from the other 49'ers as the years passed. By the mid-1980s, he had stopped attending reunions, and most of the graying veterans of the Pacific War's top-scoring fighter outfit lost touch with him. He is the last of Jerry's fellow tigers.

Bill Runey, who returned to Eugene after the war to make a home and a living, has remained one of Barbara's closest friends over the years. One morning, fifty-one years after Gerald's death, the *Eugene Register-Guard* ran an article about him. The story was unique, since Eugene rarely honors its war heroes, and in fact, has been obsessively antimilitary since the 1960s. Bill Runey, the only 49th veteran in the area, opened his paper that morning and was touched by the article. To see his friend remembered after all these years sent a wave of emotion through his heart. He was so moved by the piece that he wrote a passionate letter to the *Register-Guard*, relating his experiences with Jerry in New Guinea. The letter was never published, but one line in his letter summed up the life and exploits of Colonel Gerald R. Johnson perhaps better than anything else ever put to paper:

"He was the Luke Skywalker of my generation."

GLOSSARY

Ack-Ack: Anti-aircraft fire. This was a common term used by the pilots during the war.

Break: A sharp, sudden turn designed to shake-off an attacking aircraft.

Chandelle: An aircraft maneuver, the chandelle was a steep climbing turn.

Element: An Air Force term for a formation of two aircraft. Two to three elements composed a flight.

Flak: Anti-aircraft fire.

Flight: An Air Force term for a formation of four to six aircraft. The Navy's equivalent was the division. Each flight consisted of two or three elements.

Hit the Silk: Bailing out of an aircraft. World War II parachutes were made out of silk.

Immelmann: An aircraft maneuver generally attributed to the famous German Ace, Max Immelmann (the "Eagle of Lille"). By WWII, what he had developed during the Great War had evolved into a more complicated maneuver. Essentially, an Immelmann was a reverse split-ess. A pilot would pull up into a half-loop until he had changed his heading 180 degrees. At the top of the half-loop, he would be going the opposite way upside down. To complete the maneuver, he would roll 180 degrees and level out. It was fairly common to see the nimble Japanese fighters in New Guinea perform Immelmanns. American pilots with their heavier aircraft usually avoided such speed-draining maneuvers.

IP: Initial Point. This was the navigational point at which a bomber formation would begin its finalrun to the target area. During that period, the bombers would have to maintain a steady course and speed.

Pipper: The center dot on an American reflector gunsight.

Punching Tanks: To extend the range of its aircraft, the USAAF equipped its fighter units in New Guinea with external fuel tanks that could be jettisoned when empty. Since they slowed the fighters down and made them less maneuverable, American pilots dropped them whenever they went into a dogfight—whether they were empty or not. The pilots nicknamed this process "Punching Tanks."

Split-ess: A maneuver used by aviators to escape from attack, or to launch an attack of their own. The pilot would roll inverted, then pull back on the stick. The subsequent dive would eventually put the plane on the opposite heading from the one he was maintaining before the maneuver.

Strafer: In late 1942, Fifth Air Force bomber units began experimenting with ways to upgrade their firepower. The medium and light outfits, most notably the 3rd Attack Group, found that by replacing the bombardier's position in the nose, their aircraft could be fitted with numerous .50 caliber machine guns. So modified, the B-25s and A-20s in New Guinea wrought havoc upon the Japanese through low-altitude strafing attacks. They were dubbed "strafers" or "gunships" as a result.

Vee: A vee was a formation used by nearly every nation during the Korean War. Usually, a vee consisted of three aircraft positioned in an upside down "V" formation. This was primarily used by bombers.

Vee of vees: A squadron-sized formation composed of several flights in vee formation. The squadron's flights would then be arranged into a larger overall vee.

Zeke and Zero: The standard Japanese Naval fighter of the war was the Mitsubishi A6M Type O, or Zero, fighter. During the war, Allied intelligence gave each Japanese aircraft a code name. The Zero gained the code name "Zeke." Throughout the war, however, the A6M was called both Zero and Zeke by Allied pilots.

NOTE ON SOURCES

Almost all of the material presented in *Jungle Ace* stems from primary research I conducted between 1991 and 2000. Much of the book relies on the memories of dozens of 49th pilots, friends of Jerry, and Jerry's family. Their recollections are buttressed by the 54th and 49th Fighter Group records found at Maxwell Air Force Base's Air Force Historical Research Center, plus the Fifth Air Force records at the National Archives. Other information was gleaned from letters Jerry and Barbara wrote during the war, as well as their scrapbooks, photo albums, and other documents. Some of the flying sequences in the book trace their roots in Jerry's Form Five, found at Norton Air Force Base in the mid-1990s. Each pilot kept a detailed flight log, which was then reported monthly as the Form Five and stored in Air Force archives. Jerry's survived, though his final month's flight time is not listed, and some of the entries are damaged beyond legibility. His original logs have disappeared.

Accurate secondary sources on the air war in New Guinea and the Philippines are hard to find. Two newer volumes tower among the others. Thomas E. Griffith Jr.'s *MacArthur's Airman: General George Kenney and the War in the Southwest Pacific* is one of the best works on the subject. Steven Birdsall's *Flying Buccaneers* is a terrific classic, and Ken Rust's short book *The Fifth Air Force Story* provides an excellent overview of the units involved in the Southwest Pacific Area. Most recently, Eric Bergerud published a massive work on air combat in the South Pacific called *Fire in the Sky*, which is the closest yet to a definitive account of the air war in this oft-neglected theater. For information about Dick Bong, one cannot go wrong with his brother Carl's book, *Dear Mom, So We Have a War*. The book not only sets the record straight on a great ace, but also captures much of his elusive personality. Other works on aspects of the air war include *Protect and Avenge: The 49th Fighter Group in World War II* by S. W. Ferguson and William Pascalis. Their work is an admirable attempt at a detailed unit history, but contains many flaws and must be used carefully by historians. General George C. Kenney's memoirs, *General Kenney Reports* also must be taken with a grain of salt, as much of Kenney's penchant for exaggeration exists between its pages. For information on the Japanese side of the air war, see Henry Sakaida's marvelous, but all too-short, work *Imperial Japanese Army Air Force Aces 1937–45*. Little on the JAAF has been translated from Japanese over the years, so Sakaida's piece is truly unique in English.

INDEX

About the Author

John Bruning is an aviation historian, writer, and designer of combat flight simulators and educational CD-ROM products. A graduate of the University of Oregon, he lives in Independence, Oregon, where he served as a city councilor and a school board member.